THE
SCARLET LADY

THE
SCARLET LADY

Confessions of A Successful Abortionist

CAROL EVERETT
WITH JACK SHAW

Wolgemuth & Hyatt, Publishers, Inc.
Brentwood, Tennessee

The mission of Wolgemuth & Hyatt, Publishers, Inc. is to publish and distribute books that lead individuals toward:

- A personal faith in the one true God: Father, Son, and Holy Spirit;

- A lifestyle of practical discipleship; and

- A worldview that is consistent with the historic, Christian faith.

Moreover, the Company endeavors to accomplish this mission at a reasonable profit and in a manner which glorifies God and serves His Kingdom.

Unless otherwise noted, all Scripture quotations are from *The Amplified Bible,* Old Testament, copyright 1962, 1964, by the Zondervan Publishing House, or *The Amplified Bible,* New Testament, copyright 1958, by The Lockman Foundation.

Wolgemuth & Hyatt, Publishers, Inc.
1749 Mallory Lane, Suite 110
Brentwood, Tennessee 37027

Library of Congress Cataloging-in-Publication Data

Everett, Carol.
   The scarlet lady : confessions of an abortionist / Carol Everett
with Jack Shaw. — 1st ed.
      p. cm.
   ISBN 1-56121-073-0
   1. Everett, Carol. 2. Clinic managers—Texas—Biography.
3. Abortion services—Texas. 4. Abortion—Psychological aspects.
5. Abortion—Religious aspects—Christianity. I. Shaw, Jack.
II. Title.
RG734.E94 1991
362.1'9888'092—dc20   91-29020
   [B]   CIP

To the 35,000 mothers to whom I sold
abortions and their 35,000 unborn babies

To Tom, my unborn child's father, who
participated in our abortion unaware
he too would be victimized

To the 35,000 fathers and other family
members affected by these abortions

And to my unborn daughter, Heidi, and
all the unborn who face her fate
unless their cries are heard,
"Let me live! Let me live!"

AUTHOR'S NOTE

All of the stories in this book are true. In some, the names have been changed. In all instances, the events and conversations accurately reflect factual situations.

This is the truth. This is my story.

CONTENTS

ACKNOWLEDGMENTS

I would like to thank my parents for giving me life. Though they have not approved of all my choices, they have loved me. And now as we adjust to life without my father, my mother is one of my best friends.

I would like to thank my living children, Kelly and Joe Bob, and my daughter-in-law, Carol, Jr., who love me just as I am. Though my children have lived with my many mistakes, they have loved me through it all and are now my strongest supporters in my pro-life work.

Thank you, John and Ardelia Shoop, Nelson and Stephanie Cook, Barbara Lee, Valerie Syzmaniak, Richard and Jill Bowles, Jerry and Karen Green, and many other friends of my new life who have prayed for me, loved me unconditionally, and stood by me during my metamorphosis from abortionist to pro-lifer.

My gratitude to George Dulany, Jr., Ethelyn English, Barbara Schlapler, and Donna West, our dedicated office staff who lovingly supported us throughout the development of this book.

Thank you, Jennifer Moore, for your long hours of labor, believing in this book, encouraging me as I struggled through my emotions in committing my life to paper. Through your eyes, I saw that others could be helped by my experiences. Thank you for becoming my cherished friend in the process. Thank you, Rusty and Heather, for allowing your wife and mother to devote untold hours to this project.

Most of all I would like to thank Jack and Gwen Shaw, who have loved me, accepted me, and taught me by example and word the Christian way of life. They have been available to me since the moment I prayed that prayer of salvation, re-training me—Jack, the godly man, teaching Christian truths, grounding me in my new understanding of the love of God and helping me in the work the Lord has for me; and as I strive to be God's woman, Gwen has been and is the example of the godly woman I want to be.

As we finish this book, I would like to thank Gwen and the Shaw children, Wendy, Rhonda, and David for their patient and loving support while Jack and I have written this book.

And thank You, Lord, for redeeming me from the miry pit and for Your redeeming love that continues to work in my life.

1

THE NEIMAN-MARCUS
OF THE INDUSTRY

D r. Harvey Johnson appeared at my office door. "Carol, come back to recovery with me," he said, extending his hand to me with a quick nod.

I hurriedly joined him in the hallway where he slipped his arm around me in that familiar position we walked in so often. "What's wrong, Harvey?"

"Sheryl passed a clot. She is bleeding heavily, but she will be all right." He spoke in a low tone.

We turned the corner into the recovery room and walked over to Sheryl's bed. Becky and Connie, two LPNs, stood over her. Her pants were off, and she was lying in a pool of blood. The whole bed was soaked with blood; the privacy curtains were splashed with blood, and even the wall had blood on it. Quite honestly, I was shocked by the scene. I'm an operating room technician, but I had never seen so much blood in all my life.

I could feel Harvey's hand tighten on the back of my neck to re-asssure me and also to control my reaction. He moved to Sheryl's side, directing his comments to one of the nurses. "Connie, massage her fundus. This will close her uterus down after all the clots are out, and the bleeding will stop." As he spoke, he pushed Sheryl's small abdo-

1

men in and with a circular motion massaged the top of her uterus, called the fundus.

My medical experience kicked in, and I touched Sheryl's arm. "How are you doing, Sheryl?"

"Okay, I guess." Her voice sounded weak.

"Everything is going to be all right. I'll stay back here with you. After we get you cleaned up, we'll bring Bob back, too." I nodded to Becky who seemed relieved to have someone else in the room directing her actions.

In January 1982 we were a clean clinic, a top-notch operation. We considered ourselves the Neiman-Marcus of the abortion industry— not a single complication, not even a major infection. Harvey and I had accomplished what our competition could only talk about doing. Our confidence in our ability was high; our judgments seemed almost infallible. Our doctors were Ob-Gyn—all but one board certified. Now we faced a major complication, and we were vulnerable.

Sheryl first came into the clinic on Wednesday morning and filled out the forms stating she was eighteen weeks pregnant. The rate for an abortion at that point was three hundred and seventy-five dollars, which she paid in cash. However, in the examining room, Dr. Johnson discovered she was twenty weeks along, informing her that now an abortion would cost an additional one hundred and twenty-five dollars. Sheryl became agitated, as did Harvey, who brought the whole problem to me to straighten out.

"Carol, we need a policy for sizing patients over twelve weeks pregnant before they pay. This woman got all the way to the back having paid three hundred and seventy-five dollars for eighteen weeks, but she is twenty weeks along. She is very upset because she does not have the additional one hundred and twenty-five dollars. You talk to her and get her money so we can do her." He handed me the chart and walked away, motioning to a young woman just slipping out into the hall from an examining room. As clinic administrator, I knew what to do.

"Sheryl, please come into my office and have a seat while I look at your chart." She sat nervously in the chair I indicated, glancing up only when I spoke again. "You thought you were eighteen weeks pregnant, but Dr. Johnson found you to be twenty weeks when he did the pelvic examination. Now the cost is more, and you will have to pay another one hundred and twenty-five dollars. Do you have the money?"

"In January 1982 we were a clean clinic, a top-notch operation. We considered ourselves the Neiman-Marcus of the abortion industry—not a single complication, not even a major infection."

"No. We could barely come up with three hundred and seventy-five dollars. My boyfriend, Bob, and I live together with my two-year-old son. I have another son, who's seventeen years old, but he lives with my mother in Nebraska. Bob and I both work, but it takes everything we make. I don't know how we can get any more money. We are already using part of our rent payment this month. Can we work out some kind of payment plan? We will pay you, I swear." She kept wringing her hands as she tried desperately to convince me to help her.

It didn't work. I knew my job, and sentiment wasn't part of it. I put the chart down and looked her in the eye, allowing a sympathetic tone into my voice. "No, we are not allowed to make pay-out agreements, and we can't do the procedure until you have the rest of the money. I must stress the urgency, however, because the price keeps going up each week you wait. The charge at twenty-four weeks is seven hundred and fifty rather than five hundred. You need to find the money as quickly as you can."

I watched her shoulders slump as dejection set in. Now I got up, walked around my desk, and leaned back against it. "Surely you have a family member who could loan you the money, don't you? What about a friend? Do you have some friends who could loan you part of the money? Perhaps a family member or your friends could loan you twenty-five or even fifty dollar each."

"I can't think of anyone who could. I'm so upset. I really don't know. What are you going to do about the three hundred and seventy-five dollars I have already paid you?" Sheryl questioned.

"We will just hold it until Friday evening. I'm sure you will find the money. Go home and talk to Bob about it. I'm sure that you can come up with the money by Friday. If you can, call me back and we will be able to do the procedure Friday evening for the same price— five hundred dollars. But remember, the longer you wait, the more it will cost. Sheryl, this is such a critical time. Just come up with the extra one hundred and twenty-five dollars, and we will take care of everything on Friday." She stood up, and I walked her to the door, patting her shoulder reassuringly.

"I Have the Money"

Sheryl returned Friday as I expected. She was very shy when she walked into my office; it was after 7:00 P.M. "I have the money. Is it too late to do it tonight?"

"No, Sheryl, it's not," I said with a smile. "We can do it tonight, but before we start, I have something for you." I closed the door to my office and gave her a coupon I had clipped out of the newspaper for her. "This will give you a 10 percent discount so you will have some money to eat on until you are paid again." I hugged her and then directed her to the front to pay while her chart was pulled.

I knew Sheryl would be in recovery a long time because of the length of her pregnancy. Now I had to rush things up because recovery room nurses were not cheap. I had a date to meet later that night and a long day ahead of me on Saturday.

"We need to do this procedure as soon as possible so Sheryl can recover while the other abortions are being done. We don't want to be here all night." Our nursing staff scurried around, adjusting the schedule at my direction.

When Sheryl came back to the operating room, she said, "I'm scared. I don't know why. This is not my first abortion. I had another one some time ago, but this time I am really scared."

I had the strangest feeling Sheryl had been hurt a lot in her life. She seemed so helpless against a cruel world. Somehow I wanted to protect her, to help another hurting woman. I stopped what I was

"I held her hand and coached her through the procedure as I had learned to do in Lamaze classes. I used what I learned in those childbirth classes to coach women through the abortion procedure and help limit the screaming."

doing and held her hand. "Don't worry. Everything is going to be all right. I will go through the procedure with you. I'll be here to help you. It will all be over soon, you'll see," I reassured her.

On the procedure table I was aware of how petite Sheryl was. About five feet tall, she was a stunningly beautiful woman, not sexy, just naturally beautiful. Her skin was flawless—that creamy, white, natural blonde color. She had blonde hair and blue eyes, eyes that looked scared right now.

Sheryl was very cooperative. She slid her tiny body down to the edge of the table, hanging her bottom off the end, in just the right position for the baby's body parts to fall into the cold, stainless steel pan without making a mess.

I held her hand and coached her through the procedure as I had learned to do in Lamaze classes. I used what I learned in those child-birth classes to coach women through the abortion procedure and help limit the screaming.

"Take a deep breath, Sheryl. Everything is going to be all right," I confidently coached her.

After all, I reasoned, who better to do her abortion than the man whom I had trusted to do my own abortion? Mine went smoothly with no medical problems, and I believed Sheryl would be just fine, too. Now I was helping the best abortionist I knew do abortions on other women—yes, I guess I thought Harvey was the best abortionist money could buy.

"Take another deep breath, Sheryl. Let's count to ten before you take another one. It will help slow down your body. I'm going to pinch your elbow. Concentrate on your elbow."

I can still remember Sheryl's eyes. Even today, I'm not sure what I saw. Fear? Pain? A combination? Her eyes were haunted, almost empty; yet some emotion still deeper was reflected there.

I looked down to see how the procedure was going. Everything seemed to be all right. The arms and legs of the baby, the first parts to come out, were in the pan. Harvey reached for the body.

Usually, I was the one who held the baby motionless in the uterus for the abortion using a technique called the Hanson maneuver, in which the technician's hand is on the fundus and the contents in the uterus. This time, Leslie was assisting while I held Sheryl's hand.

Using this maneuver, the technician can tell the doctor where the body parts are, quietly directing him, "The head is here, buttocks here, and the arms and legs here." If the abortionist performs the Hanson maneuver himself, he can tell where the parts are.

I liked to help Dr. Johnson, and performing the Hanson maneuver was my way of helping him do the actual abortions. He seemed to trust my help because of a previous procedure we had done together. That time, he thought he was finished, even though I could still feel something inside the uterus. However, in order to placate me, he reached back in, only to pull out the baby's bottom. Had he stopped without checking further, we would have had a major complication on our hands at that time.

"Take another deep breath, Sheryl. Really deep. Fill your lungs. Now hold it for a few seconds. Slowly release your breath. It is just about over. Are you doing okay?" I concentrated my attention back on my patient.

Sheryl nodded her head.

Dr. Johnson had gotten the baby's body out by now and was searching for the head. The head, the largest part of the baby's body, is usually the last part to come out. The head must be located and crushed before it can pass through the cervix. Usually the head is deflated first by suctioning out the brain and all the other contents.

"Suction, please," Harvey said, but Leslie was ahead of him; the suction was in his hand almost before he asked. A good nurse/assistant anticipates what the abortionist will ask for next and is ready. She turned on the machine, and the roar of the motor startled Sheryl.

"Be still, Sheryl," I urged. That is the sound of normal procedure equipment. Take another deep breath. It is almost over."

Dr. Johnson handed the suction tube back to Leslie and once again used forceps to probe for the head. I saw the muscles of his

---

" 'Be still, Sheryl,' I urged. 'That is the sound of normal procedure equipment. Take another deep breath. It is almost over.' "

---

right arm tighten and knew what that meant: Dr. Johnson had located the head and was crushing it. Harvey used to joke about his getting tennis elbow from this technique, and his right arm was actually slightly larger than his left.

"Take a real deep breath, Sheryl, right now." I tried to ready Sheryl for the pain of the crushed head passing through the cervix.

Sheryl gasped and turned pale, but she did not utter a word, not a word.

"Suction one last time." Harvey spoke first to Leslie, then to his patient. "It's all over, Sheryl. Everything is fine."

Harvey stood up and with bloody gloves picked up the tray containing the baby's torn body. Leslie opened the door, and Harvey went to Central Supply while I pulled Sheryl up on the table.

"Put your feet down, and push back." I directed. "We'll get you dressed and into the recovery room. In a few minutes you can have a Coke."

Leslie entered and handed me a sanitary pad which I helped Sheryl place between her legs. She then helped Sheryl dress while I went to talk to Harvey.

He was in Central Supply, checking to be certain he had removed all the parts. He reconstructed the baby's body on an underpad while he talked.

"Fredi is waiting for me at Ninfa's," he said. "We are going to have Mexican food and margaritas tonight."

I didn't ask questions. It was unusual for Harvey to drink, but he had been doing it more and more lately. At that time, I blamed his girlfriend, Fredi, but now I ask myself if he might have had another reason. I wonder now if Harvey was struggling with our recent decision to do second and third trimester abortions.

I must admit we started doing late-term abortions at my insistence. You see, we needed to expand our services, and the only way to do it was to do the ones we called "bigger" abortions. I also wanted to utilize the building all week; after all, the rent was paid for all seven days. Why not use the clinic all seven days?

"You really look nice tonight, Carol. Are you dressed up for anything special?" Harvey had accounted for all the parts and now started to put the baby's body down the disposal. Sensing his next step, I turned on the disposal, so he wouldn't get blood on the switch.

"Yes, I have a date tonight with Kerry," I replied. "I hope we can get out of here early. We are going dancing." I turned the disposal off. We worked so well together; our camaraderie was comfortable and rather reassuring. "I'll see you before you leave. I'm going back to my office to finish some paper work." We parted easily, eager to finish our work for the evening.

Since Sheryl was the last big one for the night, I could get some work done without worrying about the other procedures. Leslie, Becky, and Connie all had plans for the evening, too, so they would move Harvey very quickly from room to room, finishing the rest of the abortions.

A Major Complication

So I had been in my office figuring the day's profit when Harvey had interrupted me. The amount of blood in the room scared me, and suddenly, we were not looking so top-notch. We faced our first major complication.

Medically, Harvey was in control of the situation; emotionally, he was shaken. He and the nurses continued to massage Sheryl's uterus until the bleeding slowed down. However, he did not put her back on the table for another pelvic examination to determine the source of the bleeding.

"I didn't ask questions. It was unusual for Harvey to drink, but he had been doing it more and more lately. . . . I wonder now if Harvey was struggling with our recent decision to do second and third trimester abortions."

Harvey and I stepped outside the recovery room to talk. By now we both calmed down. He looked at his watch, and then said, "I'm leaving to go meet Fredi at Ninfa's. I'll call back, and I have my beeper on if you need me. Sheryl will be fine. Just be sure to keep massaging her uterus until the bleeding stops. When her vital signs are stable, dismiss her. I'll see you in the morning." His big hand squeezed my arm one last time, and I returned to Sheryl's side.

One LPN continued to massage her uterus, and the bleeding diminished considerably. We moved Sheryl to another bed and cleaned the room as best we could. When everything was presentable, I took Bob back to be with Sheryl.

Bob hovered over her; he seemed to really care, perhaps even love Sheryl. I wondered why they weren't married. They didn't seem to have the same scars Harvey and I and the other divorced people in my world did. Somehow there was an innocence about Sheryl and Bob's relationship, no anger at the world.

For a moment I felt slightly jealous of Sheryl's beauty and their relationship. They had no heavy goals, no driving force to get rich; their lives seemed simple. Not like mine—I was alone, pushing to be rich.

Yes, they had something I wanted more than anything else—each other.

In many ways Sheryl and Bob were just an average couple having an abortion. They were having financial problems and believed abortion was the simplest way to go on with their lives with one less liability. This abortion would give them a financial reprieve. Soon they could get married and live happily ever after.

By now the front office personnel balanced the books and closed for the evening while I stayed with Sheryl and Bob. The telephones were transferred to the answering service, eliminating disturbances.

About nine o'clock we ran out of sanitary napkins. I rushed out of the clinic and called my date. "Kerry, we've had a complication at the clinic. I have to go back and make sure the patient is okay. I'm sorry."

"That's okay, Carol," he responded.

"Can you come by the house later?"

"About what time?"

"Not before eleven thirty."

"Sure."

"I'll see you later, then. I have to go." I picked up some sanitary napkins and hurried back to the clinic.

By the time I returned, Sheryl's blood pressure had dropped very low. I paged Harvey. He called, but when the answering service picked up, he just assumed everything was all right.

Sheryl and Bob were unconcerned about her low blood pressure. She pleaded with me, "Can't I go home now? My blood pressure is always low. Don't be concerned about it. I don't feel good, but I know I will feel better after I'm in my own bed. Please let me go home now."

Her blood pressure was low, but stable, and the bleeding was under control. So about eleven o'clock, I conditionally released her. "Sheryl, you can go home, but if anything—I mean anything—unusual happens, call our emergency number at once."

"We will call if anything happens," they assured me.

Connie wheeled Sheryl to the front door in a wheelchair while Bob went to get the car. I walked out with her. "Sheryl, call me in the morning to let me know how you are doing. Call us tonight if you even have the slightest question. Please do not hesitate to call us for anything. No question is foolish when it involves your health."

Relieved to be leaving, Sheryl and Bob promised they would call even if it seemed like a minor problem. "Thanks for everything, Carol. We promise to call if we need you tonight. And I'll call you when I wake up in the morning." I closed their car door and they drove away.

"'She is only thirty-two years old. She can't die. She was supposed to call if there was a problem.' I searched for something that would change what he was telling me. It just couldn't be true."

We watched them leave.

"She didn't look good, Carol," Connie commented.

"I know, Connie, but what else could we do?" I shook my head, then walked back into the clinic to lock up.

I rushed home to meet Kerry. The doorbell rang, and I forgot about Sheryl.

I was ironing my uniform when the telephone rang Saturday morning at 6:00 A.M. Harvey's voice was subdued. "Sheryl Mason is dead."

I felt the color draining from my face.

"No, Harvey, she is not dead. She can't be."

"Carol, I'm here with her at Presbyterian. She is on life support right now. We're forcing fluids, but she is going to die. It's only a matter of time. This one is dead."

"She is only thirty-two years old. She can't die. She was supposed to call if there was a problem." I searched for something that would change what he was telling me. It just couldn't be true.

Harvey's voice sounded tired. "Her boyfriend called me this morning about three o'clock and told me Sheryl was cramping heavily. I told him to put her in a tub of hot water. He called back a little later to say that she was unconscious. I told him to get her to Presbyterian Hospital Emergency Room at once, and I would meet them there.

When she arrived, fluids and a blood transfusion were started. She is on life support now, but she is gone."

"Harvey, she can't be dead. She is going to be all right." I was arguing with myself more than Harvey.

"I've seen this before, Carol. She is dead."

This could not be happening. We were helping women—we couldn't kill a woman!

Silence replaced conversation.

Finally I asked, "What are we going to do?"

Harvey was clear on that. "We are going to go on as if nothing happened. Patients are scheduled at 8:00 A.M. How many do we have on the schedule this morning?"

"Twenty-eight." I forced my mind to focus.

"When you get in, find Sheryl's chart. Keep it in your office so no one else can see it. I'll be late. It will be after nine before I can get there. I'll keep you informed. Be ready when I get there. I'll see you later," Harvey said.

"I've got to pick up groceries for lunch at the clinic, but I'll get there as quickly as I can. Good-bye."

Emptiness. A void engulfed me I cannot describe.

Like a robot, I finished ironing, dressed, stopped by the grocery store, and then arrived at the clinic. Connie greeted me in the hall, "I tried to call you at home last night, but your answering machine picked up. I wondered about Sheryl, if we should have released her. Did you hear from her?"

"No," I answered. It was the truth. I didn't hear from Sheryl; Harvey did.

"She must be all right then, or we would have heard," Connie continued.

"Yes," I lied.

Later, as Fredi, Harvey's girlfriend and our bookkeeper, and I sat in the front office, I found myself staring out the window. Connie walked in and said, "Carol, you look like you lost your best friend."

"I'm fine, Connie."

Fredi walked over and hugged me. We had never been friends, so I must have really looked terrible if Fredi hugged me!

I went through the motions of getting the patients ready for the doctor, thankful for the good help we had. I couldn't concentrate.

Finally, Harvey came in the back door. I rushed to him for protection. Yes, he looked terrible, but I desperately needed to be held, as if that would make things better. He held me for a minute, sensing the urgency in me and then said, "How many are in so far?"

"Twenty, and we are ready to go."

"Let's do it. You know I have to train John Miller today."

"We will not be able to go on. The clinic's reputation is ruined. Even if we did not close the clinic, no one will come to us for an abortion. We just killed a woman!"

"Yes, I know. He is already here." Dr. John Miller was a psychiatrist who had done abortions for another chain of clinics. But now Harvey had to teach him our way—the right way. How ironic! Today of all days!

"Let's show him how it is done." Harvey moved quickly down the hall, all business.

We entered the first room. I wasn't ready to leave Harvey yet. I needed him, his strength—something—anything—to go on just today. He was cold, offering me nothing to hang on to.

I checked the front waiting room to see how many were in. I wondered if Harvey would work so fast that I would have to worry about keeping the instruments "turned," or cleaned and resterilized after each procedure and then cool enough for him to work with on the next abortion. Today he was uncharacteristically slow training Dr. Miller. Thank heaven. I was slow, too.

Throughout the morning my mind was silently screaming. *What if I had died and left my two children without their mother? Sheryl's children don't have a mother; they are orphans.*

How am I going to make a living, now if the clinic closes? I've put all of my energy into the abortion business for the past three years, and it is just now beginning to pay off.

I have finally reached the point that I don't have to worry about money to send my children to college. Joe Bob is graduating this May. I promised Kelly and Joe Bob if they would work in high school, they would not have to work in college.

I have worked all my life to be able to afford to give them the things their father would have given them if I had stayed married to him. Now what am I going to do? I have all my eggs in this basket, and it is falling apart. There is no time for me to establish myself in another profession before Joe Bob goes to college.

We will not be able to go on. The clinic's reputation is ruined. Even if we did not close the clinic, no one will come to us for an abortion. We just killed a woman!

Reason took hold. I forced myself to think rationally. *Concentrate on today. Get through this day and deal with the future later.*

I had lunch with Dr. Miller, our new abortionist. I wanted desperately to tell him, "I need help. A woman died this morning from an abortion we did here last night." But I couldn't.

I just listened to a doctor who thought he knew it all. "Every woman deserves the right to an abortion. I grew up with Baptist parents, and they do not believe in abortion. I have had to fight for my beliefs and the rights of women." The champion of women.

Silently I thought, *If you only knew the truth. This clinic will close. We can't talk to you about a job. You are wasting your time here today.*

Maybe We'll Be All Right

Somehow I got through the day and rushed home. The phone was ringing. It was Harvey. "Are you all right?"

"I'm as good as I can be under the circumstances. How are you?" It was good to hear his voice.

"I'm fine. Fredi and I were just talking; at least we have each other to hold on to, but you have no one. How about you coming over tomorrow afternoon about two o'clock to talk some of this out?" he asked.

"Yes, I'll be there. But can you tell me more about what happened last night?"

"What do you want to know?"

"What did she die from?"

"I really don't know the cause of death right now. I have talked to the coroner's office, and he will let me know as soon as he does the autopsy."

"How is her family holding up?"

"Bob is in a state of shock. His parents were with him at the hospital. He asked me to call Sheryl's mother in Nebraska. She was upset—even angry. When she asked why Sheryl died, I told her it was from female complications. She said, 'She died from an abortion, didn't she?'"

"What did you say?" I was frightened.

Harvey answered quickly, "I told her 'No.' Bob didn't want her family to know about the abortion, and that may be what saves us. We have to support Bob now so he will help us. If we can keep this out of the newspapers, I think we will be all right.

"No one at Presbyterian will report us, with one exception. One of the nurses has a brother-in-law who is a doctor practicing in Garland. I talked to her, and I hope she doesn't tell him. If she doesn't tell him, I don't think it will get to Garland. And if it doesn't get to Garland, my

---

" 'Bob didn't want her family to know about the abortion, and that may be what saves us. We have to support Bob now so he will help us. If we can keep this out of the newspapers, I think we will be all right.' "

---

private practice won't be affected. Then if it doesn't get in the papers, it won't affect the clinic." Harvey had thought it all out.

"All we have to be concerned about is the cause of death. If that is all right, we will be okay," he said.

"Do you mean we will be able to keep the clinic open?" I asked in astonishment.

"Yes, of course. We can go on."

I couldn't believe my ears. He said what I wanted to hear with all my heart. Was it possible that we could kill a woman and go on as if nothing ever happened? Was the industry that unregulated? Could Harvey Johnson get other doctors to cover for him, even in a woman's death? Maybe my life was not over; I would be able to send my kids to college, after all. Perhaps, just perhaps, there was hope for going on, hope I did not expect.

After my conversation with Harvey, my children Kelly and Joe Bob joined me in our living room. Kelly worked part-time as a receptionist/counselor at the clinic and had worked Friday evening when Sheryl came in. She already knew we had a problem with the procedure. "Kelly, do you remember Sheryl Mason, the big one last night we had trouble with?"

"Yes."

"Well, she died early this morning. Right now we don't know why. We don't have the autopsy results, but she probably died from the abortion. We have to keep this confidential. I need you both now. I don't know what is going to happen." I was honest with them.

"What do you think will happen, Mom?" Kelly asked.

"I don't really know, baby. I hope there isn't anything in either of the Sunday papers. If we can keep it out of the newspapers, we may be all right. I'm going to meet with Harvey tomorrow afternoon and talk about everything. I'm not sure we can go on. Hug me. I love you. Thanks for standing by me."

The three of us hugged. I was so glad I could discuss the situation with my children. "They will stand by me," I reasoned.

Kerry and I had another date Saturday night. As we sat on the hearth before the fireplace, I said, "Kerry, I just don't know what happened. We're supposed to be helping women, but this one died."

"Carol, you know people die from all sorts of unexpected things. Think about it. As a policeman, I see people die all the time. Women still die from childbirth occasionally. Don't worry about it. Think of all the women you have helped. Everything will be all right," he said reassuringly.

"Hold me, Kerry."

"Everything will be all right. You will see." Oh, how I wanted to believe him.

Sunday afternoon at two o'clock, I was on Harvey's doorstep eager to finish our discussion.

"I couldn't believe my ears. He said what I wanted to hear with all my heart. Was it possible that we could kill a woman and go on as if nothing ever happened? Was the industry that unregulated?"

"What has happened since we talked?" I asked when he answered the door.

"I talked with the coroner's office. He has not done the autopsy yet, but he'll call as soon as he determines the cause of death. I told him that we would send our medical records for his chart. We have to change the blood pressure readings on Sheryl's chart to normal. Fredi and I have discussed it and think it will be easy to cut along the lines, recopy it, and no one will ever know the difference. Can you go over to the clinic with us this afternoon to do that?"

"No, I have other plans," I lied. I was pretty desperate, but I was not willing to falsify medical records. "How is Bob today?"

"He's fine. He is going to Nebraska for the funeral and will be back later in the week. If he doesn't tell Sheryl's mother, I think we will get by without a lawsuit. Bob feels pretty guilty right now. He blames himself for Sheryl's pregnancy and for bringing her in for the abortion. We can use that. We just have to be there for him for a while. His mother is with him, which will help us, I believe. She keeps telling him he did the best he could." Harvey leaned back in his chair.

"What did we do wrong, Harvey?" I asked.

Harvey shrugged his shoulders, then leaned forward. "Carol, if you deliver so many babies, a mother will die. Women still die in childbirth. We've been very lucky. We've never had a major complication before. Our number was just up. We can't worry about it. We have to go on. If we can make it without it getting in the newspapers, we will be all right."

"What about the cause of death?"

"That could be a concern; however, the coroner knows me by reputation. He will call me Monday or Tuesday with the cause of death. I'll call you as soon as I know anything."

"Could they file charges?" I had to know.

He answered quickly, "Don't even think about it. Check the newspapers in the morning. I'll call you between surgery cases and see if anything comes up. Carol, don't worry. Everything is going to be all right."

I left Harvey's house, still in shock and still unconvinced everything was going to be all right. Sheryl Mason was alive two days ago. Now she lay dead and cold because I sold her on having the abortion and showed her how to get the extra money she needed. I did not want my twenty-five-dollar commission for this one.

Monday morning there was no mention in the newspapers of the abortion-related death, not even the dignity of an obituary.

Harvey's phone call greeted me as I entered my office. "Fredi and I went to the clinic and took care of the chart. We brought the blood pressure up to normal. It really looked good. We sent a copy of the records to the coroner's office. The changed chart is in the center drawer of your desk. Hide it somewhere so no one can find it," he instructed.

"Okay, I'll put it under the files in my top, right-hand drawer," I said. Under the files—and under the Bible.

Tuesday morning, still nothing in the papers.

Harvey telephoned. "The coroner called with the results of the autopsy. The cause of death was hemorrhage from cervical tear."

I went numb.

Immediately, I thought, *We could have saved Sheryl's life! We only needed to suture her cervix. We had everything we needed in the clinic to save Sheryl's life—with one exception—a doctor willing to take the time to reexamine his patient to determine the cause of the bleeding. He had a date, and the margaritas were waiting.*

Sheryl Mason's death was unneccesary. Even a first year intern would have checked for the source of profuse bleeding, but Dr. Johnson diagnosed without a physical examination—wrongly.

This doctor I had trusted with my life is not trustworthy. Yes, it was only one mistake, but a deadly one. I purposed to watch him in the future.

I regained my composure and continued the conversation.

"Harvey, what is going to happen?"

"Nothing, I hope. You might get out your prayer rug on this one."

Nothing in the paper Wednesday. So far, so good.

Papers clear Thursday.

"I think we are okay, Carol."

Okay! But, we were still not the Neiman-Marcus of the abortion industry.

I wondered now if such a thing were even possible.

2

COMPLICATIONS AND THE COVER-UP

Jenni was beautiful—tall, model thin with brunette hair. At twenty-one, she loved attention and knew how to get it with her body. That was obvious the moment she danced into the clinic on a Wednesday afternoon in May 1982.

I took her back to the examining room for her pregnancy to be sized by a doctor before she paid for the procedure. "Take your clothes off from the waist down, and have a seat on the edge of the table," I directed.

Unashamedly, she raised her multi-colored sundress to reveal she was wearing no underwear, hopped upon the table, and lay down. I draped her with a sheet, opened the door, and told Harvey, "We're ready."

Harvey came in, patted Jenni on the leg, and said with a reassuring smile, "Hi, baby. We're just going to check you to see how big you are. It won't hurt."

I handed him the glove, squeezed the K-Y jelly out for him, and watched him proceed with the examination.

"It looks like you're twenty-two weeks along," Harvey commented as he finished the examination. "The pelvis is normal, so the procedure can be done without any problem. The fee will be seven hundred and fifty dollars if we put you to sleep, and it will be easier on you if we do. Do you have the money?" Harvey removed and tossed the glove into the wastebasket.

"Yes, and I have enough to be put to sleep—seven hundred and fifty dollars. Connie said it is much easier if I can afford to be put to sleep. I hate pain. I have a fifteen-month-old daughter living in Nevada with my parents. Her birth nearly killed me. I just can't stand pain." Jenni spoke quickly, her voice sounding young and carefree.

"Yes, Jenni, it is much easier on you. I will be in the room with you. Everything is going to be all right," I assured her.

Harvey patted her on the leg again. "I'll see you later," he promised.

"Let's go up to the front desk, so you can pay," I continued. "Have a seat there, and you will be called soon."

I went to check out the operating room to be sure it was ready. The instruments had to be prepared—large dilators, sterilized yet cool enough; a #16 cannula, a tube to insert into the uterus; and Bierhoff forceps, to remove the pieces of the unwanted baby.

It took a little while for us to get everything ready. I checked on Jenni several times, to make sure she was okay, that she wasn't getting too nervous. "Where do you work, Jenni?" I asked conversationally.

"I work at a local Ford dealership," she answered as she flipped through the pages of an old magazine.

"And where do you live?"

"With my grandparents."

Without her telling me, I knew she had run away from some problems back in Nevada. We discussed her leaving her daughter with her parents. She did not seem to miss her, although she talked about her; it was as though the child was a part of her history, not a part of her. She talked to me about several of her lovers, but never about the father of her child.

"Jenni, everything is ready now," I called. "This won't take long."

"I don't have on any underwear," she announced as she danced into the room acting very vivacious and pulled up her dress for all to see. "Let's get it over with." She jumped upon the table and waited for us to give her a sheet.

The other nurses watched with amazement. I had seen similar acts before; she was scared!

After the anesthetist put her to sleep, I placed my hand on Jenni's abdomen. I felt movement, one of the only babies I can ever remember feeling move inside the mother during an abortion.

Harvey proceeded as normal: He cleaned off the cervix with Beta- dine, dilated the cervix, and suctioned briefly to break the bag of am- niotic fluid surrounding the baby. The baby did not move again after

---

"After the anesthetist put her to sleep, I placed my hand on Jenni's abdomen. I felt movement, one of the only babies I can ever remember feeling move inside the mother during an abortion."

---

he finished suctioning. The next step required Harvey to crush the baby inside Jenni's uterus and then remove the baby piece by piece using Bierhoff forceps.

The first time Harvey reached in, he pulled out placenta. The sec- ond time he reached in, he pulled out the lining around the colon. Immediately, I saw the shock on Harvey's face. I really couldn't see what he had pulled out, but the look on his face told me it was seri- ous.

His face was ashen as he spoke, "It's over. I pulled out omentum." He frantically tried to push the bowel back into the uterine cavity, but to no avail. "We have to take her to the hospital, Carol."

"It can't be over. The baby is not even dead. It is still intact. We can't take this woman to the hospital with a live baby still whole inside! It can't be over. Surely, there is something we can do." I knew my voice sounded hysterical, but I couldn't believe this was happening.

"No, Carol, there isn't." Harvey pushed back from the table. He leaned toward me looking very dejected and said quietly, "We have to take her to the hospital."

Harvey knew he had blown this one badly. He was scared to death, and it showed.

"Where will we take her?" I asked. Garland Memorial was out of the question; lately we had taken so many botched abortions there. Dr. George was now checking every one of Harvey's charts trying to catch one of his botched abortions.

Harvey stood up, picked up the pan for the body parts, and walked out of the room. I followed him into Central Supply where he slowly removed his gloves. I silently waited for his decision.

As we headed to his office, he said, "I am going to call Lloyd. He will help us."

Harvey always seemed to have a list of people who owed him a favor. He called them in at times like this.

My mind raced ahead with what I knew of the medical procedures. I thought to myself, *If her bowel has come out through the vagina, the uterus has to be perforated. With the baby alive and a bowel resection needed, this will be quite a surgical procedure requiring several specialists. Harvey cannot do the bowel resection. And what will they do with the baby's body in a hospital surrounding?*

I had things to do. I hurried to the front desk to tell the staff I would be gone for a while. Something in me wanted my daughter Kelly to go with me to the hospital. I needed someone to go with me, but the twisted truth is I wanted her to experience the ordeal of taking a woman to the hospital. She had to be trained and tested.

"Kelly, we have a problem in the back. I have to take someone to the hospital, and I want you to go with me to hold the IV bag. Please take my keys and move my car to the back door of the recovery room, and be ready to go," I directed quietly. Of course, we had to use my car; an ambulance is terrible publicity in front of an abortion clinic.

"What's wrong?" I could see Kelly trying to read the answer in my expression.

"Jenni has a problem. I really don't know all the details, but we have to go. Come on. Move the car, baby," I pleaded.

By now the supervisors and employees were becoming accustomed to our frantic moving of a botched abortion to a hospital. They ignored us as best they could.

I checked again with Harvey to be sure everything was set with Lloyd. "What are we going to do?" I asked.

"Let me think about this . . ." he hesitated.

Harvey made some more telephone calls and then finally said, "Move her to your car, and take her to Garland Humana Hospital. For some time they have been trying to get me to use the hospital. Take her to the emergency room entrance, and Dr. Lloyd will meet you there."

"By now the supervisors and employees were becoming accustomed to our frantic moving of a botched abortion to a hospital. They ignored us as best they could."

He dropped his hand on my shoulder and looked directly into my eyes. "Do not tell anyone what happened. I told Lloyd that I was taking care of another doctor's problems. Don't even mention my name," he emphasized.

"Don't worry. I won't." I hurried to the back. "Leslie, put Jenni into my car."

Leslie had helped me move women before, so she knew exactly what to do. She moved the wheelchair next to the operating table and locked the brakes in place.

"Jenni, can you sit up? We are going to move you now."

"Is is over, Carol?" she mumbled.

"Jenni, there has been a problem. We have to move you to the hospital for additional surgery. We can't do it in the clinic." I was calm and matter-of-fact.

"I can't go to the hospital. I don't have any insurance."

"We have to take you to the hospital. You must be treated. We can't stop now."

"What about money?"

"Jenni, I can't answer you. Help us get you in the wheelchair and out to the car. Is there anyone you would like for us to call to have with you?"

"Yes. Call Sharon. Tell her what has happened. See if she can come to the hospital." As we wheeled Jenni out the back door, she asked, "Are you taking me to the hospital in a car?" She sounded confused.

I took over. "Yes, and Kelly is going to ride with us. Leslie and I will lift your arms while you stand up. I hope it doesn't hurt, but we have to move you to the car."

Kelly held the IV, her eyes wide open in shock. She had never seen anything like this before. I had protected her from a few things, it seems, but very few actually.

I started giving orders. "Jenni, I'm going to recline that seat as far as I can. Kelly, I'll hold the IV while you go around and get in the back seat." Obediently, Kelly hurried around the car and got in. "Here, Kelly, hold it up over her head. Keep it running."

Jenni wanted to know, "Which hospital are we going to?"

"Garland Humana."

"I've never heard of it. Where is it?"

"It's a good hospital in Garland. My son was operated on there."

"I hurt. Where is Dr. Johnson?"

"He will meet us at the hospital."

"How much longer? I can't stand the pain. Hurry. Why is it taking so long?"

"We are going to a good hospital with the best doctors. It is in Garland and takes a little longer to get to. You will be well cared for. It will be a few more minutes." I tried to keep as calm as possible, much calmer than I actually felt.

Jenni screamed in pain all the way to the hospital. Every time I looked at my daughter, I wished I had not brought her. Kelly was definitely shocked, nervous, and very scared.

I realized that for some time I had wanted Kelly's validation of abortion and what I was doing, but she was noncommittal. I felt she was acting pro-choice just to win my approval.

If Kelly was going to be good in the business, she had to learn it all. I had recently forced her to watch a big procedure, her first one. She did not like it at all; instead, she kept trying to get out of the room. I insisted she stay throughout the entire procedure, however, and afterward she was very upset and refused to talk to me about it.

Now this plan was backfiring on me, too. Kelly seemed to be putting herself in Jenni's place; she did not seem confident about what her mother was doing at all.

Riding to the hospital, I too began to identify Jenni with Kelly. I kept thinking, *This could be Kelly in trouble. How would I feel if this were happening to my daughter?* I didn't like the answer.

"Kelly, how is that IV doing?" Back to reality.

"I realized that for some time I had wanted Kelly's validation of abortion and what I was doing, but she was noncommittal. I felt she was acting pro-choice just to win my approval."

"It's still running."

"Good. Thank you, baby, for helping me." I concentrated on driving and was very relieved when the entrance to Garland Humana appeared ahead.

"Jenni, here we are. Let's find the Emergency Room. There it is." I pulled into the parking spot reserved for ambulances and jumped out of the car. "Kelly, I'm going in to get a stretcher. Stay in the car."

A nurse stepped out into the hall as I entered. "May I help you?"

"Yes. I have an emergency admission in the car. We need a gurney."

"Does the patient have a doctor?" she asked as she rounded a corner to get the stretcher.

"Yes, Dr. Lloyd is supposed to meet us here."

An angry Dr. Lloyd came out of nowhere. "Carol, come here. I'll tell you I am not covering for Harvey this time!"

The nurse returned with a gurney and Jenni was quickly moved to a room. Suddenly the nurse yelled, "There is pitocin in the IV. Is she an abortion patient?"

Jenni screamed, "Where is Dr. Johnson?"

"Did Harvey do her abortion, Carol?" Dr. Lloyd questioned.

Before I could answer, Harvey walked up, slipped his arm over
Dr. Lloyd's shoulder, and the two walked toward Jenni's emergency
room. Dr. Lloyd was arguing, but I could tell Harvey would win him
over, as usual.

I hugged Kelly and sent her back to the clinic in my car.

We've Got to Protect the Clinic

Harvey reappeared briefly to direct me to the doctor's lounge to wait
while Jenni's surgery was performed. I went through hell in that room
while I waited on Harvey. Painful as it was to admit, I knew we were
not helping women have safe abortions; instead, we were maiming and
even killing them. How had this happened?

Over the past five months, we had experienced too many botched
abortions. We were maiming at least one woman a month; one out of
every five hundred had to have major surgery; we had even had one
death.

One of our patients, Lisa, was a twenty-one-year-old single mother
with a two year old, and twenty weeks pregnant.

Dr. Burney did her abortion which proceeded uneventfully until
he said to me, "Carol, she has a polyp on the back of her uterus, and I
think I will pull it off."

He pulled and pulled, but he couldn't get it off.

He called Dr. Johnson from across the hall where he was doing
abortions. "I think this woman has a polyp on the back of her uterus. I
have tried to pull it off, but I can't. Could you help me?"

"Yes," Harvey replied.

Both doctors pulled and pulled, but they could not get the polyp out.

They finally gave up and sent Lisa to recovery. I believe they
pulled Lisa's uterus wrong side out.

Her vital signs became erratic. About four o'clock, Dr. Johnson
called me to the recovery room with that now familiar sick look on his
face. "Carol, Lisa is hemorrhaging. We are going to have to take her to
the hospital. I have called Garland Memorial. We have a room scheduled for surgery at five o'clock. Pull your car around, and I will drive."

On the way, Harvey was angry that he was having to cover for Dr.
Burney's botched abortion, but we both knew we had to protect the
clinic.

What will happen to Lisa, I wondered. *She will have a hysterectomy now, so she cannot have any more children. She'll miss at least a month's work. How will she and her two year old live?*

When I saw Lisa six weeks later, she had changed from a thin, beautiful woman to an overweight woman whose eyes had lost their sparkle.

"Painful as it was to admit, I knew we were not helping women have safe abortions; instead, we were maiming and even killing them. How had this happened?"

I remembered another patient, a twenty-seven year old from a small town in Arkansas who came in with her parents. She thought she was about twenty weeks pregnant at the time. Dr. Johnson, who examined her, determined he could do the abortion.

Using local anesthesia and a small dosage of Valium, Harvey started the abortion, but he discovered the baby was too far advanced. Its muscle structure was so strong that the baby would not come apart. After almost an hour on the table with six nurses holding and pulling the woman away from Harvey, the baby's body finally separated from the head and came out. Then Harvey worked and worked to crush the head and remove it. It was a very long ordeal for both the woman and Dr. Johnson.

One of the nurses, Becky, who never reacted to anything, rolled her eyes back in her head; I thought for a minute she was going to faint.

After the procedure, Harvey measured the baby's foot. He tried to hide the measurement from me, but I saw it—the baby was about thirty-two weeks, probably old enough to survive outside its mother.

The baby's body was too large to go down the garbage disposal, so Harvey suggested I take it to our competitor's trash receptacle so that if it were found, it would be in his trash—not ours. Dutifully, I wrapped the baby in a paper drape, put it in a brown paper sack, and planted it in the other clinic's trash that night.

Harvey had to hospitalize the woman. His dismissal diagnosis: some sort of heart problem.

The more I reflected on our botched abortions, the sicker I felt inside because of all the pain we were causing. All of our doctors were botching abortions, but Harvey—my beloved, trusted Harvey—was the doctor with most of the major complications. Yes, he did perform most of the big abortions. However, the other doctors handled these cases without the complication rate Harvey had.

I asked myself, *What am I going to do about Harvey botching so many abortions?* Harvey was very important as the medical director of the clinic. He was the one we needed when a major complication occurred; his help was vital in all facets of the cover-up. I also needed Harvey personally; he was such an important part of my support system. *What am I going to do? And how can I keep my plans a secret from Harvey as long as Fredi is in the clinic?*

I forced my attention to the problem at hand. *I just know the legal forces are going to come out of the woodwork on Jenni's botched abortion. We have really blown it. We are going to be sued for everything we are worth and more—and we deserve it!*

Get hold of yourself, Carol. Go check to see if Jenni's friend is here. Find out if she is going to be friend or foe.

I left the doctor's lounge and found the surgery waiting room. A pretty blonde woman in her early twenties was nervously sitting on the edge of the couch. "Are you a friend of Jenni Richardson?" I asked.

"Yes. Who are you?" I motioned for her to stay seated and I joined her on the adjacent couch.

"I'm Carol Everett from the clinic. Jenni is in surgery and will be out soon, but she will be in the recovery room for a time before she is taken to her room. How well do you know Jenni?" I kept my voice level.

"I met her at work, and we have been out together several times," she responded.

"Are you close to her?"

"Are you asking me if I knew why she was at the clinc?"

"Yes, I suppose I am," I admitted.

"I know she was having an abortion today, and she had mixed emotions about it. She was scared but happy that it was about to be over," she said.

"Do you know her family?"

"Jenni lives with her grandparents in Plano, and her parents live in Nevada. I don't think she gets along with her grandparents. They have

---

"The baby's body was too large to go down the garbage disposal, so Harvey suggested I take it to our competitor's trash receptacle so that if it were found, it would be in his trash—not ours."

---

some old fashioned ideas. I have never met them, but I did telephone them a little while ago."

"Are they going to come to the hospital?" I asked.

"Not today."

"Did they know Jenni was having an abortion today?"

"I'm not sure. They do wonder what really happened, but I don't know what Jenni told them," she answered honestly. "How long do you think it will be before I can see Jenni?"

"I really don't know, but it will be at least a couple of hours before she is back in her room, and she will be groggy then. Are you going to wait?"

"I don't think so. I will call back later tonight." The young woman stood up.

"I'll talk to Jenni tomorrow. I'll tell her that you were here. What is your name?" I asked.

"Sharon Clark." She extended her hand to me, which I clasped with relief.

"It was nice to meet you, Sharon. I'll see you later."

"Good-bye." And she headed toward the elevator.

Looks like we are safe with her friend and family.

I went back to the doctor's lounge. The waiting seemed like an eternity. A lot was on my mind—my daughter Kelly, Jenni, Harvey, botched abortions, the business. Finally, Harvey appeared in the door looking rather haggard. "Carol, we don't have a problem now."

I couldn't believe my ears. How could we not have a problem? We had really blown it on Jenni. We could be facing a major lawsuit here.

"I'll tell you about it later. Let's get out of here. Did any of her family come?"

"Only a friend, and she left."

As we walked out of the hospital, I realized I didn't feel the usual pride walking with Harvey.

The Perfect-Harvey Balloon
Springs a Leak

We drove to Harvey's house to pick up Fredi before they could drive me home. On the way, he commented, "I have to talk to Dale, the pathologist, in the morning to work out a few things, but I'm sure the abdominal pregnancy was the cause of the colostomy."

I kept my mouth shut, but I certainly talked to myself. *Abdominal pregnancy? That was not an abdominal pregnancy. You examined her before the abortion. You would surely have picked that up in a physical examination of a five-and-a-half-month pregnancy. No competent doctor would have started an abortion on a woman with an advanced abdominal pregnancy.*

So, this is how you choose to cover up this one. Have all of the doctors who operated with you on this agreed to write up the records as an abdominal pregnancy? Will the pathologist write up his records the same way? You are going to lie to keep us from being sued, and all of your doctor buddies are going to support your lie.

I couldn't stand it any longer. "Harvey, we have just ruined a young woman's body and her life. Jenni has had a colostomy. What if she were one of our children? What if she were Kelly, or even your daughter Jan? How would we feel?"

Harvey ignored my question. He calmly continued with the details of the surgical procedure. "I wrapped the baby in a disposable sheet and threw it with the trash in the surgical suite. No one will think it anything other than a disposable sheet."

You really covered your tracks, I thought.

"Lloyd thinks he can resection the colostomy in about six months, so the colostomy will not be permanent," he told me.

"Thank heaven for that. Jenni is such a beautiful woman."

"The hospital administrator at Humana has been trying to get me to move my surgery over there for some time. I'll go see him in the morning. Maybe I can get him to write off the bill," Harvey added.

"Do you think he will?" I asked.

"They need the business, and I'll do a few cases over there."

We pulled up to Harvey's house and Fredi joined us. "How did it go?" she asked when she got into the car.

"Everything is all right," he answered. "She had to have a colostomy, but Dr. Smith checked her urinary tract, and everything is okay. It was an abdominal pregnancy."

I screamed inside. *He is lying to us—Fredi and me—the people who protect him from everything and anything. He can't even tell us the truth—that he blew it.* I couldn't stand it. I had to let Harvey know I knew he was lying. My hand had been on that baby, and it was perfectly in place inside her uterus.

"Are you going to change the records at the clinic to reflect abdominal pregnancy?" I asked manipulatively.

"Do you mean it wasn't an abdominal pregnancy?" Fredi shot back, looking first at me, then at Harvey.

On the hot seat, Harvey did not directly answer, but said tersely to me, "You will need to pull that chart and keep it in your office. I will make some notes about the surgical procedure the next time I am in the clinic."

"Harvey, what happened?" Fredi demanded.

"Everything is all right, Fredi. Jenni had an abdominal pregnancy; that's all. It's always critical when we hospitalize one from the clinic, you know that."

As we turned the corner off Marsh Lane to take me home, I knew what I had to do about Harvey and his botched abortions. In the future I would make sure Harvey Johnson did not do any abortion over fifteen weeks, which clearly seemed to be in his safety zone. I didn't know exactly how I was going to accomplish this without Fredi knowing, but Harvey Johnson was not going to do another big abortion if I could help it—and I could help it!

I had other doctors who could safely do big abortions, and quite frankly, I felt it would relieve some pressure on Harvey when he didn't see a big one on his schedule.

We pulled up to my house, and Harvey insisted on walking me in. Inside we were greeted by wall-to-wall kids—my kids and their friends.

The men I dated were never good enough for Harvey, and now my kids didn't measure up. He left after some cutting remark about the children. He really was stepping into dangerous territory putting my kids down.

All the events of the day considered, my Harvey Johnson "perfect man" balloon, which already had a slow leak, was losing air much faster now.

The next morning when Harvey made his regular call to check in, I asked about Jenni.

"Jenni is complaining about the pain, but she is fine this morning. She wants to know when she can go home. She asked about you, Carol. Call her soon," he insisted.

"I will, Harvey," I assured him.

So he continued, "I went to pathology and talked to Dale. Everything is fine. Now, back to business. How many do you have scheduled today?"

"Nine," I responded.

"Have a good day, baby," and he was off.

"You too, Harvey." I hung up also, thinking, *How superficial we are while women are being maimed.*

As promised, I called Jenni. "Hi, Jenni. This is Carol from the clinic. How are you feeling today?"

"Terrible. I hurt all over. I don't understand why my back is hurting so much." She sounded extremely weak.

"You had some pretty extensive surgery," I explained. "That abdominal pregnancy affects your entire abdomen, and you will be sore all over for a few days. Ask the nurse to give you something for the pain. I'm certain Dr. Johnson ordered something for you. Is there anything I can get you, Jenni?"

"Not now," she answered softly.

"Call me if you need anything, and I will get it for you. I'll talk to you later. Good-bye."

I could hardly wait to talk to Harvey that night to get a complete update.

"All the events of the day considered, my Harvey Johnson 'perfect man' balloon, which already had a slow leak, was losing air much faster now."

"I talked to the hospital administrator, and he agreed to write off Jenni's bill," he said. "I will do a few cases there, and hopefully, when the colostomy is reversed, he will write that bill off, too. None of the other surgeons will send her a bill, so I think we will be okay.

"When Jenni gets out of the hospital, I will take her out a few times. And, Carol, you need to stay in touch with her. She seems to like you. Maybe you can take her to dinner a few times. I don't think Jenni will sue us if we take care of her."

I did not share Harvey's vision of befriending this young woman to keep her from suing, but I would do anything to keep this out of the news and reduce the risk of a lawsuit. I privately wondered how many other women Harvey had affairs with to keep them from suing him.

I thought, *Another leak in the perfect-Harvey balloon. I'm not sure how many more leaks it can stand.*

"How long will she be in the hospital?" I asked aloud.

"Lloyd will dismiss her, but probably no more than five to seven days," he answered.

"How long before she can go back to work?"

"That depends on her, but probably a month to six weeks."

"Looks like we have lots of babysitting ahead then. You know, Jenni is just a little younger than our own kids, Jan and Joe Bob."

"She's twenty-one years old." Then he changed the subject. "How was the day?"

"We did all nine, but Leggett took three hours to do them. He just talks too much. We have twenty-eight scheduled for tomorrow, and you know how Dr. Fisher moves. Also Dr. Mosely is going to come by to do a big one on his lunch hour. He has inserted laminaria for two days, so her cervix should be dilated sufficiently for the baby to come right out." It helped to keep my mind focused on the clinic.

"Do we have a good weekend scheduled?" he asked.

"I don't remember how many are on for Saturday, but I know it's over thirty. June is starting off with great numbers. We could have a really good month." I sounded more confident than I felt.

"Let's make it a good month. I'll talk to you in the morning. Love you, baby."

"I love you, Harvey. Good night."

What is real love, anyway? Many have said those words to me, "I love you." I've discovered there's not much difference in those words and no words.

Playing the Game

After Jenni was released, she called me regularly at the clinic.

"Carol, I don't feel pretty with this thing hanging out of my side."

My heart answered, *I don't feel very pretty either with that thing hanging out of your side, Jenni,* but I had to play the game. "It won't be long now, Jenni, before it can be removed. Think of how pretty you will look then."

I kept Harvey informed of all my contacts with Jenni.

Once Jenni mentioned, "Carol, Dr. Johnson calls me all the time. He says he wants to take me to dinner. I'm very excited about seeing him." It was hard listening to her eagerness.

"I'm sure he will call soon, Jenni. I know he is excited about spending some time with you."

Jenni finally called me with more good news, "Dr. Johnson has asked me out to dinner. I am so excited. I can hardly wait."

3

THE CHILDHOOD LESSONS OF LITTLE CAROL NAN

Mother wanted to surprise Daddy with the good news. "Sonny, I'm pregnant. We're going to have a baby in December."

Daddy was not surprised. "I know you're pregnant; you've missed two periods. It's going to be a girl."

"She'll be arriving near Christmas, if not on Christmas!" Mother exclaimed.

"Carol should be her name, then," Daddy concluded.

"I'd like to name a girl after my sister, Nan. What do you think about the name Carol Nan?" she asked.

"I like it. That will be her name."

On December 22, 1944, Sonny and Dorothy Gage received their daughter, Carol Nan Gage.

Carol in Latin means "strong and womanly." In old French the name means "joyous song." Both the Latin and French meanings of my name become very significant as my story unfolds. My middle name, Nan, means "graceful one" or "beauty walking." I did not like that name for years; with such a beautiful meaning, I can't imagine why. Today, I wish I had appreciated it more. Maybe if I had, my story would be much different.

My parents were married on October 30, 1942, in Belton, Texas, several miles away from their home and their parents. My father was a cook in the Navy stationed in Orange, Texas; my mother worked while Daddy played sailor. Two days before my birth my father was shipped out to sea, so he was told of my birth over the ship's loudspeaker.

While Daddy was overseas, Mother and I went to live with her parents and my Aunt Nan and Uncle Max in Houston, Texas.

Mother stayed at home with me while the other adults worked. I was a breast-fed baby, watched over very carefully by my mother and grandparents.

Always dressed perfectly, I was the center of attention and the family entertainment especially when everyone arrived home from work. Adored by all, I was given everything I wanted.

Through the years I've often heard, "You were such a good baby. We didn't need to correct you because you were so good!" I am sure I provided a lot of "joy" as the "graceful one" and "beauty walking" for a family longing to have their hearts lightened, especially during the war.

Mother often showed me a picture of Daddy to make sure I would know him when he returned from overseas. "This is your Daddy. Isn't he handsome? He loves you so much. When he gets home, you'll love him, too."

He returned on December 11, 1945. When he was discharged from the Navy, we returned to Mother and Daddy's hometown of San Saba, Texas.

Life seemed good then. Daddy and I were busy getting to know each other. I soon learned that all I had to say was, "Daddy, Daddy," and I captured his undivided attention.

But I was unaware that a storm was brewing. Mother was feeling left out—not so much because of Daddy's developing relationship with me, but because of his sense of responsibility to his own family.

When Daddy was seventeen, his father had died. To help support the family, Daddy quit school and got a job at a grocery store making seven dollars a week. When he returned from the Navy, my grandmother was still on his dependent list. She was getting something my mother felt like she should be getting. Not only was Mother sharing Daddy with me, but she also shared him with his mother and family. She was not getting the attention a young bride expected to have from her returning, conquering hero.

I don't think she blamed me, but I am convinced she did blame my father's family. From early childhood and throughout my life, Mother often said to Daddy, "You always put your family first, ahead of us." Jealousy was creeping in, taking deep root for future expression.

"But I was unaware that a storm was brewing. Mother was feeling left out— not so much because of Daddy's developing relationship with me, but because of his sense of responsibility to his own family."

By the age of two I felt like a real "queen." That year I was asked to be the little "queen" of the May Fete along with two-year-old Sonny Berrien who would be the little "king." I was full of life.

Everyone, including me, made sure that life revolved around me. I was "so good" and a "joy" to my family, but I was spoiled rotten. My daddy's philosophy was, "You don't start correcting children until they are two. You don't tell them 'no' until then." So I established my own boundaries.

Children have ways of controlling their parents and their world. I had mine, an imaginary playmate named Rezin.

"Rezin wants to eat with us. Set him a place by me. I love to eat with Rezin."

"Clean your plate, Rezin," Mommy chimed in.

Sometimes when we left the house, we forgot Rezin.

"Oh, no! We left Rezin at home. We've got to go back and get him," I would cry.

My parents did everything I told them we had to do for Rezin. I would talk to Rezin, and he would tell me what to say to them.

"Stop the car! Rezin needs to tee tee."

Parents are so gullible!

The time finally came when my big "king" hurt his little "queen" for the first time, however. I was only two years old, and we lived in our duplex next door to Daddy's brother and his family.

"Carol Nan and I are going outside for a walk," Daddy informed Mother as she was cleaning the kitchen. Standing in the sun and holding my father's hand made me feel very happy.

Some friends drove by and stopped for a visit. Suddenly a wasp came out of the shrubbery and stung my eyelid. I turned and reached out, screaming, "Daddy, Daddy."

He slapped me!

Confused and hurting, I screamed louder.

Hearing my screams, Mother rushed out of the house and rescued me. "What happened? Move your hand and let me see your eye. Oh, Carol Nan, you've been stung. It's okay. It's going to be okay. Let's go inside and put something on it."

I felt pain from my eye, but I felt much deeper pain within my heart.

Strength Is Power

Years later I recognized attitudes that formed in that brief childhood encounter with my father. I thought I had been Daddy's perfect girl. Even though I tried, I failed. What did I do wrong? Maybe I would just try harder to please him.

I also learned that the strong endure pain. They do not cry out. I would show my daddy the Latin meaning of my name—I would be strong!

In San Saba Daddy worked in the same grocery store where he had worked before he went into the Navy. At night he butchered cattle for the meat market to make extra money. Mother and I often went with him.

We watched him put the animals in a building with a concrete floor that sloped to a drain in the center. He closed the door and shot the cow. Then we went in and watched him pull the cow off the floor and hang it from the ceiling. I can still see the blood running down that drain. Daddy dressed each cow, quartered it, took it to the grocery store, and hung it in the cooler.

Mother always felt uneasy being at the butcher barn. "How much longer will this take, Sonny? Hurry! Can't we go home now?"

When I was three years old, I had a white cat named Kitty Cat. Kitty Cat stayed in the garage with her new litter of kittens. As we drove into the garage one night, Mother screamed, "We hit Kitty Cat!"

Daddy calmly got out of the car, picked up Kitty Cat, and disappeared behind the house. I heard a shot in the night air. When Daddy came back, he said, "Kitty Cat is out of her misery."

I loved to be in charge and win when I played with my cousin, Nancy. I can remember standing far on her side of the driveway dividing our family's duplex and insisting, "Stay over on your side of the driveway, Nancy. The driveway is mine to this line."

Of course 75 percent of the driveway was always mine!

Nancy stood there and cried. I loved it.

All my possessions had to be bigger and better, including my swing set. Daddy built mine out of pipe set in concrete. It was taller so I could swing higher and enjoy the thrill of conquering new heights.

I told Nancy, "Since you don't have a swing set, come swing on my big swing set." Then I pushed her as high as I could, hoping to scare her.

When I was six, my parents told me, "You're going to get a baby— your very own baby." They did not want me to be jealous so they told me it would be mine.

Mother said, "If it's a boy, his name will be Calvin Jefferson after your daddy and grandfather. But if it's a girl, you get to choose the name."

"I'll give her a good name—one she will like. Her name will be Diane." Two weeks before my sister was born, someone in San Saba named their baby girl Diane so I changed her name to Anita Jo.

The baby came on August 7. As Daddy and I were looking at her through the window of the nursery, Daddy asked, "Do you remember the Golden Book story, 'Big Toot and Little Toot'?"

"Uh-huh."

"Well, just like the trains, you will be 'Big Toot' and the baby will be 'Little Toot.'"

Little Toot, or Tooter, was "my" baby. I quickly learned to change her diapers, even the dirty ones. I loved to take care of her. When she cried, I tried to be the one to help her. The adults praised, "Look, she takes such good care of her little sister." I needed that attention, and even a smelly diaper could be endured to get it.

When Tooter was one month old, I started school about three-and-a-half blocks from home. The year had its trying moments, not because I had to leave Tooter or because of the other kids in school, but because of my parents.

"Sonny, Carol Nan is not old enough to walk home by herself. She's just a baby," Mother explained. So I was the only child whose mother took her to school and picked her up in the afternoon. My father even picked me up for lunch.

I begged, "Please, let me walk by myself. I'm big enough."

Finally, one day Daddy was late. He was not at the door to meet me when I came out; I hid behind a tree when I saw him coming. He returned home without me, and I got to walk home alone! I declared my independence.

After this event Daddy convinced Mother to let me walk to and from school. But, she stood in the middle of the road and watched until I got to school and was there when I returned home every day. She was deathly afraid I was going to get run over.

After I finished first grade, we moved to Goldthwaite, Texas, an even smaller town twenty-two miles from San Saba, because of Daddy's new job as a route man for Mrs. Baird's Bread—a step up from a grocery check-out man.

The time came for that typical childhood request, "Daddy, I want a bicycle."

"We can't afford one right now, baby. We don't have enough money."

I was not happy.

Weeks later Daddy came home and said to me, "Sister, go sweep out the back of the bread truck for me."

When I opened the door, there was a twenty-six-inch girl's bicycle—a big bicycle! My heart's desire. "Oh, Daddy, thank you! Help me get it out of the truck. Let me ride it!"

Like the swing set, my bicycle had to be bigger and better than anyone else's. I nearly wrecked a dozen times trying to master it, but I did get a lot of praise when I did ride it.

In the second grade I represented my class in the annual bathing beauty contest. Mother excitedly announced, "We're going to get you a new bathing suit." She made me try on every bathing suit in the store.

> ## "On the day of the contest, she curled my hair perfectly, powdered my nose, and blushed my cheeks. I got the shock of my life when the judges picked someone else the winner!"

"I want the red one with ruffles on the bottom."

"Okay, we'll buy the red one."

On the day of the contest, she curled my hair perfectly, powdered my nose, and blushed my cheeks. I got the shock of my life when the judges picked someone else the winner!

Goldthwaite was a new, strange place, and I felt very alone and isolated. I felt no one cared about me. I did not dare cry where it would be noticed, but I remember crying a lot and wandering around by myself. That's when I met the "horny toads."

A neighborhood boy cautioned me, "Horny toads can spit blood on you and kill you, especially the big fat ones."

I talked to the horny toads. "Get away from me. You can't spit on me." I was still scared of them, but I defended myself by throwing rocks and using sticks and a hoe to chase them away or kill them.

It's My Responsibility To Make Things Right

Life must have been dull in Goldthwaite because we went to the drive-in movie every time it changed. We always parked beside a woman with two boys whose husband travelled all the time. She was very friendly.

Accusingly, Mother would say to Daddy, "You're having an affair with that woman, aren't you?" Mother constantly screamed at Daddy about this woman, but he always denied her accusations.

I tried to intercede between them on many occasions when they fought, using every weapon I could. Following my appendectomy, whenever they started to argue, I bent over as though I were in excruciating pain and screamed, "My side is hurting! Stop fighting."

"Your side is not hurting," Daddy replied. "I know what you're trying to do."

Maybe parents aren't so gullible after all.

By the third grade, things picked up for me in Goldthwaite. Butch Schuman and I were elected to represent our class at homecoming. When Butch shyly asked, "Carol Nan, can we go to homecoming together?" I wholeheartedly agreed.

Excitedly, I dressed in my little formal and waited for Butch to arrive. His parents came to the door with him and met my parents.

Handing me a corsage, Butch said, "You sure look pretty in that dress."

"Thank you." I replied.

We were off on our night of royalty and the applause of the crowd.

Daddy and Shorty Schuman (Butch's dad) became friends and went into the trucking business together with plans to make a lot of money. Butch and I became playmates.

Butch's mother warned us, "If you go in the hen house, don't touch the eggs." In spite of her words, we sneaked into the hen house taking eggs and throwing them. We also played cowboys and Indians and fed the animals.

Butch's older sister, Tootie, took us swimming. She sunbathed by the deep end where the teenage boys were and restricted us. "You two stay in the shallow water and keep away from me." We loved it.

Daddy's new business required him to travel with the road construction crews, providing the water trucks used in highway construction. Mother, Tooter, and I were home alone at night. We all slept together in the same bed—safety in numbers, you know.

One night, someone tried to break in our front door.

Mother frantically shook me. "Carol Nan. Wake up! Wake up! Shhhhh. Do you hear that? What is it? Is someone trying to get in the front door?"

My heart began to race. *What should I do? Someone's trying to get in.*

"I've got to get help. Hold your sister while I call the neighbor," Mother whispered.

Hearing the activity in our house and seeing the lights come on at our next door neighbor's, the prowler ran away.

"I tried to intercede between them on many occasions when they fought, using every weapon I could. Following my appendectomy, whenever they started to argue, I bent over as though I were in excruciating pain and screamed, 'My side is hurting! Stop fighting.' "

I shall never forget feeling responsible for my mother and sister that night during Daddy's absence. I was only nine.

Every Sunday afternoon at four o'clock, darkness in the form of depression fell over our home. It was time for Daddy to leave for his work week. We started to pack Daddy's things, and the weekly departure ritual began.

"Sonny, I hate for you to leave me and the girls. Are you sure you have to go?" Mother quizzed.

"You know I have to go. I've got to make a living," Daddy answered.

"I wish you could find something to do back in San Saba. I hate it when you're gone," reminded Mother.

Tooter began to beg, "Daddy, don't go."

"Daddy, be careful," I cautioned. It was awful to see him go—I felt responsible again.

Each one of us kissed him good-bye, and he climbed into his pickup. Then, all of the women—Mother, Tooter, and I—started crying and waved to him until he was out of sight. The crying continued in the house for some time.

For most of my life on Sunday afternoons at 4:00 P.M., I got depressed. I dreaded each week at that time, but I didn't recognize why until I was forty-one.

Things were not easy for our family during those start-up years in the trucking business. Soon, however, we moved back to San Saba into our old duplex so Mother could go to work as a telephone operator.

Granny Gage was there to take care of Tooter and me. She made us clothes out of scrap materials including Daddy's old bread uniforms. It was good for me; she was a fantastic cook and taught me a lot about cooking. She also told me stories as long as I would listen—mostly stories about her years as a midwife delivering babies.

"Carol Nan, I remember when babies tried to go up instead of down. I'd put a towsack around those women, just above the baby, using safety pins and gradually push that baby out. You know, I delivered half of the babies in San Saba." I could listen for hours.

Mother resented her even more now and said nasty things about her. But it didn't matter. I loved my Granny Gage, and I knew she loved me.

I asssumed responsibility for keeping the house clean, taking care of Tooter, doing some cooking, and buying the groceries. I knew Mother was angry with Daddy for making her go to work, so I thought if I could help with housework, things would be better for her.

Tooter did not share my vision and did not cooperate with me. As a matter of fact, Tooter became very angry with me when I tried to make her do something to help.

"Tooter, I'll wash the dishes, and you dry them."

"You can't make me."

"Tooter, help me fold the clothes."

"I don't want to."

"Tooter, go clean the bathroom."

"I'm going to tell Mommy on you when she gets home."

Boy, was she stubborn. They told me she was "my" baby when she was born, but they forgot to tell her!

"Tooter, why won't you help me do anything?"

"You're not my mother. I don't want to."

Picking up a butcher knife, Tooter often chased me saying, "I'm going to kill you," and I feared she would. I ran to the bathroom, shut the door, sat on the floor, put my feet up against the door with my back to the bathtub, and prayed she wouldn't break the door down.

Hitting the door repeatedly with the butcher knife, Tooter continued to threaten, "I'm going to kill you. I'm going to kill you."

"We need to keep this house clean," I reminded her.

"I hate you. I hate you."

"You need to help me, Tooter."

"Leave me alone," she demanded.

"I asssumed responsibility for keeping the house clean, taking care of Tooter, doing some cooking, and buying the groceries. I knew Mother was angry with Daddy for making her go to work, so I thought if I could help with housework, things would be better for her."

"I'm going to tell Mommy what you're doing to that door," I warned her.

"She won't care. She won't do anything to me."

That old wooden door had so many gashes in it.

Once Tooter worked out her frustration and was convinced she couldn't get to me, she left, dropping the knife on the floor. I rushed out and got the knife along with all the other knives and scissors I could find and hid them. Then I resumed my responsibilities.

Each day Mother worked from 8:00 A.M. until 12:00 noon and returned at 4:00 P.M. to work until 8:00 P.M.

I waited each noon for her, so proud I had cleaned the house well and cooked her lunch—anything to make her happy. Those four hours between noon and four, however, were filled with anger and complaints.

"You only cleaned the surface dirt. You didn't even look at the closet except to hide something in it."

"Your daddy finally has enough clothes so I don't have to wash them on the weekends while he's here. But I still have to work to pay for that car he bought and wash and iron his clothes during the week."

I began to wash and iron Daddy's clothes, hoping to relieve the pressure off of Mother.

I remember clearly at 3:30 P.M. each day, just before Mother had to go back to work, she made me sit in a chair in the kitchen and screamed, "You bitch. You can't do anything right. You half-clean the house. You put too much garlic in the food, and you wash the dark clothes with the white clothes. Can't you do anything right?"

I especially remember her calling me a "bitch" over and over, day after day.

Nothing I did was right. If I got recognition outside the home, she complained more about my work at home never being right. In her mind I could not be doing things right outside the home when I was botching my chores at home so badly.

I had gladly taken on those chores to help relieve her pressures at home. Now they were my responsibilities, unfinished and botched according to my mother.

I felt so worthless. I wanted her to affirm me, to love me, but I couldn't do anything right in her eyes. I tried everything, but instead she kept a running list of all the things she thought I was doing wrong and reminded me of them often.

I was the one under pressure, and I was only eleven years old.

Pleasing Daddy

Finally, things started to improve for us financially. Daddy bought some acreage seven miles north of town. He loved that farm, and I loved the time we spent together there. He raised cattle and hogs which meant more hard work. I did it right along with him.

Animals meant exposure to the miracle of birth. However, for some reason Daddy would never let me be there when the actual birth of an animal took place. It didn't seem fair. I was introduced to the death of animals as a child but couldn't participate in the birth of animals even though I was eleven.

I grew up in a man's world. My mother idolized my father and taught me to idolize him. I grew up believing all little girls idolize their fathers, and their fathers are supposed to love and cherish them.

It was a source of pride to me that Daddy always brought in the first deer whenever he went hunting. He killed more deer than anyone regardless of the limit.

I often bragged to my cousin, Nancy, "My daddy got the first deer. Your daddy hasn't killed a deer yet."

She sobbed. I won again. Inside, I felt so good.

Daddy also let me hunt with him. Almost every afternoon during deer season, just before dusk, he put Tooter and me in the car, and we drove slowly down the road, hunting deer. I played a game trying to spot the deer first, hoping to gain Daddy's approval.

"Daddy, Daddy, there's a deer."

"Shhhhh. You're right, Carol Nan. That's a big buck. Be quiet and roll down the window. I'm going to put the gun over you, out the window, and look through the scope. Shhhhh. It's a twelve pointer!" he whispered.

My heart raced with the thrill of knowing I spotted the deer first.

"I felt so worthless. I wanted her to affirm me, to love me, but I couldn't do anything right in her eyes. I tried everything, but instead she kept a •running list of all the things she thought I was doing wrong and reminded me of them often."

Bang. The sound of the gunfire echoed in my ears. The deer dropped.

"You got it, Daddy!" I squealed.

"Shhhhh. Now remember where he is. Help me watch for the game warden."

We left the scene and made several passes to be sure the coast was clear. Convinced it was, Daddy stopped near the scene again.

"Carol Nan, sit here and keep watch. Don't honk if you see anything. I'm going to bring the deer up to the road, and I'll be watching, too."

I sat there, breathlessly watching.

He jumped out of the car, hurried toward the deer and dragged it to the side of the road, still hidden. I was always relieved when I heard Daddy near the car again.

We made another pass to be sure it was still safe. When Daddy stopped at the scene this time, he opened the trunk, threw the deer inside, and we took off.

Relief! We had not been caught. What an exciting adventure for me with Daddy.

I was learning to win at all costs, regardless of the rules.

Daddy made some incredible shots, once killing a thirteen-point deer at over three hundred feet, a trophy deer. We ate venison year 'round.

Road hunting with Daddy was great until he started taking a friend named Vance and his daughters with us. Now I was relegated to the back seat to play with the other girls. I lost my job as the spotter. I hated it.

At other times Daddy brought home several water trucks used in his business, parked them in the back yard, and cleaned them. I was so glad to see him, so eager to prove myself to him that I worked hard cleaning those trucks.

"Sister, you're small enough to get inside those tanks," he directed. "Get in there and clean them out. Take this flashlight and go all the way to the back to the third compartment, and get all the black stuff out."

I was scared inside those dark tanks, but I did it to please him.

Inside the tank working, I could often hear Tooter outside, playing around Daddy. I always knew Tooter was Mother's favorite, but I wondered, maybe she was Daddy's favorite, too. Why shouldn't she be? She was really cute, acting cute. On the other hand, I felt so awkward like other eleven-year-old girls do, I am sure. I began to feel rejected, like the family Cinderella, unloved.

Jealousy began to build its root system deep inside my heart, like inside my mother, but mine was directed at Little Toot. I tried to act independent, grown up, hoping to hide the hurt I was feeling. My mother and daddy had no idea of the struggle going on inside me. Daddy never knew how to express affection, to give me the affirmation I needed. Maybe my act was convincing.

The glow was leaving my cheeks, and the sparkle was diminishing from my eyes. My jealousy toward my sister was silently growing,

---

"Relief! We had not been caught. What an exciting adventure for me with Daddy. I was learning to win at all costs, regardless of the rules."

---

while my mother's vindictiveness was directed toward me. I felt that my mother hated me: She didn't just want to destroy me; she wanted to annihilate me. And I wanted Tooter to get what she deserved, whatever that was.

Working alongside my daddy, just like a man, my appreciation for gentle, soft femininity diminished. Daddy's silence was easier to accept, while Mother's constant complaining made me feel like a failure.

I helped Daddy with the farm chores, then went home and helped Mother clean house, cook, and iron. Working alongside my mother, listening to her complain, strengthened my resolve not to be a weak woman.

I patterned my life after my father rather than my mother. Watching and listening to Daddy, my feelings and attitudes about women were skewed badly. The picture of the woman as a total failure, weak and teary-eyed, solidified in my young mind and heart. Two pictures were formed in my mind: my father was ultrasuccessful and in control, while my mother appeared a total failure and out of control.

My father was always making fun of my mother. I can remember one stormy night there was a clap of thunder and the sound of rain on the roof.

"Is it raining?" Mother asked.

"No, it's snowing in July," Daddy matter-of-factly answered.

Tooter, Daddy, and I laughed uncontrollably.

"Shut up," Mother screamed. "Don't make fun of me. I hate you all."

We were on a rare family outing one Sunday afternoon when Mother asked, "How many cows are in this pasture?"

"Thirty-two."

"How many bulls are in this pasture?"

"Cows and bulls do not marry, Maw. Only one bull for the bunch." Daddy winked at Tooter and me. The three of us hollered.

Mother screamed, "I don't appreciate your treating me like I'm stupid. Shut up. I know bulls and cows don't marry."

In my perception, she was always made to look stupid. A female was inferior and could not match up to a man. Men were smart, strong, positive; to be female was to be second class. Every time my father showed disrespect to my mother, it made being a girl less attractive to me.

I was conditioned to identify with masculine qualities and to abhor feminine qualities. After all, why would I not want to be like my daddy—smart, aggressive, controlling, competitive, hard working, and the person with the money. Mother couldn't handle the pressure. I learned well what not to become.

It all began very innocently as a little child, but with each insult to my mother, I buried a little more of my femininity. I lost touch with how to relate to females as I learned more and more about how my father functioned.

Mother and I drifted farther and farther apart. We competed for Daddy's attention and affection and ultimately his praise. The only arena where my mother did not compete with me was in the bedroom.

How does it happen? How did a little blonde-haired, green-eyed beauty, the apple of her daddy's eye, suddenly grow out-of-date and style? How many young girls like myself, enjoying so much attention in their first years, suddenly feel they no longer deserve the hugs and kisses they once needed from their father.

I loved my daddy. He was my idol, and I needed his attention, but I couldn't tell him. How many young girls face this same fate—the loss of needed involvement and attention, hugs and kisses, from their fathers at such a vulnerable age. I know it was unintentional, but the effects were devastating.

"Mother and I drifted farther and farther apart. We competed for Daddy's attention and affection and ultimately his praise."

How did a little baby girl so prized by her mother when she was born become her mortal enemy? I did not want to fight with my mother. I wanted to love her and be loved by her.

How much did being around so much blood and killing of animals as a child desensitize my feelings about blood and death?

How did 'Big Toot' become so jealous of 'Little Toot' in five short years and begin to feel like the family Cinderella rather than the queen?

Most of all, how did Carol, "strong and womanly," so powerfully overshadow Carol, "joyous song"? And, how did Nan, "graceful one" and "beauty walking," become "beauty working" in just eleven short childhood years?

4

THE POWER OF SEX

G rowing up is not easy. Puberty came, and I developed quickly and abundantly.

My thirteenth birthday, one of our first boy-girl parties, was celebrated at the home of my friend, Cheri Mays. I was the center of attention as thirty kids gathered around the cake to sing "Happy Birthday."

"Happy Birthday to you. Happy Birthday to you. Happy Birthday, Carol Nan . . . "

But over all the other voices Dwight sang, "Happy Birthday, Dear 'Chesty' . . . "

Embarrassed and humiliated, I ran out of the room crying.

I had done everything to play down my new shape. In spite of my trying, the growth process continued along with the relentless and open teasing. The boys even accused me of wearing falsies. It is a wonder my back isn't deformed from slumping over, trying not to show.

These are the times that try girls' souls.

The living conditions at home made it even worse. Living in a one bedroom—total of three rooms—duplex afforded little privacy for a family of four.

I hated the situation. Four of us slept in the same bedroom containing two double beds. I did not want to be in the same room with my parents at night. I was too old to be there. "Let me sleep downstairs," I begged. "I want to sleep in a room alone."

"You don't need to be downstairs, Carol Nan. We wouldn't be able to hear you if you needed us." Mother's fearful nature again.

I complained until they finally let me. However, whenever I acted up, my punishment was the loss of my downstairs privilege.

I will always remember their making love at night. I hated it so much. One night I covered my ears and tried to stop the sound, but couldn't. I finally screamed, "Stop it."

Daddy jumped over on top of me and screamed, "Shut up," as he beat me through the cover. It really hurt, but I kept quiet.

They never made me sleep upstairs again.

I still had the responsibility of taking care of Tooter most of the time. She had to go everywhere I went. Of course, I blamed Mother for not taking care of her as she was supposed to. Crowded in a three-room duplex was tough, but having my seven-year-old sister along with me everywhere I went was too much.

I longed for freedom with my friends and complained to my parents, "No one else has to take their little sister with them. Can't Tooter stay with someone else? Why do I always have to take her with me?"

"Tooter doesn't bother you and your friends. It doesn't hurt you to take her with you," Mother usually answered.

"I am the only person I know who has to take care of her little sister. I hate it."

They refused to listen and warned, "Carol Nan, you better take care of Tooter and treat her right," while never telling her to mind me. I felt violated.

Tooter probably longed to be my age. She tried to talk and act like us; at the same time I think she needed to be with children her own age.

My little sister was a real "Tooter." When I did something wrong and told her not to tell, she couldn't wait to tell on me. "Mommy, Sister and her friends had some cigarettes. They smoked and hid the rest under the car seat. Do you want me to show you where they are?"

Mother acted too busy to investigate. She actually already knew what we were doing. She smoked our "hidden" cigarettes when she ran out of her own, without saying a word to me.

Operating on my limited knowledge, however, I falsely accused Tooter of getting our cigarettes. "What happened to our cigarettes, Tooter?"

"I don't know. I certainly didn't smoke them."

I never could figure out what happened to those cigarettes. Years later Mother told me what she had done.

How did I truly feel about Tooter? Can you love someone and hate them at the same time? Do sisters ever feel that way?

"I longed for freedom with my friends and complained to my parents, 'No one else has to take their little sister with them. Can't Tooter stay with someone else? Why do I always have to take her with me?' "

I know I was jealous of her. She looked like the Gage side of the family, tall and slender, with her dark hair and dark complexion. Daddy seemed to shift more of his attention toward her. And she was Mother's favorite.

I was hurt; at the same time, however, I did love my sister. I say "did" because she died in a swimming accident when she was twenty-four. I even felt responsible for that, as if somehow I could have protected her. She left a six-year-old son behind for whom I still feel some responsibility. I cherish her memory now.

Did I love Tooter? Yes, indeed! And I still do!

Somehow, my first dating experiences were not hampered by Tooter's presence. The boy's family arrived and took us to the event, and then picked us up and delivered me back home.

When we went to a Baptist youth group party, we would lock out the leaders and start dancing. I was always the ringleader. "Turn up the record player. They can't get in until we unlock the door!"

"If we slow dance, they'll get upset. Let's jitterbug."

"Look, they are outside knocking on the window. What are we going to do?"

"Keep dancing. They will think we don't hear them."

You know how Baptists feel about dancing—that's why I went to the Methodist Church.

I guess Mother wasn't a good Baptist either because dancing brought her to life and even helped our relationship. She was more than happy to teach me and my friends (especially the Baptists) to dance.

I had a lot of close friends—Mary Lou, Cheri, Jo, Jonibeth, Kay, Brenda, Nancy, Terry, Margaret, Sylvia, Loy Nell, and Karen. We did everything together. Our house was small so we couldn't have parties there, but Mother chauffeured us everywhere to try and make up for that. Those were the good ole days!

Early Conquests

I was a young teenager before I knew it. The boys were giving me lots of attention. The awkwardness of early physical development and the nicknames faded away. Older boys noticed me now. I was on center stage again, and I loved the recognition. What I had lost from my daddy, I found in young men.

In the seventh and eighth grade, I met boys at the movies to sit together. I had several boyfriends, always the popular boys. I especially liked Franklin, but Mother didn't approve. Dwight and I talked so much on the phone Daddy called him the "telephone kid." I started "going steady" with him to break up with Franklin.

Dwight was the one I wanted. He was very popular and handsome, blonde and tall enough to be a good dancer. We learned how to dance together, even the jitterbug.

Most of the boys were too shy to learn to jitterbug, but Dwight had a lot of self-confidence. My mother and Aunt Joyce and Uncle Pudge taught a group of my friends how to dance. Dwight's parents were close friends of my aunt and uncle so Dwight was very comfortable with the adult teachers and quickly learned all the steps.

"Come on, Carol Nan. Let's dance."

I loved to dance with Dwight.

Dwight was very special to me for another reason; he was the first boy I kissed. It was on my first hayride; I was so excited. Even though we met the boys at the hayride, everyone had a "date" and Dwight was mine.

We rode the entire evening under our blankets, many of us hoping we would be kissed for the first time that night. Sitting cramped between other couples, we talked through our blankets. At the end of the evening as we knew we were pulling back into town, everyone was very quiet. An eternity of silence later, Dwight put his arms around me, pulled me close, and kissed me on the mouth!

"Wow!" Dwight said.

Wow! I thought. *This is neat!*

"I could not see that I had developed a basic character flaw: I was willing to compromise to get what I wanted."

I was learning to compete for boys. It was great fun. The more unavailable they were, the more I was challenged.

My friend Cheri was always talking about John Richardson. "John works for my dad at the feed store. He is so cute! I would love to go out with him, but my parents wouldn't let me even if he asked. They think he is too old."

John was definitely not desirable from my parents' standpoint either, but he was the best looking boy I'd ever seen. I thought he was gorgeous. He was dark, with auburn hair and brown eyes and at least six feet tall. Every girl in high school wanted to date John, especially some of my girlfriends. Their parents would not let them go out with him; I knew I could manipulate my parents.

Like my daddy, the hunter, I was on a hunt. He always came in first; I wanted to be first, too. So what if the rules had to be bent a little. Didn't I learn that from my daddy, too? I could not see that I had developed a basic character flaw: I was willing to compromise to get what I wanted. And I wanted John because he was untouchable. What compromise would I have to make to have him?

At the end of the summer just before I was to start high school, John called.

"Carol Nan, this is John Richardson. Would you go to the drive-in with me Friday night?"

"Yes, I would love to. What time will you pick me up?"

"7:30."

"I'll be ready."

John was a senior; I was fourteen. He was supposed to be out of reach. When I was younger, I always felt inadequate, especially around popular boys. I hated that feeling then and determined to change it. When John asked me out, I knew I had accomplished my first goal. I was attracted to John by the challenge to win him over all the other girls; to have the untouchable; to be with a popular senior and receive the resulting attention.

By this time, the distance between my father and me was so great I wasn't concerned about what he thought. In fact, I wanted to date John just to show Daddy I could. John reminded me of my father in so many ways. In a sense he was taking my daddy's place, giving me the attention I was not getting from him.

When I started dating John, things at home were very stormy. Mother was very unhappy and complaining constantly about Daddy. After he had been home one weekend, Mother confided in me, "Your father slept with another woman."

"He what? Who would Daddy sleep with?"

"Some woman he picked up on a trip."

"How did you find out?"

"He told me."

"You mean he confessed?"

"Yes. He feels guilty about it."

"You don't have anything to worry about then. It won't happen again."

But Mother did not agree with me. "I'm thinking about divorcing him," she declared.

I thought to myself, *Mother is building her case, preparing for divorce. Why is she so upset? What difference does his having sex with another woman make? After all, he came home to her as usual.*

Another black mark on her invisible slate. I didn't even think it strange that she would confide in me. Couldn't she see that my role model could do no wrong in my eyes? He set his own rules. I did too.

My only curfews were self-imposed; my parents continued their unrestricted ways with me.

John cared a lot about me, or so it seemed. The more time we spent together, the more explosive our attraction became. He was much more experienced than I was; he had played around a lot, or so it seemed to me.

After months of dating, he made his move. "When are you going to loosen up, Carol Nan?"

"What do you mean?"

"We have been dating for some time, but you won't let me even unbutton your blouse. Relax a little," he drawled.

"John, I'm scared."

"Trust me, Carol Nan."

It was quite clear that we were going to be more intimate, or he was going to stop dating me. I didn't want that! I now knew the price tag for keeping John.

It was compromise time, time to bend the rules.

I wanted John for the prestige. I understood his reputation was not good, but I didn't care. He wanted me. The exchange would give both of us what we wanted.

About eleven o'clock on a cold night, parked on top of Chapel Hill, in the back seat of John's car, I gave what I had to give to keep him. I was nervous, but ready for all those things that are supposed to happen at your first sexual encounter.

Control by Manipulation

My expectations of bliss and that special bonding were short-lived as the pain of intercourse seemed endless. John seemed oblivious to my pain. Where was the ecstasy? Where was the pleasure? This was hard, cold pain—nothing more. How those "first" experiences set patterns for our lives!

I controlled my emotions outwardly that evening, but once alone I grieved over the loss of that one thing a girl reserves for her special troubadour—the gift she can only give one time. I surrendered my innocence that night but I also learned how to use my resources to manipulate people, especially men, to get what I wanted.

John felt more guilty than I did. The next day he was remorseful. "Carol Nan, let's just forget that last night ever happened."

"How can I forget last night?" *The damage is done,* I thought. *Now he wants to walk away.*

"I am sorry for pushing you into having sex with me." Oh, so that was it. He felt he had wronged me, without knowing I had used him, too.

I now suspected that last night was also the first time for John, and I saw a weakness—a weakness I could use. I knew John enjoyed our sexual encounter, and I was going to be sure there were more—no matter how painful it was for me.

I saw something more. I could also use his sense of guilt to control him. If we continued to have sex, he would feel obligated to stay with me. This first time I realized the powerful tool sex can be in a relationship. I knew I could control John with sex—and I did for two and a half years.

However, the sword cuts both ways. Once at a party with our friends, John grabbed me. "Carol Nan, you were flirting with Charlie. You'd better straighten up."

"I wasn't flirting with Charlie or anyone," I responded.

"Yes, you were," and he slapped me.

His jealousy was too much, along with the physical abuse and embarrassment. A lot of other boys wanted to date me; I didn't need him. I broke it off with him.

I was sixteen. A boy named Mike invited me to homecoming. Jim Bob Everett was there. Mike and I danced a few times; then Jim Bob approached me. "Carol Nan, would you like to dance?"

"I would love to, Jim Bob." We glided out on the floor. I was determined to impress him.

"How is college?" I asked.

"Fine. I like San Marcos."

"What is your major?"

"Pharmacy, but I will have to transfer to the University of Texas in order to get that degree. What are you doing tomorrow night?"

"Nothing."

"Would you like to go to the drive-in with me?"

"Yes."

"I'll pick you up at 7:00."

Jim Bob was an even better catch. He had graduated from high school fourth in his class, was a member of the National Honor Society, captain of the football team, and very popular.

Jim Bob and I continued dancing throughout the evening. Mike pretended not to notice, or at least he didn't say anything. At the end of the dance, Mike took me home and never asked me out again.

Jim Bob and I started dating immediately. Here I was dating a very popular guy, plus I was doing all right in the popularity arena myself. That December I was selected as a princess in the local Pecan Queen Contest.

Daddy was out of town on business at the time of the contest and called out as we walked in the door, "How did you do?"

"I am a Pecan Princess."

"That is great for your first entry. You'll be the Queen next year!" I beamed with pride.

And Then It Happened

Jim Bob and I made a very cute couple. Even Jim Bob's mother, Catherine, was proud of her son for dating a Pecan Princess. "I heard you were beautiful at the Pecan Queen contest. Congratulations. I am proud of you." Catherine Everett smiled.

Jim Bob enjoyed necking, but he always stopped short of anything else. Once I helped him unbutton my dress, and he caught on quickly! I went back to using sex to control a relationship. Soon we were having sex every weekend.

"Are you sure you won't get pregnant now?"

"This is supposed to be a safe time."

We had been dating for three months in late December 1961 when I first suspected I was pregnant, just two and a half weeks after being named a Pecan Princess.

What a turn of events. This was certainly not the kind of attention I was looking for.

I was scared. Would Jim Bob believe the baby was his? Almost paralyzed with fear of rejection, I told him. "Jim Bob, I have missed my period. I think I am pregnant."

"How do we find out for sure?"

"I can go to the doctor in Goldthwaite. No one will see me there."

"When can you go?"

"Saturday."

He struggled with the news, especially since others were telling him that I was still seeing John, which wasn't true. He finally believed me.

What does a sixteen-year-old girl—living in a small town, popular in high school, holding a student body office—do when she thinks she's pregnant?

I didn't know the first thing to do. I was so scared, but I was excited, too, in a strange way. The thought that I could have a baby was unbelievable, and I could feel my body making changes. I was going to be a mother. I think Jim Bob was even excited he was going to be a father.

Since Jim Bob was home for Christmas, I took his car and some money, dressed in adult clothes, and went to the doctor in Goldthwaite. I borrowed eyeglasses and changed my appearance as much as I could, hoping no one would recognize me there.

I checked in Dr. Childress's office under the name of Sonia Sears, telling him I was sixteen and married. As proof, I wore a pearl ring that John had given me upside down.

I was thrilled with the news of my pregnancy. Dr. Childress kindly asked if I needed any help. I said, "No, everything is all right."

I rushed back to San Saba to tell Jim Bob. "I am pregnant. The baby will be born in August," I exclaimed.

"We will get married right away," he assured me.

"I love you, Jim Bob."

"I love you, too."

When he said we would get married, I was really relieved. We had talked about getting married, but not under these circumstances.

Now, we had to face our parents. Jim Bob didn't mind telling his parents, but I feared telling mine. I could not stand the punishment I thought I would have to face and the conditional love I knew was there. I decided to just tell my parents we wanted to get married at semester break.

Jim Bob was lucky. His father, Sam, was at deer camp hunting, so he told his mother first. She was somewhat upset but handled it well. We then drove to the camp together and told his father.

"Welcome to the family, Carolyn Ann." Sam kissed me. Sam never got my name right, but I loved him because he was so sweet.

He was encouraging at that time, but changed when he got back home to his wife. By this time Catherine determined "Jim Bobby" was being trapped into marriage; and she blamed me for the pregnancy.

I don't know to this day how Jim Bob stood up to his mother. I guess he really loved me.

I could not and did not tell my parents the truth. Mother had always stressed, "Don't have sex before you are married. Remember,

---

"What does a sixteen-year-old girl— living in a small town, popular in high school, holding a student body office— do when she thinks she's pregnant?"

---

you are like a rosebud. If you force a rosebud open, it is ugly. If you let it open naturally, in its own time, it is beautiful."

"Good" girls did not get pregnant; only girls who weren't smart did. I told my parents, "Jim Bob and I are going to get married between semesters in January."

"You can't get married! You are too young. I will not sign for you," my mother screamed.

"Married? If you are that stupid, I will sign for you." My father helped me without even realizing what he had done. I didn't have to tell them the truth. I was relieved beyond words.

"Why do you want to get married? Are you pregnant?" Mother later quizzed.

"No. I'm not pregnant. Jim Bob and I love each other. We have just decided that we do not want to wait."

"You have your whole life ahead of you. This is such a mistake."

Inside I thought, *If you only knew how much I do not want to get married now. I do not have a choice.*

As the wedding date drew near, Scott Benson, the president of the Student Council and a dear friend, came to see me. As a sophomore I had been nominated for president of the Student Council. My junior year I was elected to the Student Council and served as secretary. Scott was certain I would be elected president my senior year.

"Carol Nan, you ought to reconsider getting married," he said. "You're throwing away some honors in your senior year that will look good later." Then he point-blank asked me, "Are you pregnant?"

Of course, I said, "No." At that time how I dearly wished the only thing I had to worry about was being elected president of the Student Council my senior year rather than being a mother.

One day just before the wedding, I telephoned Jim Bob. Somehow, the operator plugged me into the wrong circuit where I overheard a conversation between the florist and Jim Bob's brother.

"Is Jim Bob there?" I recognized the florist who was handling our wedding.

"No. This is Billy Don. Can I help you with something?"

"Well, you know, it's customary for the groom to pay for the bride's bouquet and some of the corsages. I needed to see if Jim Bob wanted to help here."

Immediately his brother said, "No. Just let the Gages pay for everything."

I didn't say a word, but I was crushed. I felt I couldn't say anything then because Jim Bob might not marry me if I caused any problems. I was trapped now, and I knew it. *I* was the one who was trapped into marriage—not Jim Bob. Honestly, at that time I know I wouldn't have married him if I had not been pregnant—I wonder now if I ever would have.

I had such mixed emotions about getting married. Although the prospect was thrilling, this was such a final step out of a world I was not ready to leave. By my own manipulation I had prematurely enlarged my boundaries into an adult world with adult responsibilities. I saw Jim Bob as a way of escape from all the griping, complaining, and condescending every day at home.

But even at the last minute, I would have backed out if I had not been pregnant.

I even felt that I was letting my parents down. In the back of my mind I thought, *Who is going to be there to help Mother cook and clean the house?* What a thing to be thinking about. My home, as bad as it had seemed to me, was more of a security blanket than I ever dreamed.

Rules are made to be broken, aren't they? But I didn't realize the high cost when you get caught. And Jim Bob and I were just beginning to pay for our mistake.

5

FOR BETTER OR FOR WORSE

My name changed from Carol Nan Gage to Carol Nan Everett on Friday, January 26, 1962. For better or for worse, Jim Bob had a strong young woman on his hands, one who needed a lot of attention and a firm hand to rein her in. Only time would tell if he could.

We married on Friday night at the First Baptist Church in San Saba with just the family and close friends present. As we drove to Austin later that night for our honeymoon, I asked, "Jim Bob, where are we going to stay tonight?"

"I thought we would find a cheap motel on the expressway."

"How much can we afford?"

"We need to find as cheap a room as possible."

I spotted a nice motel that I wanted to stay in, but Jim Bob said, "Let's go to the one next door. It looks cheaper."

We drove in. Jim Bob went in, registered, and came back dangling a room key from his hand. "Only six dollars for the night," he exclaimed.

The lovemaking wasn't any better than the room. The marriage had started.

Saturday morning my parents helped us move into the married student housing at the University of Texas at Austin—six hundred old

71

army barracks from World War II which had been converted into apartments.

Daddy was not happy with our first home. "Is this where my daughter is going to live?" he asked Jim Bob.

"Yes. We'll only pay twenty-eight dollars per month plus half of our electricity. This is all we can afford, but we will be around a lot of other married students here. We will move to a nicer place as soon as we can afford it," Jim Bob explained.

"Well, this looks like a cedar chopper's village. I can't believe you are going to live here," Daddy said to me, in a loud enough voice for Jim Bob to hear.

As we started to move in our furniture, Daddy got a little happier. Jim Bob's father owned a furniture store and had given us new furniture. Now the apartment looked very nice.

"Not many newly married couples start out with new furniture," Daddy commented. Little did I suspect, however, this was a short-lived honeymoon with the new furniture. We had to turn our furniture into the store at the end of the semester; we were reissued old, used furniture when we returned to Austin for the fall semester.

I really loved my new home. We received so many shower gifts that we didn't need anything but a broom to be ready for housekeeping. My parents supplied a nice one. It was fun having my own home, and I enjoyed the freedom of being independent.

The following Monday morning after our wedding, Jim Bob started the spring semester at the University of Texas, and I enrolled in Austin High School to finish my junior year. I took six courses that semester and two more by correspondence. I graduated from high school without having to go my senior year.

We went to school all week, studied at night, and on the weekends rushed home to San Saba. We both felt guilty about what we had done to our parents, so Jim Bob worked at his father's service station while I cleaned my parents' house. I also got our clothes clean for the next week.

My parents gave us twenty dollars a week and gas credit cards. Jim Bob's father gave us one hundred and fifty dollars a month—the same amount he had been giving him before our marriage. I do not remember lacking for anything. We actually seemed to have more than enough money to live on.

Sometimes, during those first months, I was very sick; I often thought I was going to lose the baby. The thought that a baby was growing in me was exciting, and I never doubted it was going to be a boy.

I was seventeen, newly married, and pregnant. Today the world would say to a young woman, "You can do anything you want to except have a baby in a crisis situation." Thank God, I did not hear those voices then. Abortion, which was to become my career, was unthinkable at that time.

Aborting a child violates everything a woman's body wants to do, is supposed to do. I was alive. A baby boy was alive in me. Sure, it was tough; yes, I was sick; of course, finishing school was difficult; but it was all worth it.

Old Problems Resurface

We had been married two months when I first felt rejection. Just as my mother had experienced as a young bride, I was sure Jim Bob preferred his mother over me. And I wanted to have first place in my husband's life.

"Today the world would say to a young woman, 'You can do anything you want to except have a baby in a crisis situation.' Thank God, I did not hear those voices then. Abortion, which was to become my career, was unthinkable at that time."

One Sunday afternoon when returning to Austin, we argued. It had been a rough weekend for me, and I could not understand Jim Bob's casual attitude. "Your mother is so nasty to me. There is no one in the world that can get along with her. I do everything I can to help her, and she still hates me," I pouted.

"My mother doesn't hate you," he insisted.

"Yes, she does. She blames me for your having to get married. Well, I didn't do this by myself." The old martyr routine.

"You will just have to overlook my mother for a while."

I couldn't believe what I heard. "Overlook your mother? What about me? Why don't you make her be nice to me rather than me overlook her?" I demanded.

Jim Bob threatened, "You overlook my mother, or I'll take you back to your parents and leave you. I mean it. Shut up about it."

I was crushed! It seemed Jim Bob loved his mother more than me; I couldn't express my feelings or I would be alone and pregnant. I felt controlled, stomped on.

That very day I started to build my case against my husband and his mother. I would get back at him for rejecting me and her for being the apparent reason. After experiencing rejection at home growing up, now rejection was going to be a permanent part of my marriage. I was devastated! I never expected this from Jim Bob; I never dreamed he would choose his mother over me.

The web of jealousy within me had now spread to my husband and my mother-in-law. I began to relive the nightmare my mother had lived before me.

Today, I realize that I was wrong. I was not rejected as a child nearly as much as I was *told* by my mother that she and I were rejected. There was no rejection then; I chose to believe a lie. And in the early stage of my marriage to Jim Bob, as well as in most other relationships, I continued to believe that lie.

As a result I chose to follow destructive paths that assured my rejection for many years. Throughout my life I have been responsible for doing more than enough, on my part, to destroy many potentially wholesome relationships or to run away from them. My relationships with Jim Bob and his mother were no exception.

Before we married, I dreamed we would have a huge home with a master bedroom that had a window overlooking the cattle on our ranch. We would have three or four children. I would be able to dress nicely, and we would be members of San Saba society. That was my dream, and it was so far from reality that I couldn't appreciate what I did have.

A relationship between Jim Bob and me seemed irrelevant. I just did not see happy marriages, at least none that I knew. Everyone seemed to be unhappy, fighting all the time, or having affairs. I really thought the way to keep a man happy was to please him sexually. I would make certain I did that, even if it was mundane.

"A relationship between Jim Bob and me seemed irrelevant. I just did not see happy marriages, at least none that I knew. Everyone seemed to be unhappy, fighting all the time, or having affairs."

Joe Bob, our first child, was born September 12, 1962. He was truly my baby. The struggles I had endured were worth it to have our son. I really hoped the birth of our son would finally make us a family, and we made a promising start.

We put a lot of energy into him, for we both were crazy about him. He slept with us. Both sets of grandparents really loved him, too. He was also sick a lot which gave me more reason to hold him.

The euphoria of new life wore off fast, however. Soon it was back to my old ways, to the "war zone" with the Everett family. Only now, there was another reason to fight with them and another weapon to use against them—my son.

Joe Bob was only five months old when his ten-month-old cousin bit him. At the time, we were driving around Austin with Jim Bob's brother's family. As I comforted Joe Bob, I said in everyone's hearing, "That's okay, Joe Bob. In a few months you will be old enough to bite Devin back."

Neither Billy Don nor Pat apologized for their son biting mine. They just silently got out of our car when we returned home and left. Soon the whole Everett family knew how "hateful" I'd been.

I wanted Jim Bob to say something to them; but he wanted peace at all costs. He actually told me to be quiet. "Just be nice around my family. It sure wouldn't hurt if you tried to be quiet around them."

I felt he was making a choice—them over us. I could not believe he would not take up for his own child.

As soon as I finished high school, I started to business college. My plan was to prepare for a job so we could stop taking money from Jim Bob's parents. And then we would not have to go back to San Saba so often. But before I finished business college, I was pregnant again.

Our daughter Kelly Kay was born on August 27, 1964. We moved out of the married student housing into low-income housing to get more space. How I wanted us to be the perfect American family; we certainly had a good start—a firstborn son and a beautiful daughter.

I actually thought of Kelly like a toy doll. I wanted to dress her up in ruffles and keep her that way. I dressed her in very feminine clothes until she started walking; then I started finding her and her brother matching outfits.

Joe Bob was very proud of his little sister, and he really tried to take care of her. Of course at two years old, his care was questionable: he would help her eat her ice cream by stuffing the cone in her face, getting it all over her. Kelly loved her brother; they played together all the time, surprisingly without many arguments.

Catherine Everett and I were not speaking to each other by this time. Even I knew that had to change. Things were so strained between us Jim Bob could not even ask his family to visit us. I finally extended them an invitation to come to our home, hoping to help matters. It did, and we slowly began to rebuild our relationship. Sadly to say, it was only a short fix.

The Battle for Control Rages

I completely disregarded the hurt Jim Bob must have felt. I did not understand the "old tapes" that were playing inside him regarding his mother. I was too busy listening to my own "old tapes." I was buried in selfishness, wanting recognition for myself and my children.

I looked to Jim Bob for praise, unaware that he too needed praise for he too suffered rejection. When he was born, his dad was away in World War II. His mother, I am told, had a nervous breakdown and rejected Jim Bob. His dad was called back home from the service to be with her. Catherine's sister moved in with them and took care of Jim Bob and his older brother, Billy Don. Aunt Tommie loved Jim Bob very much and still does.

I can see now that he was also struggling with rejection from me, adding to his problem with his mother. I wish we could have understood the inner struggle each of us was going through back then. I know things would have been different.

I focused on Catherine as the problem. I resented her and the way she treated my kids, trying to control them. I resented her for "causing" our marriage problems. My energies went into getting back at her through Jim Bob.

The poor guy never had a chance. At the time I didn't realize that Catherine and I were so much alike. I'll admit to being very selfish, trying to control my family. I only knew then that she was competition. I was going to win or be gone myself.

Our marriage had a lot of potential, but I did my best to destroy it. We both started out with the same goal in life: Jim Bob wanted what I wanted—a loving family. We just could not make it work.

To me Jim Bob grew weaker with each passing year. He failed some of his courses and spent time out with his friends drinking and gambling. He sometimes lost as much as two hundred dollars at a time in poker games; we had to borrow money to pay the gambling bills. Things were becoming unbearable.

Seven months after Kelly Kay was born, I went to work as a secretary in an insurance company. I did really well and was promoted. Jim Bob continued to party with his friends to the detriment of his grades.

One evening in the fourth year of our marriage, we had a big argument. I had had enough of his lifestyle, while I was working all the time.

That night I demanded, "Why don't you ever come home? You are either at school, work, out drinking with your friends, or playing poker. You never spend any time with me and the kids."

"I need some time to relax," was his answer.

"Why not relax with us? I need to relax, too. It's not relaxing at all for me when you are out drinking until all hours of the night. And another thing, every time you're playing poker, I wonder how much money I've lost. You never bring the money home to me when you win, but if you lose, it's my loss too. If you have to borrow money to pay your gambling debts, I have to help pay it back."

I was worn out by now with the same old things. Would things ever improve? "I just want a divorce," I said finally.

"Just stay with me until I get out of school, and then if you still want a divorce, I will put you through college," Jim Bob promised.

But I put no stock in that promise. I began planning to divorce him that night, never dreaming it would take him another three and a half years to graduate. It took him a total of eight and a half years to get his diploma. Seven of those years he was married to me. He got "our" degree.

I knew when I divorced Jim Bob, I would have to make more money than I was now making to support myself and my two children. It would be my responsibility to make as much and more money than their father would make when he became a pharmacist. This became my challenge! I did not see that as a problem, only an opportunity to compete with men as I had been trained to do by my father.

I was recruited by Tupperware and jumped on it. I became the youngest manager in the southwest region at age twenty-one and quickly climbed into the Top Ten in sales. I received the first check for three hundred dollars written by my distributorship up until that time. I was furnished a car and had forty-two women working for me. I was rolling!

Jim Bob perceived my success as a further threat to our marriage. "Carol Nan, you need to quit Tupperware and get a day job so you can be home with me and the kids at night," he insisted.

"How will we live if I give up this good job with Tupperware? We'll have to buy a car. I can't make this kind of money anywhere in an 8 to 5 job."

"I'll be getting out of school soon and will get a raise at the highway department. I'll take care of it."

Deep inside I guess I was confused so I quit Tupperware. I wanted to believe him. A part of me wanted to divorce Jim Bob, but another part still wanted the marriage to work.

I went to work for less money at Austin Diagnostic Clinic. This was my first, but not my last, exposure to the medical world. I started as a bookkeeper and soon became credit manager for the clinic.

Life with Jim Bob continued to get worse. The more he stayed away and did poorly in college, the more we fought and the greater my desire was to strike back at him. I tried to warn him, to get his

> **"It would be my responsibility to make as much and more money than their father would make when he became a pharmacist. This became my challenge! I did not see that as a problem, only an opportunity to compete with men as I had been trained to do by my father."**

attention. I punished him every way I could think of for neglecting me and the children. Nothing changed in his life; I was so frustrated that I used every weapon I had.

I stopped keeping the house clean, especially washing the dishes. He just bought a dishwasher. The poor guy certainly wasn't a mind reader, but how could he be so blind? Didn't he realize that I needed him, not appliances? Maybe we were both just too young.

Getting Even . . . and Getting Free

Early in the sixth year of our marriage I began to have thoughts of having an affair. And if I did, it would be someone close to Jim Bob so that when he found out, he would hurt just as he had hurt me.

The idea of an affair became very appealing to me. I could set my own boundaries; besides the hunt would be fun. I had been free to make up my own rules all my life; no boundaries were set for me in the past.

My mother always called me a "bitch." Since being nice to Jim Bob was not working, I decided to change the rules and be a "bitch" to see if he would respond differently. Of course, I did not consider myself a bitch, only a woman doing what a strong woman has to do to get her husband to do what she wants him to do. I did not see myself as doing anything terribly wrong.

I had watched Daddy treat Mother similarly. His having an affair had gotten a response from her; maybe it would work with Jim Bob.

I picked my first target—the right time, place, and the perfect prey. This affair went on for the remainder of our marriage. I picked other targets to go after. Each time Jim Bob and I fought or he stayed out late, I had someone waiting to spend time with me who would give me the attention I wanted. This game I played was very destructive.

In the early spring of 1969 Jim Bob tried to act responsible, like a real husband and provider. He was close to being out of school, and I guess he wanted to show he was ready for the real world. He went about it the wrong way, however.

I had worked very hard to help us get ahead. We had been able to buy a house because of my work. Suddenly without telling me, he cut off all the charge accounts.

I stormed into the house and confronted him. "I went to the French Bootery today to buy some shoes. They wouldn't let me charge; they pulled my account. It had a note on it that said, 'Account closed at husband's request.' Do you have any idea how embarrassing that was? If you were going to close my account, the very least you could have done is told me so I wouldn't have tried to charge."

"I knew you would be mad," he said calmly.

"Didn't you think I would find out?"

"Yes. I knew you would."

"I've paid that account myself for years. You had no right to close it."

"I've closed all of our charge accounts."

"Without discussing it with me?"

"Yes."

"I thought when you said you would take care of everything that you meant you would take care of the bills. I didn't know I was going to have to cut down. You have no right to treat me this way."

He refused to answer me. End of discussion—because he was the boss. Well, it was shades of our honeymoon motel again. Jim Bob hadn't learned after six years I was not a cheap date. I wasn't going for that. He had no right to take charge now. I had worked to put him through

"I had watched Daddy treat Mother similarly. His having an affair had gotten a response from her; maybe it would work with Jim Bob."

school, and now he wanted me to be the weak wife and let him be the strong one in the family. No way!

The war was really on now. Later that night, I reminded him, "Jim Bob, you'll be through school in August. I agreed to stay with you until you were out of school. In three months you will be out. I want a divorce then."

"Things will be so different when I'm out of school. This is no time to get a divorce." Just like that—as if I believed his promises.

"I've lived with you too long; things aren't going to be better when you are out of school." So I promptly took the kids to San Saba for the summer and started having fun, living a life apart from him.

While we were separated, he tried everything to get me to come back. He even said what I never expected to hear: "We will stop going to San Saba every weekend. I'll never go back there again if you will come back to me."

He finally said it. Jim Bob finally said he would put me before his mother. But, it was too late. By now I didn't believe him or care anymore; I was through trusting him.

Jim Bob even followed me once on a date with an admirer. He caught us at the lake together and followed me home. I went to my parents' house. He came in and began yelling a familiar name at me, "bitch."

"Kick him out of here. Get him away from me," I pleaded with my father.

"No, Carol Nan. We're not going to ask him to leave. These children belong to him, too," he responded.

I turned around. "Get out of here or I'm going to kill you."

He kept calling me a "bitch." I went to my father's closet to get his gun. Jim Bob left.

I filed for divorce immediately. I just wanted out.

He promised again we would never have to go back to San Saba if I would change my mind. But what I perceived as seven years of rejection was too much for me to overcome.

In the divorce settlement Jim Bob had "convenient memory lapse."

"You promised me that if I helped you get through school, you would help me get through. I need to go to college now. I want you to help me," I reminded him.

"I never said that, Carol Nan."

"It doesn't surprise me you don't remember your agreement. I've taken care of you all this time. I couldn't depend on you before; why should I be able to depend on you now?"

Jim Bob finally signed the divorce papers when I agreed to pay my own attorney's fees. The divorce was final in November 1969.

I guess Jim Bob wasn't strong enough to handle me. Or was I too weak to face myself?

6

A PROMISE KEPT
...A LIFE LOST

M y divorce attorney gave me some "free" advice when my divorce with Jim Bob was final. "Consider yourself a rabbit in a large carrot patch. Be selective; you don't have to take the first carrot you see," he said.

I was a twenty-four-year-old, free bunny in a whole patch of big juicy carrots with all the university students in Austin, Texas. It was the end of the sixties when the free love movement was going full blast.

I knew what men wanted and how to control them: sex was my weapon. Those once embarrassing breasts were now a big part of my artillery. I saw them all as weak, only desiring sex and not caring about the whole person.

Whenever I did run into a strong man, I didn't stay around long exactly because he couldn't be controlled. He might want a "stay-at-home housewife and mother," not a strong partner in marriage.

Earlier, Jim Bob helped a friend get a job at the Texas Highway Department where he worked while he was in school. In early 1970 after our divorce, I once called Jim Bob at work. On that day, my telephone line was crossed to someone else by mistake.

"Hello. This is Tom White," his strong voice answered.

Tom and I originally met when he and his first wife, Susan, lived in the married student housing next to Jim Bob and me at the University of Texas. His wife babysat for me sometimes while I worked with Tupperware. I had recruited her to sell Tupperware, but that did not work out. Our families had limited contact after Jim Bob and I bought our own house and moved.

"This is Carol, Tom. Carol Nan Everett. I was calling Jim Bob. Something must have happened," I apologized.

"I just dialed out. I guess our lines got crossed."

We had a brief conversation, and he told me he and Susan were divorced and asked, "Are you busy tonight?"

"No."

"Would you meet me for a cup of coffee?" he suggested.

So we met at a local restaurant and talked about our families and our lives. Then, he also shared that his father was dying with cancer.

Tom was more physically and intellectually attractive to me that evening than I had remembered. He was the fraternity man I always wanted. I did not hear from Tom again for several months, however.

In the meantime, I self-destructed at Austin Diagnostic Clinic. I was fired for constantly being late and for having a running conflict with a co-worker.

I decided to go back to San Saba, that dreaded hick town where I was raised. I moved into the other half of my parents' duplex. Granny Gage had moved out of the duplex into her own little house across the street. It was peaceful and quiet there, and the children quickly settled into kindergarten and first grade.

The carrot patch in San Saba was almost empty; it had been picked over real well. This bunny rabbit was about to starve to death in San Saba, with no carrots, when Tom called from Austin.

"Carol Nan, this is Tom White. Did you move to San Saba?"

"Yes, about a month ago."

"Do you ever get back to Austin?"

"About once a week so I can keep my sanity!"

"When are you coming back to town?"

"Tomorrow."

"How about dinner tomorrow night?"

"Great. I'll call you when I get to town to find out where to meet you." I was ecstatic! A big, juicy carrot!

That evening Tom told me, "I decided not to call you until I was absolutely certain Susan and I were never going to get back together."

That made sense, but I also knew he was living with a nineteen-year-old girl and her mother, sleeping with the daughter while desiring her mother.

Of course he mentioned that he remembered how I looked flopping across the parking lot. He just had to call me, he said.

How could I have been so blind and gullible to have believed his line? The bunny was too hungry to take the lawyer's free advice, I guess. Instead, Tom trapped me at my own game.

Tom and I started seeing each other every weekend in Austin, and I stayed in his apartment. Early one Friday afternoon, he called to break our weekend date. "I won't be able to see you this weekend; my dad just died."

I felt so cold, identifying with his loss. I didn't know what to say, but I blurted out, "I'm sorry about your father's death. When are you going to Monahans?"

"My plane leaves in about two hours."

I knew he was alone, and I longed to be with him. He sounded so empty when I hung up the phone that I called him back. "I don't

---

"How could I have been so blind and gullible to have believed his line? The bunny was too hungry to take the lawyer's free advice, I guess. Instead, Tom trapped me at my own game."

---

know what to say, but I feel so sad. I just want you to know I truly care. Is there anything I can do?"

"No. Thanks for calling. I'll call you when I get back." He seemed relieved to hear my voice.

Two weeks after the funeral we both went to see his mother in Monahans. Faye White was quite a lady, beautiful, very poised and adjusting to her husband's death gracefully. However, I knew by the time we left her home that weekend, she did not want her son to marry a woman with two children. I also knew that I was not on the same social level with them. In San Saba we only had two levels— those "with it" and those "not with it." In Monahans there was another level, "the uppercrusts."

The Whites were "uppercrust."

Faye White didn't think she had to worry about a marriage between Tom and me. So marrying Tom became a real challenge for that reason.

While I was seeing Tom, Daddy was planning my future in San Saba. "Baby, I've been thinking about getting you a few hogs and putting them out north of town. I think you can make a pretty good living raising hogs," he suggested one day.

My response to his good business venture? "Can I borrow three hundred dollars to move back to Austin?"

"Yes," he replied.

I don't know if he knew the hogs would get rid of me, but it worked. I was sure Daddy wasn't aware of the fact that "uppercrusts" in Monahans look down their noses at female hog farmers from San Saba.

Married in Red

I moved back to Austin leaving the children in San Saba until I got settled. I went to work as credit manager at Holy Cross Hospital and moved into an apartment close to Tom's apartment. He kept his apartment, but his clothes stayed in mine.

Tom was sexually exciting to me, and we spent most of our free time in bed. I wanted Tom to be my husband. I wanted us to live together the rest of our lives.

The time came for the children to rejoin me in Austin. Tom didn't think it was a good idea. "Carol Nan, why don't you leave the kids in San Saba with their grandparents?" he asked.

"Jim Bob will try to get custody of the kids if I do. There is no way I am going to give him the opportunity to get my children."

When I brought them home, Tom and I continued to have the same living arrangement. Despite the fact that I liked him, I did not like the impression my children were getting about a family, especially a husband/wife relationship. I gave him an ultimatum, "Either we marry or we break off the relationship," I said.

When he did not respond, I decided to set up a date through a friend of mine with a man from Houston. I told him, "Tom, I'm going on. There are other men out there. You don't intend to marry me. So I'm going to Houston for a date this weekend."

"Cancel the trip to Houston and spend the weekend with me visiting my mother," he pleaded. That was it. We took the children with us to meet his mother in her new apartment in Ft. Worth. Suddenly, my hopes of marriage to Tom looked bright.

After we returned from being paraded before Faye White, I knew we were "lowercrust," and had failed to meet her "uppercrust" requirements.

Visiting his mother, I realized how much he struggled with pleasing her just as Jim Bob struggled with pleasing his mother. I could see the rejection Tom felt inside. I knew he was confused about marrying me, knowing it would displease his mother. I wasn't sure Tom would choose to go against her. I had to go on with my life.

The following Monday I went to see my counselor I had been seeing for some time, and Tom went with me. As we got started, I stated my feelings, "I have reached the point where I am ready to go on with my life. Tom does not want to get married. I see no reason to stay in this relationship if we are not going to get married. I want out," I explained.

Steve looked at Tom. "How do you feel about that, Tom?"

"I don't want to get married, but I am not ready to call it off either."

"Tom, you know that Carol is a strong woman. This relationship will not wait. What are you going to do?" Steve asked.

"I don't like to be pushed into anything," Tom admitted.

I answered him, "Tom, I am not pushing you. I am just finished. I am going on. I love you, and I want to build a life with you. But, you don't want that with me."

"I am not ready to remarry," he said, more to himself than to us.

Steve said softly, "I don't think Carol is questioning that. She is ready to leave you behind if that is how you feel. She understands. Tom, I don't know you, but I have been seeing Carol for some time.

This woman is not going to wait for you. If you want her, you are going to have to make a move now."

"I see."

After the session, we left in silence. Tom wasn't talking and I felt I couldn't say any more. Sitting in the car at the red light, I was both relieved that I had made a decision and sorry that our relationship was over. I had to get on with my life.

"Carol Nan, will you marry me this afternoon?" came Tom's voice out of the blue.

Without hesitation, I answered, "Yes, Tom. I will."

"I'll call a Justice of the Peace when I get back to the office. Let's do it as soon as possible." And he kissed me.

I was on cloud nine! I skipped back into the office but did little work. A bouquet of flowers was delivered; it really was true. The telephone rang in about an hour, and my husband-to-be asked, "Can you meet me at the court house at 4:00?"

"Yes, and thank you for the roses. I love you very much."

"I love you, too."

I took the rest of the day off, bought a red dress (I loved red because of the childish rhyme Mother used to tell me, "Married in red, you'll wish you were dead!") and met Tom at the courthouse. We signed the marriage license, and the county judge married us in his office. Tom's University of Texas graduate ring was turned upside down and used for my wedding ring. It was 5:00 P.M.

It was late when we picked the children up from the babysitter. We went home and told them. "We got married today."

Their response was typical. Joe Bob said, "Let's eat." Kelly cried. And Trey, Tom's son, got up to go with Joe Bob.

We had a grilled cheese sandwich with a bowl of tomato soup and settled in to telephone our parents.

"Hi, Mama. Tom and I got married this afternoon."

"What color dress did you wear?"

"I got a new red one to wear."

"Married in red, you'll wish you were dead!"

Faye White refused to talk to me. Her silence spoke a thousand words. This was shades of the past, reminding me of my relationship with my first mother-in-law, Catherine Everett. The die was cast between us. It would be a stormy relationship between Faye White and Carol Nan.

Tom and I took off work the next morning, went to the jewelry store and bought a gold wedding band with black etching for me. Tom promised, "In the future we will add a diamond for each year of our

---

"I took the rest of the day off, bought a red dress (I loved red because of the childish rhyme Mother used to tell me, 'Married in red, you'll wish you were dead!') and met Tom at the courthouse."

---

marriage." The ring remained diamondless throughout our four years of marriage—another promise unfulfilled by a man in my life.

An Agreement Is Sacred

Tom White and I were married on November 9, 1970, exactly one year after my divorce from Jim Bob—because I was a strong woman, strong enough to make a good living for two children and myself. I loved Tom and wanted to prove myself to him in every way; he would see he had made a wise choice in marrying me.

Tom and I had a premarital agreement, and negotiations were settled long before the wedding. In the bedroom after sex, over a period of months before the marriage, we defined the parameters. I often visualized Tom pulling out his little black book and recording another negotiated point.

Agreements are sacred to Tom White. If you renege on an agreement, you're weak, and Tom doesn't like weak people—certainly not a weak woman. "I felt trapped into the marriage with Susan because of the pregnancy," he said often. "I just don't want to be trapped again. You have two children; I have one; we just don't need any more children."

"I'm not going to get pregnant, Tom."

"If you do, will you get an abortion? I don't want another child."

"Sure, Tom. I'm not going to get pregnant. But, if I do, I'll get an abortion," I agreed.

Because I saw the pain inside Tom, I believed he had been married to a weak woman. So it was okay for Tom to be demanding. I could also see how much rejection he felt from his mother. It would be an honor to be a strong woman standing beside this strong man. The other women in his life had always fallen into "a heap" as soon as he committed to them; I would not.

When he married Susan, his first wife, she was perfect. Later their marriage fell apart because she didn't do many of the things she had promised him. I knew our marriage would not fall apart because of my weakness.

I wanted Tom White so badly I didn't care what the premarital agreement said. The final negotiated terms were clear:

First, I would pay all the household bills; he would give me one hundred dollars per month and pay the phone bill.

Second, if I became pregnant, there would be an abortion. My two children, along with Tom's son, Trey, were enough. This part of the agreement I considered rather lightly simply because I never thought it would happen.

Third, my two children were my responsibility. He did not want to be called Daddy by them—he was Tom. I was to take care of them by myself.

Fourth, if we ever divorced, I had to pay all the legal expenses and ask nothing from him. He had been cleaned out once by Susan and wanted to be sure that never happened to him again.

Proving myself to Tom was very important; whatever it took for me to be the perfect wife and strong woman, I would do.

My life was work as usual, cooking, cleaning house, and taking care of three children each day. Trey stayed with us a lot during the week because one of Tom's old neighbors told him Trey was being left alone at night.

I tried hard to parent Trey in hopes Tom would want to parent my children. At my urging, Tom filed a suit to get custody of Trey, but the neighbor refused to testify and we lost. Trey would have been a wonderful addition to our family; I thought he would be the glue to seal us together as a family.

Professional opportunities were limited for Tom in Austin, so he began to search for a job elsewhere. We were married for about two years when Frito Lay hired him.

We moved to Dallas in June 1972, and lived in an apartment for three months until we bought our house. Tom settled into his job, and

---

"Because I saw the pain inside Tom, I believed he had been married to a weak woman. So it was okay for Tom to be demanding. I could also see how much rejection he felt from his mother."

I went to work for Dr. Howard Wisner as his office manager and operating room technician. Dr. Wisner used Garland Memorial Hospital as his primary hospital.

I loved Tom. Whenever I saw him, something inside me quickened. I stayed busy trying to keep things running just the way he liked it, giving little thought to myself.

He reminded me of my father in so many ways, making me want to please him like I did my daddy. The only kind of love I had ever known was conditional, dependent on what I did and how well I did it. In my mind Tom kept a little black book with all my pluses and minuses, just like my mother did.

For Tom to love me I had to be the perfect wife, the perfect woman. But, when could I be sure he knew I loved him, and when would I be assured of his love for me?

The Unexpected Happens

Between December 10 and 12, 1972, I got pregnant.

Deep inside I wanted to have Tom's baby. It was my third pregnancy but the first one I was old enough, and in love enough, to truly enjoy. And yet, I feared Tom would reject me if I did not honor item two of our prenuptial agreement—abortion.

I experienced some bleeding, but the intensity of the mental and emotional struggle within me during the first weeks of my pregnancy was almost unbearable. I agonized over how to deal with Tom regarding the abortion part of our agreement.

My thoughts about the child were very warm. It was like a joyous song inside me playing in the midst of a storm.

You are two weeks old, and I know you are there. I can feel you growing. All my hormones are changing in my body to let you grow and live. The changes are making me sick. You are going to be so special.

My other children are blonde and look like me, but you will have a dark complexion, like your father. You will have dark hair and dark eyes, too. I love you already.

I can feel you inside me, protected by my body, growing silently. I know you will be special. Your sister is eight and your brother is ten, and you will be the baby, the last of my children. You and I are lucky; I am twenty-eight years old, finally old enough to have children, and I can be the mother to you I have never been able to be to your brother and sister.

You are my secret. There will be problems when your father finds out, so you just grow quietly, and I will take care of the rest. I will protect you.

I am making room for you in my body, even starting to glow. You know, women are supposed to be prettier when they are pregnant. Some people even say I look pregnant—but it is so early—no one can know but me.

I love your father so much, and because of our love you will be so loved. You will have a home with a mother and father that love you, like I was loved when I was born. You have a sister and a brother who will be so excited to hear about your coming into our home. Yes, there will be others who will wonder why I am pregnant again, but you are a gift of the love I have for your father.

Your coming will make us a family—the family I have longed for us to be all along. You don't understand this, but your sister and brother are mine from another marriage, and your father is their step-

father, but you will make us a family. Yes, our lives will change because of you, but for the better. You will be the rallying point of so
many good things. You will be special in so many ways!

I hold my hand over my abdomen where you are growing to let
you know that I love you, and I want you very much. I can't wait to
hold you in my arms. I will breast feed you just so I can spend extra
time with you, and I will tell you all about this world that will be so
new to you.

I can really be a mother to you, a luxury I didn't have with your
sister and brother. I am going to really enjoy you. . . . Will your daddy
be as excited as I am?

You have fingers, toes, and yes, you are alive. Your heart is beat-
ing, you have brain waves, and everything is growing according to
plan, and you are perfect. I just know it!

I also had some very strange thoughts, for me, about work and
career. Somehow the "good job" and the work-a-day world seemed so
humdrum compared to being a real mother to this baby. I couldn't
wait to be "just a mother, a housewife," to invest in my new baby, my
daughter, and my son. Was I becoming weak or truly strong?

"You are my secret. There will be problems when your father finds out, so you just grow quietly, and I will take care of the rest. I will protect you."

The time had come to test our love for each other. Hoping for a
miracle, I worked up the courage to tell Tom.

"Tom, I think I'm pregnant."

"What about the IUD?"

"It's still there, but I think I'm pregnant anyway."

"Are you going to the doctor?"

"Yes. You know I've been bleeding for over five weeks."

"Well, what about all that X-ray you've been exposed to in surgery?"

"I don't know; that's not good. There could be something wrong with the baby."

The conversation was over.

It was a very trying time wondering if he would push to abort the child or abort the marriage. The agreement I had entered into so lightly now weighed so heavy on my heart.

It may sound strange coming from me now, but I was hoping for a miracle, yes, a miracle from God. After all, birth is a miracle, and out of the act of love life is formed. And how special, the main thing Tom and I really had to keep us together—sex—was the avenue for this miracle.

I needed some support to encourage me, to help me deal with Tom, and to stop the consequences of our agreement. Where I grew up in San Saba, Texas, country town, USA, babies were babies at conception; abortions were out of the question.

During Christmas I told my Aunt Nan I was pregnant; she would help me. But she was sick at the time and wasn't able to muster up any support for me. I told my mother and her mother, Grandmother Taylor, hoping they would encourage me, but they seemed indifferent. And my husband still wasn't saying another word. He had always said children were a liability, referring to my children, Joe Bob and Kelly Kay. Why did I think he would consider another one, even ours, an asset?

What if he walked out on me? Running through my mind constantly was the thought, *How will I feel living without Tom, with three children? How can I make it alone with three children?* And I wondered how soon he would leave me if I did not abort the child.

The bleeding continued into the sixth week. I finally went to see Dr. Harvey Johnson, a roommate of Dr. Wisner's, for a check-up to confirm I was pregnant. I had met Dr. Johnson while working at the hospital and chose him to be my personal doctor because of his good reputation. Dr. Johnson examined me and told me my IUD was perfectly in place, that I was not pregnant, and what I needed was a D and C to remove the IUD to stop the bleeding.

I can't tell you how relieved I was that I did not have to decide on an abortion. The expert had spoken, and besides, if I were pregnant and he did a D and C, I would not be responsible for killing my child.

Surgery was scheduled for 7:00 A.M. the next day. I left Dr. Johnson's office, returned to work for a few hours, and then checked into the hospital. The lab work was done that evening in preparation for my D and C the following morning.

> ## "It was a very trying time wondering if he would push to abort the child or abort the marriage. The agreement I had entered into so lightly now weighed so heavy on my heart."

Early the next morning the nurse informed me Dr. Johnson needed to examine me again. *What in the world is going on?*

I was wheeled into an examining room with Dr. Johnson.

"Carol, you are pregnant," he announced soon after his examination.

"I told you I was."

"I cannot do a D and C."

I began to ride an emotional roller coaster. My thoughts focused on my baby again, *We have been given a reprieve. See, no one listens to me. I knew you were there. Now, they know. You're not safe anymore.*

But, who was my baby not safe from?

A Choice Is Made

A choice—would I choose my child or my husband?

After being discharged from the hospital, I called Tom at work. "I'm not having surgery today."

"Why?"

"The pregnancy test is positive. I am pregnant."

There was silence . . . not a word . . . only silence.

I told my friends at work I was pregnant, and they kept asking me, "What are you going to do?"

"Have an abortion." *How did those words, that word—abortion— come out of my mouth?*

I started to build my case to justify my future action. I reasoned, *I have been bleeding for six weeks now; that must mean there is a problem with the pregnancy. And what about the X-rays I've been exposed to? Wouldn't the baby be deformed?* I hated myself, and there wasn't anyone to rescue me.

I cannot do it; the abortion has to be stopped. Dr. Johnson is my way out. He will save me from myself. I'll go ahead and ask Dr. Johnson his opinion of abortion, and he'll just say, "No, abortion is wrong." After all Dr. Johnson has a good reputation.

I will be safe then, with Tom. I'll just tell him I can't have an abortion. Dr. Johnson said so. Tom will see that I am not weak; that I am not reneging on my agreement.

For the second time within the first six weeks of my third pregnancy, "my rules" allowed me to turn to recognized authority to put traditional bounds on me. First, I turned to God in prayer for a miracle; then to my highly professional doctor and traditional life values. A *doctor who lives by the Hippocratic Oath would say, "How could you think of such a thing,"* I reasoned. Doctors are supposed to give life, protect and support life, not take life, aren't they?

The Hippocratic Oath has been the ethical guide of the medical profession since late in the fifth century. It states, "To please no one will I prescribe a deadly drug, nor give advice which may cause his death. Nor will I give a woman a pessary to procure abortion." A more modern version states, "I will maintain the utmost respect for human life from the time of conception; even under threat, I will not use my medical knowledge contrary to the laws of humanity. I make these promises solemnly, freely, and upon my honor."

But, there are doctors, and then there are abortionists.

I called him. "Dr. Johnson, what do you think about abortion? Tom wants me to have one. I hear they are doing them in New Mexico."

I was shocked beyond words when I heard Dr. Johnson respond, "You don't have to go anywhere; I do them all the time." He was a "secret" abortionist, and I didn't know it. He continued to explain, "It's not a baby yet; it's only a glob of tissue."

That was not what I needed to hear. I was stunned. "Oh, well, we surely can't talk about this over the telephone because it is illegal. Do I come to your office or where do we meet to talk about this?"

Dr. Johnson said, "Oh, no problem. Just bring in the father's urine; we will give it to the lab for the pregnancy test, and it will be negative. I'll call it a D and C, and your insurance will pay for it."

Actually, on January 22, 1973, the Supreme Court ruled in favor of abortion in the Roe vs. Wade case, allowing a woman the right to privacy, the right to choose an abortion. Several states were already allowing abortions to be performed, but I did not know it at the time.

But did the "secret" abortionist know it? Was Dr. Harvey Johnson afraid of being found out by his existing clients, unless they secretly needed his "hush, hush" service?

Harvey Johnson made abortion sound so simple, so easy. After all it was just a glob of tissue—my baby by the man I loved, the product of precious intimacy, was just a glob of tissue.

I struggled with Dr. Johnson's "expert" opinion about abortion. Inside my thoughts went wild. I talked to the "glob of tissue" but really to myself as never before. *I really want to be your mother. I want you to have a father that loves you, a brother and sister who will love you in a heartbeat, love you so much they will carry you around and show you off to everyone.*

" 'You don't have to go anywhere; I do them all the time.' He was a 'secret' abortionist, and I didn't know it. He continued to explain, 'It's not a baby yet; it's only a glob of tissue.' "

Your dad won't talk to me about this. He doesn't want you. You will only mess up the picture; we'd have diaper bags and 2:00 A.M. feedings and things like that. I know you are not just a glob of tissue; you are growing inside me. I know, too, the growth has to stop, or else—I'll lose my husband, your dad.

I have to pull myself together and be happy about this abortion. I will just tell the children something went wrong with the pregnancy, so they won't find out the truth.

My last hope was gone; I saw no way out.

I did not trust my relationship with Tom enough to challenge the agreement. I wanted the child, but I loved my husband. It was a choice between the baby I wanted and the husband I worshiped. If I told Tom I wanted the child, I would be showing weakness and breaking our premarital agreement; and agreements are sacred to Tom White.

The hour of decision had come. The time was close for the ultimate sacrifice—a blood sacrifice—to prove my love for Tom. He would be sure of my love for him when the sacrifice was made. But would I be assured of his love for me?

I told the child, *No matter how much I love you, your father doesn't want you. If I keep you, he won't want me. You are so little; it really won't hurt you. I'm so sorry.*

I made my final decision consoling myself with this fact: *Agreements are made to be broken, but love doesn't break them.* I love Tom. He wins this time.

I made the phone call of a lifetime. "Dr. Johnson, let's do it as soon as possible. When can I go in? Tomorrow? Yes, I'll be there."

When I checked into the hospital Thursday evening, February 15, 1973, Tom went with me and did his part; he provided the urine Dr. Johnson requested for insurance purposes, guaranteeing a negative pregnancy test. By that act, if by no other, Tom cast his vote for the abortion. Whether he wants to accept involvement, his participation by that act alone, guarantees to me he will face his judgment as surely as I will.

Later that evening I was alone, just me and the baby. I never felt so heavy or such numbness in all my life. *We are alone, now. I don't know what to say. What kind of mother am I to voluntarily take your life from you? I wish your dad would call me and say, "Stop it," and release me from the promise I made.*

I want you, but if I violate my promise, your dad will leave me. I still love him so much, and I really don't know you; please try to understand.

Although there is room for you in my heart, there just isn't enough room for you in our home.

As I lay there preparing myself for the abortion, I wanted Tom to change into my knight in shining armor, race through the door of the hospital room, and rescue us. I wanted to call Tom and say, "Please don't make me do this."

"As I lay there preparing myself for the abortion, I wanted Tom to change into my knight in shining armor, race through the door of the hospital room, and rescue us."

Those words remained unspoken. What a tragedy for the unborn, for Tom, Joe Bob, Kelly, and for me.

As they wheeled me into the operating room, I asked Jodie, the surgical supervisor, "How is the procedure listed on the schedule?"

"It's posted as 'incomplete abortion,'" which is the term for a spontaneous miscarriage that has not completely discharged all the pregnancy.

The operating room doctors and nurses were my co-workers at the hospital. Jan Batson, Dr. Johnson's scrub nurse, patted me and said reassuringly, "We're going to get this taken care of and get you back to work."

As the anesthesiologist put me out, he jokingly said, "I'm going to have to put you to sleep so I can finally see your boobs!" Men are the same everywhere, aren't they?

My third child was aborted at 7:00 A.M. Friday morning, February 16, 1973.

Friday had always been mine and Tom's special day during our dating time and throughout our marriage. It was a time I always looked forward to with much joy and fondness. There was no joy that Friday, only heaviness and shame. Fridays would never be the same again.

When I woke up, my womb was empty. I felt the emptiness where my child had been safely tucked away only a few hours earlier.

Depression overwhelmed me; guilt engulfed me; tears were everywhere. I felt too ashamed to call my mother, Grandmother Taylor, or Aunt Nan for comfort.

My heart was broken. The joyful song that had been created by the life forming and growing within me was gone, along with the excitement and anticipation. I had nothing to sing about anymore.

Tom's strong woman honored their sacred agreement. Carol, the strong one, did not show weakness and renege on the deal. The price was paid in full with the sacrifice of the life of our innocent, helpless child.

Death is so final. The Grim Reaper won that time, not Tom or Carol.

7

A VICTIM OF THE BIG LIE

L ike many others, I bought the big lie: It is only a glob of tissue—not a baby.

I was a victim of all the other lies: *Abortion is all right. After all, I do them all the time. It's only a glob of tissue. It will be so simple. We'll do it at the hospital and your insurance will pay for it. There's really nothing to the procedure; it will only take a little while and then everything will be fine. You can have the abortion on Friday morning and go back to work on Monday.* And Dr. Harvey Johnson, my personal Ob-Gyn, the one I turned to for help, was in reality a secret abortionist, an abortionist for profit. I was a victim of his lies.

Friday morning, February 16, 1973, I voluntarily joined the post-abortion women's society. We were a very secretive society then, with one thing in common—the killing of our unborn children.

In 1973 not much was known about abortion and its effect on the other victims of abortion—the aborted child's mother, father, living siblings, grandparents, and other family members. Because of the secrecy surrounding these events, there was no way of knowing the impact abortions were having.

However, I can tell you my abortion served to further destroy my self-worth and compound my destructive ways toward my family, in my workplace, and ultimately toward society as a whole.

I take full responsibility for voluntarily aborting my child, yet at the same time I consider myself a victim of abortion. Because of my own lack of self-worth, I made Tom White my idol and my excuse for aborting my child. I was also a victim of an abortionist and a budding new business in the marketplace, a business that has experienced phenomenal growth since 1973.

Post-Abortion Syndrome

In the recovery room that glob of tissue, the impersonal product of conception, was my aborted child. I killed my baby, my child by Tom. I was supposed to nurture and protect that baby, but I killed it. Back in my hospital room my mind and emotions were like a runaway train headed for a big crash.

What is it with me; why do I hurt so badly? I was told abortion is not supposed to be this painful or bother me this much. Why do I feel so depressed now that I have liberated myself from motherhood—no 2:00 A.M. feedings, no dirty diapers. I thought the "freedom to choose, the right to choose" was supposed to make me feel better, even make me feel more like a woman. Why do I feel raped?

My mind and emotions continued to race, *The baby and I are the only ones who got hurt in this abortion. Tom escaped again. I must have a sterilization procedure right now so I will neither get pregnant again nor hurt so badly again. I will really be liberated then.*

Then I imagined God would somehow punish me. *Oh no, God will take away Joe Bob or Kelly now because I have killed my unborn child.*

How do I deal with what I have done? Get it together, Carol Nan. You have a good track record; you have always been able to work your way through your problems. Don't think for a minute Tom will be able to help you through this. Stop thinking about the pain, and start thinking about all the work waiting for you when you get home. On and on my mind wrestled with what I had done.

Growing up, my father always set invisible boundaries. They were invisible because he never told me what his boundary was until after I had crossed it. "Carol Nan, I *was* going to get you a car, but since you used my pick-up for such a long time, I'm not going to," he'd say.

I'd want to ask, "Why didn't you tell me, Daddy?" but instead, I silently accepted my punishment.

His punishment, like his invisible boundary, was always a secret. When I had my abortion, something inside me said, *You have crossed an "invisible" boundary again; now you must face your punishment.*

I want to talk to someone. Someone who loves me. Someone who cares about me. Who can I call? I can't call my mother and say, "I just killed my baby." Oh, I'm depressed. I want to be comforted by someone, anyone, but I can't bring myself to tell anyone the truth. Tom knows. Surely Tom will feel this same remorse at the loss of our child. I will be with him soon.

"What is it with me; why do I hurt so badly? I was told abortion is not supposed to be this painful or bother me this much. Why do I feel so depressed now that I have liberated myself from motherhood?"

I left the hospital feeling guilty, confused, and ashamed.

On the way home I picked up shrimp for our regular Friday "funday" dinner. In my heart I had mixed emotions about facing my two living children. I wanted so badly to hold them and tell them how much I loved them and needed them, but what if they knew what I had just done? Could they tell by just looking at me? I picked them up at the babysitter's house.

"Hi, urchins. How are you?" I hugged them, one on each side, holding on too long for Joe Bob's comfort; he wiggled away so I almost crushed Kelly hugging her.

"Fine, Mommy. How do you feel?"

"I feel fine. I'm glad to be home with you."

"How was your day, Kelly?"

"Okay."

"Joe Bob, how was your day?"

"Okay. Can I go out to play?"

"Sure. Kelly, what are you going to do?"

"I want to see if Jennifer is at home and wants to play."

"That will be fine."

Normal conversation. The children didn't suspect that I had just killed their brother or sister. Life was normal for them, so I had to try to be normal, too. *Will they ever discover just what kind of mother I really am? They just can't. I am determined they will never find out from me what I have done.*

The first thing I wanted to do was reach out to Tom to help me fill the emptiness I felt inside after the abortion—the emptiness created by the loss of warm, tender affection I had been experiencing with the attached baby in my womb. The natural, instinctive love I had for our baby, a love that grew each day I carried our unborn child, somehow had to be replaced.

While preparing Tom's favorite shrimp dinner, I wanted him to make the first move, to hold me, thinking maybe now he would really love and comfort me. After dinner my perfect performance required cleaning the kitchen quickly and efficiently and getting the children to bed. Then, I went to our bedroom, our room of love, hoping Tom would want to strengthen our bond of love, to fill the new emptiness within me. Would he, even though we could not have sex?

"How do you feel?" he asked.

"I'm all right."

"How long will it be before we can make love again?"

That is all he wants from me. He doesn't love me, doesn't respect me, but most of all, he doesn't understand what I have just done for him. Aloud, I answered, "No sex for a week. Tom, I feel terrible and so depressed."

"What is on TV tonight?"

Does he even hear me? I suppose I should be happy he doesn't go outside to one of his beloved projects. At least he is staying inside with me. I feel so alone right in this king-size bed with this man, this man I love, but who really doesn't seem to care about me.

"Tom, I am really upset about this."

"What do you mean?"

"The abortion."

"I could not see that the power we selfishly crave as human beings is the doorway for deception which leads to destruction. I still could not see abortion had sabotaged our relationship; what was supposed to fix it was about to destroy it."

"Carol Nan, we made the best choice we could, and we need to go on with our lives."

There was no reassurance or comfort from him.

I felt very remorseful and thought Tom was feeling the same way, but he wasn't. I could not believe he said, "We made the best choice we could, and we need to go on with our lives." At least this was the first admittance of his part in the decision. Thank God! But "the best choice"? He didn't feel remorseful at all; he felt relieved.

I quietly cried myself to sleep while the father of my aborted baby watched television because he couldn't participate in his regular Friday night sport—making love. In spite of his insensitivity that evening, however, I kept wanting to bond with Tom. I was looking for him to affirm me for honoring my end of the agreement, but there was no acknowledgment of anything special I had done. It was all in a day's work.

I honored my "covenant duty" by aborting our baby. *Surely the act of abortion will open a new level of love, trust, and communication between us,* I reasoned. At the time, our child was not as important to me as the act of pleasing Tom, proving I was a strong woman worthy of him.

Now, I thought, *I can have true happiness—Tom will share that unrevealed part of himself that he's been withholding from me.* It was so clear to me—the abortion of our child was the crowning act that proved my love for Tom—proved my reverence for him and my gratitude to him for marrying me. No woman had ever loved him enough to put him first, before herself, by upholding her agreement at all cost. Surely, he would reciprocate by freely giving himself to me.

I felt a strong need to be a greater part of Tom, a new sense of dependence; I needed him more because of my loss. Surely, Tom needed me and loved me, too. I had passed the supreme test; now I was worthy of his special attention and devotion.

Somehow, I believed this act of love on my part would cause Tom to commit to me, give me the recognition, the attention I craved; then, I would be in control. I could not see that the power we selfishly crave as human beings is the doorway for deception which leads to destruction. I still could not see abortion had sabotaged our relationship; what was supposed to fix it was about to destroy it.

I kept wanting Tom to change and be a real husband to me and a father to my children. Somehow, I thought the price I had paid in the abortion would buy that change.

It didn't work.

"Are you going to work on your car again tonight?"

"Yes. My new project is to cover the dash with leather. This will complete the restoration on the Mercedes."

"What is the next project?"

"I am going to start to work on the Jaguar."

"Is there ever time for me? I think you must have orgasms working on your cars. Those cars come before anything."

Out the door he silently went to his cars—his projects.

I needed a family unit more than ever before. More than anything else I wanted to get pregnant again. I wanted a child with Tom, the only man I spontaneously loved. Maybe our child would bring us together. But Tom had other things on his mind, as usual—his beloved cars and other projects.

Tom and I just could not bond. The emptiness, the hurt, and the depression helped me make the decision to have the sterilization procedure done. I finally accepted the fact Tom did not want to have children; that there would be no other children from our union.

As soon after my abortion as Dr. Johnson would do the surgery, I surrendered the life-giving part of my femininity to my strong, destructive self. Pain on top of pain, I now could not have another child.

I made two big sacrifices for Tom—my child and my ability to give life. My attitude toward him changed, hardened. He knew he controlled me now. He had to be smiling inside at the good deal he made in our premarital agreement and the silent power he exerted over me. Well, I didn't want to be humiliated every day by his knowing that he had the upper hand, that he had won. I had to show him another aspect of my strength. I would hide the pain; I would cry no more.

For the very first time I realized the horrible state our marriage was in. I didn't have a husband; I had a live-in lover with a license, and a very smart one at that.

He had negotiated a deal no man would walk away from—a house to call home, a live-in maid and cook, sex upon demand with a willing participant who would reproduce no "liabilities"—all for the price of two hundred dollars a month (raised from the one hundred dollars I received before we moved into our house in Dallas) plus the telephone bill.

I realized I hadn't loved too much—I just had a rotten self-image.

My whole life is a lie! I am not strong. I am weak, stupid, just exactly the kind of person my dad thought my mother was. And what's more, Tom White is not strong, either. He's weaker than I am.

How could I have ever been so deceived by such false strength? True strength stands firm in the face of responsibility. What greater responsibility do a husband and wife have than to graciously accept the gift of the unborn, the fruit of their love-making, to nurture and protect it? Tom and I rejected our responsibility—or what would have been my responsibility—and refused the gift of life which had so much to give us.

The thrill and excitement of being with Tom White was gone. The spark that once ignited my fire for him was not there anymore. The joyful song inside me that our love had created was silenced, and in its place were cold, hard facts about our relationship.

Someone once said, "Love is blind," and when the blinders were taken off, Tom looked totally different to me. He looked like a man who deserved to be humbled, to be punished, and I was just the woman for the job.

My Path of Destruction

Now it was time for Tom to worship at my shrine and prove he loved me. Tom and my mother weren't the only ones who kept a list. My "invisible black slate" with a fast-growing list was going to be hard, if not impossible, for Tom to erase.

But he had to erase it to prove himself to me, to prove he was wrong about the way we had been living. If he cared enough to erase it all, then I would know he loved me.

There were four big items on my invisible black slate:

1. Tom's belief that children are liabilities rather than assets had to change. He had to become a father to my children.

2. Tom had to accept responsibility for his part in the abortion. He had to acknowledge his guilt and show remorse for his silent consent and the provision of his urine specimen. He had to take his punishment like a man. The baby's suffering was over; his suffering was just beginning; mine would never end.

3. Tom had to admit he was insensitive to my needs, demonstrated by his never asking me if I wanted the child. He had to apologize for it.

4. Tom had to admit that our marriage was only a business deal with selfish pleasure thrown in, that he was not a husband to me—just a sex partner and good negotiator. The business deal had to be dropped and a new deal struck on our marriage relationship, whatever that meant.

The rules of the game had to change because the deal had gone sour.

Tom White would begin to experience my unforgiving, vindictive, destructive side. I would inflict as much pain and punishment as I could on him until he hurt as badly as the innocent child and I did, until he acknowledged his rejection of us, admitted his guilt, and sought my forgiveness for his cold, calculated, loveless actions.

I would be the judge as to when the slate was clean and when he was sufficiently humbled.

Two weeks after the sterilization process was done, I started planning an affair. I had to find someone who cared about me. I had to prove to myself that I was lovable, to find someone to fill the emptiness I felt. At the same time, I had to punish Tom.

What a mess I was in emotionally—unloved, unlovable, but desperately trying to prove otherwise; feeling guilty, yet unforgiving, and at the same time acting so self-righteous in meting out punishment on my partner-in-sin against our innocent, helpless child.

Poor Tom was caught up in something like a west Texas sand storm that had come out of nowhere.

I began to have an affair with a co-worker, right on the job.

Once Tom took the call, "The telephone is for you, Carol Nan. It's Max from the office."

"Tom had to admit that our marriage was only a business deal with selfish pleasure thrown in, that he was not a husband to me. . . ."

I was relieved when Tom went to the garage so I could talk to Max without reservation. "Hello, Max."

"Could you meet me at 7:30 in the morning at the hospital for breakfast?"

"Yes. I'll be there. I can't wait to see you."

Tom returned right after the telephone call was finished. I thought, "That is strange behavior for him. How did he know I was off the telephone. Tom is so strange sometimes!"

On another occasion I made a call to another old boyfriend. Tom asked, "Where is Cathy's Kitchen?"

"What do you mean?"

"I heard you say something about Cathy's Kitchen."

I hadn't mentioned Cathy's Kitchen, but the person I was talking to on the telephone did. "Tom, are you listening in on my telephone conversations?"

Silence. I knew the answer. He was running to the garage everytime the telephone rang so he could listen in on my telephone conversation. I couldn't believe it. He was violating my privacy. My telephone calls would change. They would certainly be more interesting to him now!

I had many affairs, each one designed to hurt Tom even more. He appeared to be taking his punishment like a man, or so it seemed to me. He assured me he was not running around on me. After all, agreements are sacred to Tom. He even started taking more interest in caring for the children. Maybe my plan was working.

My destructive pattern was not limited to Tom's and my relationship. I was subconsciously punishing myself, too. I began to change as many patterns in my life as I could.

Drinking had always been a man's thing; I had only had a few drinks my entire life. But now I had some new liberated friends who went drinking after work. So, at least once a month I joined them and got really drunk.

The first time I joined them, I did not call Tom until after half past eight in the evening. "Tom, I had to work late with John, and I forgot to call you. I'm sorry. Can you go get the children?" Surely he heard the music in the background.

"I picked up the children when I realized that you were going to be late."

What a shock! Tom picked up the children by himself. I was delighted I had not called him. Now he knew how I felt when he didn't come home. "Have ya'll eaten?" I asked.

"Yes. We've eaten."

"I'll be home soon," I lied. I wanted to finish the evening with my friends, and I did. I don't know what time I finally got home, but it was early the next morning. I was so hung over the next day, but I showed Tom what it was like when he went out drinking. *At least I called at 8:30 to tell him. He never calls me,* I rationalized.

Work became my real "mister," and spending money became my new "mistress." I found solace in buying a new outfit when I got really depressed, which was more and more often. I loaded up all my credit cards and soon got into a financial pinch.

I took a second job as a waitress at the Knights of Columbus. Waiting tables was a job I looked upon with disdain in the past. Now the job became part of my low self-esteem punishment. There was a side benefit, however; men noticed me, complimented me, and asked me out. My life with Tom was so negative, and the attention of men opened new doors for me. Perhaps there was life for me after Tom White.

Separation would be my final act to hurt Tom; nothing else I had done brought him to me remorseful and broken. I felt strong enough

"My destructive pattern was not limited to Tom's and my relationship. I was subconsciously punishing myself, too. I began to change as many patterns in my life as I could."

now to separate from him for a while, maybe six months; by then he would come around.

"Tom, I think we should separate for a while," I suggested one evening.

"That would probably be good. I'll move out."

This is too easy, I thought. *If Tom takes his punishment like a man, he can then move back in for the summer while the children are with my parents, and we can have the honeymoon we never had.* I had it all worked out.

Even Tom's mother called me. "Carol Nan, if he moves out, you will never get back together. Isn't there some way you can work it out and still live together?"

My thoughts screamed, *If you only knew what your son has done to me. I killed our baby, my baby, for him, and he didn't even notice. I hate him for that. If he doesn't change, I don't want him to move back in.*

My last step before separation was to buy a new car. I picked out a color I hated, yellow, and financed it at a San Saba bank without Tom's help.

We separated in February 1974. If he took the final phase of my punishment and humbled himself, we would get back together; if not, then I would divorce him. After all, he had proven he was weak, not strong, by tapping the telephone, not fighting for me and with me.

Surprise! Tom had a plan of his own.

I Hit Bottom

I came in from a date about two o'clock in the morning and called his apartment, but he did not answer. I called again. No answer. So he wasn't suffering.

"Come on, kiddos. Let's go to Tom's apartment," I roused the children with determination.

"Mommy, I'm sleepy."

"You can sleep in the car. Come on."

I beat on Tom's apartment door, but no answer. What do I do? A man walked by. "Are you looking for Tom?"

"Yes. Do you know where he might be?"

"Probably at Mary Wilson's apartment."

"Where is that?"

"She lives in 2202. It's at the end of that building, second floor."

I ran to 2202. The lights were on, so I knocked on the door. Tom answered. "What do you want?"

"You come out here."

He threw open the door and screamed, "You can't do this to me."

"Look what you have done to me," I screamed back.

He pushed me toward the car; I turned and stabbed him in the chest with my keys. I hated him. He was not a man at all—in any respect. He physically fathered my child but would not be a parent, and now he would not take his punishment either. I saw Tom White as weak, my kind of man—outwardly strong, inwardly weak.

He wasn't playing by my rules, my game.

On a downward spiral, Tom and I became really destructive with one another. Oh, we continued to have sexual relations regularly. But when we did, we wound up talking about what it was like with other sex partners. It was all right for me to play that game, but when he did, I exploded with anger. I erupted in a second with the slightest provocation.

There were no tears now, however; Tom only saw my anger. Anger became the emotion I used to protect all of my other emotions. I hurt so deeply from the destructiveness in our marriage, and Tom's unwillingness to humble himself devastated me even more.

My destructiveness manifested itself in other ways.

It is hard to explain, but I fought being a woman. I fought femininity, wearing mostly black pants or jump suits. The only time I wore a dress was to go to church occasionally or to a funeral. I changed my hairstyle from "puffy" to a short, straight look.

I wanted to use men the same way men use women, just as I felt the men in my life had used me. There was no way a man was going to get close to me; I protected myself from every gentle, yield-ing feeling.

It became a source of pride to me I could sleep with a man and not care for him. If he tried to get close on his terms, I managed to find something to be angry at him about to keep him from hurting me.

I wanted to compete with men, to compete for control of the rela-tionship. I saw them on my terms, on my own turf.

My spending habits worsened. When my credit cards reached the limit, I started borrowing money from individuals until my friends reached their limit also.

All of my destructive ways drove Tom farther away. In the early spring of 1974 when it finally became clear to me that we were not going to get back together, I sunk into a deep depression.

Suicide would be my way out. A car wreck would be the way to do it; that way no one would ever know I was weak. Of course, I had to be certain that the wreck was fatal.

Some other details had to be worked out as well. Who would take care of the children? I called my sister, "Tooter, if something happens to me, will you take care of my children?"

"Yes, I will. But how will I support them?"

"I have a life insurance policy; they will get my social security, and Jim Bob will continue his child support." Oh, I had it all figured out.

Except for one thing. If my sister kept the children, they would be raised in San Saba. No way was I going to let Jim Bob Everett have the children. And Tom would not raise the children; he saw them as a liability. Three strikes and you're out; suicide was not an option for me, after all.

I still wanted Tom to rescue me. "Tom, I am going to kill myself. There is no reason to go on."

"You won't kill yourself."

He did call my psychiatrist to see if Dr. Blair thought I was really suicidal. Finally I went to see Dr. Blair.

"Your husband called to ask if I thought you would really kill yourself."

"What did you tell him?"

"I don't think you will kill yourself."

"How can you be so sure I won't kill myself? I just might." I hated anyone telling me what I was or wasn't going to do.

In our sessions Dr. Blair kept asking me how I felt about him. I told him he was the doctor for my mind and nothing more. He seemed to act jealous when I told him I was dating a psychologist. He began to prescribe "mood elevators" so strong that when I took one at bedtime, I slept through the night and floated through the entire next day.

I saw Dr. Blair for about four months, seeing him every day the last month. It finally became so expensive I couldn't afford to see him anymore. By that time, I was hooked on Tofranil and kept taking it for two more years with Dr. Johnson providing the prescription.

After a year of focusing my attention on Tom and the list on my black slate, I gave up my warped plan to restore him.

At the very bottom of the deepest pit of depression imaginable, I turned to Joe Bob and Kelly to help fill the emptiness in my life. I felt like such a failure as a mother; subconsciously I was too ashamed to feel I deserved their love.

Joe Bob and Kelly had witnessed their mother falling madly in love with Tom and had lived with the excitement between us for four years. They also witnessed the anger and hatred between us after the abortion, not knowing why those feelings were there. They watched their mother run wild with other men without any explanation. Why should I expect them to be so receptive to me now when I had neglected them so long.

At the age of thirteen and eleven, they were living with a drugged-up, mood-swinging, workaholic mother who was trying desperately to cope with depression and fighting off suicide. They watched their mother—once a good cook and housekeeper who took great pride in keeping their clothes so nice—stop doing those things. Those were a woman's job, and I just couldn't do them anymore.

I'd come home in a fog and remark, "How nice that you cooked dinner, Kelly. It smells so good. Who cleaned the house?"

"I did," Joe Bob piped in.

"It really looks nice. Thank you."

I can just imagine now how Kelly and Joe Bob felt trying to cook and clean house, as I had once done, trying to help their mother thinking, hoping, praying it would somehow help things between Tom and me. Oh! God, what webs we weave!

How could I, at this stage, reach out for their love expecting it to be there without an explanation? I was not going to reveal my secret; no way could I tell them the truth about their mother.

The sad truth is I rejected motherhood and neglected my children's need for love at the same critical time in their lives that my parents neglected me, so unknowingly. And I was selfishly doing it because of my own need for love.

"I bought a dozen small pizzas for dinner. Just pop one in the oven when you are hungry. I have to go to work. I love you. Get to bed early. I'll see you in the morning. I'll kiss you when I get home. We are going shopping this weekend with the money I make tonight." I'd run in and out of the house with barely a glance their way.

Neither of them asked me to stay home with them, but I knew they did not want me to work at night. I reasoned that I needed the extra money to buy them things their father would have given them if I had stayed married to him.

At the same time they were reaching out to me, I was reaching out to Tom, to other men, and to my work. They had so much love to give me, the same as I had wanted to give my parents. How do we miss the acres of diamonds in our own back yard and go searching elsewhere, only to wind up penniless and despondent?

"The sad truth is I rejected motherhood and neglected my children's need for love at the same critical time in their lives that my parents neglected me, so unknowingly. And I was selfishly doing it because of my own need for love."

Joe Bob and Kelly got a double whammy. Not only did I neglect them but Jim Bob, their father, was busy with his third wife and her children. And Tom just wanted to be Tom, not Daddy to them. It was part of the premarital agreement for me to be totally responsible for them—loving them like a father, too, as well as a mother. I failed miserably at one, and the other I could not do.

Since they deserved better than me as a mother, my function became the provider role, the father's role. I gave them the money they needed. And I continued to work at two jobs so I could keep my mind occupied.

I noticed changes in the children. Joe Bob was quiet, but very opinionated about adult issues. He acted as if he were responsible for Kelly and me, that he was the head of the house. On the other hand, Kelly was much quieter, developed poor eating habits, and started to drink in high school. My daughter picked up on my self-destructive tendencies.

It was so painful to spend time with the children that I limited my involvement with them. I feared getting too close to them. If I did, they might discover my secret.

Our weekly routine consisted of getting them ready and taking them to school each morning. They stayed home after school until I came home. Almost every Friday afternoon I met my parents halfway between San Saba and Dallas so the children could visit for the weekend.

The children were out of my hair, and I convinced myself they were much better off because they were with horses and animals and grandparents who doted over them. I know their grandparents loved having them every weekend, but I'm sure it made my parents wonder about me as a mother.

With the children in San Saba, I worked and slept when I wasn't partying. On Sunday afternoons I met my parents halfway between San Saba and Dallas to pick up the children.

"Hi. Did you have a good weekend?" I asked without listening to the answer.

"Yes. I won first place in barrel racing. I got a blue ribbon!" Kelly handed me her first place ribbon for inspection.

"Ganmaw had some pictures made of us barrel racing. Action shots they call them. What do you think?" Joe Bob shoved the pictures at me.

"The pictures are great. I am so proud of both of you."

How could I not believe they were better off?

They say hindsight is good—20/20. I long to see the good in what my children were put through by the "adult" behavior of their key role models. Today I cringe inside when I think of the dysfunctional behavior they grew up with and what they accept today as normal, adult behavior, as a result.

"It was so painful to spend time with the children that I limited my involvement with them. I feared getting too close to them. If I did, they might discover my secret."

When the pressure built until I could no longer stand it, I had tantrums. As the children got older—and bigger—Joe Bob sat on me to hold me down so I could not throw things.

"I can't stand it anymore. Nothing ever goes right," I yelled while throwing pots and pans, as if breaking something would ease some of the pressure.

"Stop throwing things, Mother," my grown-up-sounding son would demand.

"Joe Bob, leave me alone. Don't touch me."

"Mother, you've got to stop tearing up the house." He'd hold me down and sit on me until I had no choice but to calm down.

Recently, Joe Bob told me, "It is hell to raise your mother." I understood. I understood both as a child and as a parent.

That June, as soon as school was out, I took the children to San Saba to stay with their grandparents for the summer. This gave me the opportunity to get my act together, to get out of the depression I was in and away from the psychiatrist.

Finding the Answer in Work

Something my father always said helped me: "Get out there, sister, and go to work. Work hard; don't sit around and gripe, pout, or cry.

Sister, you know where the money is. You know sometimes I work twenty-four hours a day if I have to. You can do it, too. You have responsibilities. You have two children to raise by yourself. Your mother and I always put you kids first. Take good care of your family."

Work was my answer, hard work and a lot more of it. What I needed was a challenging new job and a new career. My children needed a change also.

"Mother, will you change your name back to Everett when you divorce so it will be the same as ours?" they begged.

"Yes, I will, kids." I started using my old name even before the divorce was final.

I still respected Tom's business mind, so I sought his advice about a career change. He was honest with me, "You will never be happy until you are back in sales. That is where your real talent lies. Find yourself a job selling medical supplies. You understand the needs of doctors."

The next job had to be one where I could really compete with men, bury them, and make a great living for myself and the kids.

I approached Chuck Osborn, the owner of Physician's Supply Service, who sold medical supplies to us at the doctor's clinic. "Chuck, I have some sales experience, and I want to get back into sales. I would like to talk to you about a job."

He shook his head, "Carol, you know I can't talk to you as long as you are working for Dr. Wisner. That would be a conflict of interest." Then he winked and said, "But, let me know when you leave. I think I can put you to work."

After I gave my notice, I called Chuck. "Now I am unemployed and want to talk to you about a job."

"Come on over. You need to meet my partner, John. Can you be here at ten o'clock today?"

"Yes. I'll be there."

In the interview, Chuck remarked, "Carol, you know there are no other women selling medical supplies in this area. You should be able to get a lot of business just because you are a woman."

I was not planning on making my living based on my femininity, but if it would help, why not?

"I'm sure you will be a good salesperson aside from being a woman, but that asset will not hurt you," he continued.

If they only knew how I felt about my femininity.

"We only have one other employee, our sales manager, John Scott. We can give you a draw of four hundred and fifty dollars per month, plus 40 percent of your gross profit from sales, much higher than any other comparable company in the area. Most companies pay only 30 percent to 33 percent of gross profit. You can make a lot of money, Carol, if you are willing to work."

Work was symbolic of my name. *Get your checkbook ready, Chuck.*

I continued to scrub for Dr. Wisner for several months part-time and to work for the Knights of Columbus as a waitress.

As I began my new career, I had to close the final chapter of my old life. My divorce with Tom had to be finalized in order to finally close the door on the past four and a half years of awful destruction. I had to honor the fourth part of our premarital agreement that said if we divorced, I would pay all of the legal expenses and get nothing from him in the way of a settlement.

My marriage to Tom finally ended in August 1974. I called him and tearfully told him the divorce was final. "Tom, you are a free man. Our divorce was final about half past nine this morning. I paid for everything. I held up my end of the agreement."

Tom's voice was strange. I didn't know if it was relief or sorrow, but he only said, "Thank you for calling. I love you."

"I love you, too."

How did all of this happen? Yes, Tom was legally free, but always in my private heart the door remained open for him to enter again.

It had been a real roller coaster ride emotionally, for both of us, I am sure. As for me, I had never experienced such a high in loving a man, nor such a low in hating a man. And the anger between us was filled with painful venom, mine outwardly expressed and Tom's more suppressed and passive-aggressive.

The loss of two loves, my unborn child and my "heart-stopper" husband, along with the loss of my female, life-giving ability created an unbearable emptiness. The hurt incurred by reaching out to the wrong sources to fill the emptiness set me up to be even more destructive.

What next? How many other victims of my abortion would there be?

8

THE ABORTION
BUSINESS BECKONS

As I began a new chapter in my life in the fall of 1974, I had no idea how my past would play such a significant part in my future. Someone, an unseen hand, had written a script just for me, and designed a leading role for someone with just my credentials—in a role that assured stardom.

It was like the director of the play studied the script carefully, screened several actresses, and finally chose me for the lead part. The potential leading lady was ready to wreak havoc on her helpless audience. The big payday seemed so close now. It was as though I had never had an abortion and had forgotten all the pain caused by having been victimized myself.

In my wildest imagination I could never have fathomed the door that opened to me, one that could make me rich, and enable me to do all the things I ever dreamed of doing for my children and myself.

The leading role required a leading lady with just my special qualities:

1. A woman with an insatiable craving for attention; a woman who loved the limelight.

2. An unscrupulous woman with an ability to bend the rules, if the situation warranted it, to get what she wanted.

3. A strong woman with a tireless work ethic who needed to make a lot of money.

4. A woman who understood doctors, who knew how to work with them, and who had experience in running a doctor's clinic.

5. A woman who had a relationship with a silent abortionist who wanted to go public for the bang of the big buck.

6. A feminist, a silent member of the post-abortion women's society, who had a lot of destructive patterns in her life.

7. A woman who understood marketing and knew how to sell; who could relate to women and victimize them into having an abortion.

8. A woman with a strong dislike for men and a desire to use them, even to punish them, but most of all, with an insatiable desire to control them.

It seemed too good to be true, "a play made in heaven," as they say, just for me. My heritage and past life experiences were to merge with a phenomenal, money-making opportunity, to open the door for me not just to dream, but to be rich.

I was thirty years old and single again, living in the midst of a sexual revolution spearheaded by the Women's Liberation Movement. Women were talking openly to each other about a deeply ingrained sense of feeling less valuable than men . . . emotional weakness, a characteristic of our sex, which keeps us from winning . . . if we react with feelings, we are weak, and if we think clearly, we are unwomanly . . . the man does the real work of the world.

I was ahead of the game. I could teach women a lot to help them. I was on the cutting edge of something big. I was also in a very lonely spot, not really able to identify with men or women. I was having a real identity crisis, struggling to be somebody.

In my new search for significance, I focused on becoming the top sales person in the medical supply field. I continued to help Dr. Wisner in his office and to work as a waitress for the Knights of Columbus to supplement my income. The drug Tofranil was my special friend while I tried to live with myself and keep up my work schedule.

The kids were getting everything they needed, except attention from their mother.

My income from medical supply sales grew from a base of four hundred and fifty to one thousand five hundred dollars per month

"My heritage and past life experiences were to merge with a phenomenal, money-making opportunity, to open the door for me not just to dream, but to be rich."

over the next two years. There was more money to be made at J. D.'s After Dark, a bar on Harry Hines, so I left Knights of Columbus and went to work there in November 1975.

I continued to see Tom, my ex-husband, while using other men. The children continued to get more attention from their grandparents than from me. And I continued to prove my worth in dollars like a man.

In the meantime, John, Chuck's partner in Physician's Supply Service, acquired a new account, one that paid top dollar for our equipment and supplies without questioning the price. John and Chuck investigated the business and soon discovered it was an abortion clinic.

A Lucrative Business Opportunity

The Women's Center, located in a high profile Dallas location, was owned by Dr. Sam Greene. Abortionist Greene got his start doing abortions on women referred to him by the East Texas Pastoral Council long before Roe vs. Wade. In February 1973 he opened his clinic and started to do legal abortions.

Dr. Greene was not the only secret abortionist to go public after Roe vs. Wade. Most of the back-alley abortionists opened clinics, along with profiteers. Billboard and newspaper advertising began to scream *abortion,* always with a telephone number to call. Women lined up for this newfound freedom that was revolutionizing sex and womanhood.

Chuck and John established a good rapport with the operators of the clinic, gained an understanding of the abortion business, and found it to be very lucrative. The money was too good to pass up.

Finally, late in 1975, they went into the abortion business themselves, using Chuck's Aunt Sue, an R.N., as the front person. They opened their first clinic in Ft. Worth, Texas. Within a year they owned three abortion clinics in Ft. Worth, Lubbock, and Beaumont.

During the first year Chuck and John operated their abortion clinics, I was not involved in any way. I was concentrating my efforts on medical supply sales. One of the first persons I set up an account with was my personal Ob-Gyn, abortionist, and drug prescriptionist, Dr. Harvey Johnson. His door was always open to me; I looked forward to seeing him because he made me feel so good.

I continued to feel a strange attachment to Harvey. And he did have a way with women; he could sense what I wanted. He touched a lot, using terms of endearment and made me feel very special and desirable.

One Friday afternoon Chuck approached me and said, "Carol, I need a doctor to do abortions tomorrow morning in Ft. Worth. Do you know any doctors who might be willing to do abortions for me?"

Of course, I immediately thought of Harvey Johnson. I called him. "You know Chuck Osborne, don't you, the owner of the medical supply company? Well, he owns several abortion clinics and needs a doctor to help him in Ft. Worth tomorrow. Are you interested?"

"Yes," he quickly agreed.

"Here he is. I'll let you talk to him," and I put Chuck on the phone.

Dr. Harvey Johnson's career in free-standing abortion clinics was thus launched by yours truly.

On June 12, 1976 I received a sudden phone call from my mother. "Tooter is gone. She got caught in a trotline while swimming and drowned. How soon can you get here?"

"I'll leave just as soon as I can get my car out of the shop."

We were later told she broke her neck. She dived into an area of the San Saba River we had dived into all our lives. This time it was tragic.

The loss of Tooter really affected both of my parents, so much so, I felt we all would have been better off if I had been the one who had been killed. She left behind her six-year-old son, Cal, for my parents to raise. It was as though Daddy finally had the son he always wanted. I felt even more displaced than ever, and I felt my two children were being pushed back as well.

Just before Tooter's death I had finally gotten off Tofranil. The news of her death and the guilt I felt inside for the jealousy I had nursed through the years gave me the excuse I needed to go back to using it.

I struggled with her death for several months and was angry at her leaving me with unfinished business between us. I never got to tell her I was sorry for being jealous of her, nor was I able to tell her how much I truly loved her. How do two sisters grow so far apart and finally find themselves separated so suddenly by one's death, never to truly resolve their differences?

I really got mad at God when Tooter died. I had been sending my tithe regularly for about two years at the time of her death, but for some reason I had quit the month before. I had so much guilt inside me, that I even believed for a long time that God was playing the same old game of "invisible" sin Daddy played. I thought God was punishing me because I stopped sending my tithe to the church.

After Tooter's death, I spent a lot of time in San Saba taking care of her grave, planting grass and flowers. I lost touch with everything including my work ethic. Then Chuck messed with my commission structure so I quit and went to work at J. D.'s After Dark on my own schedule. I spiraled into debt and depression, using Tofranil heavily.

Finally in September, Chuck called me. "Carol, I would like for you to come back to work. I'm sure we can work everything out."

I swallowed my pride and went back to work for him.

Later that year Chuck gave me a new opportunity. "Carol, how would you like to make some extra money? For any abortion referral you get from doctors, I will pay you twenty-five dollars."

"Chuck, you know I can sure use it," and so I took my first step toward claiming my role as the leading lady in the abortion industry.

The web between Harvey Johnson and me spread. Right after my sister's death, he made me a new offer. He and some other doctors started North Texas Doctor's Radio, a beeper and answering service.

"How would you like to sell beepers for me? You can sell our service to all the doctors you presently call on. It will help you and us," he offered.

"It's a natural addition to my portfolio, plus a nice way to make some extra money. Okay, Harvey," I agreed. I sold beepers for several years supplementing my income. Harvey tried to get me involved in other business ventures with him, but I declined.

He finally made the big pitch. "Carol, how would you like to go out to dinner with me?"

I was stunned. "Sure, Harvey. When?"

"How about Friday night?"

I was anticipating a big evening when he called late Friday afternoon. "Something has come up at the hospital. We'll have to postpone our date to another time."

"That's okay, Harvey. Some other time." I thought he had decided to reserve me for "business only" purposes, and that was fine with me.

Harvey fit many of my criteria for my next mate—good provider, tall, sensuous—but with all those qualities came the possibility of losing him. He had too many opportunities with other women. A romantic interlude was not worth the risk if I was going to build a future working relationship with him.

The strange attachment I had with Harvey strongly resembled my attachment to Tom. It was as though I was still connected to both of them.

Maybe that's the way it is; people with hidden, shameful pasts who collaborate in wrongful acts have to stick together. Maybe we know we are accepted with each other, that we are just as good as our cohorts. We feel so unclean and disgraceful around other people because we know nothing of their dark side. Maybe if we knew their secrets, we could all get together and stop feeling so badly about ourselves. Maybe then we could be free from our bondage to a limited "guilty" few.

As time passed, I found myself wanting to please Harvey. I knew he would reward me; he owed me. Harvey could be my ticket to big money without the price tag of sex.

Harvey's business consultant, a man named Wayne Byles, ran North Texas Doctor's Radio. I first met Wayne in 1976 when I started selling for them. I made sure I got along with him because I wanted to use Harvey to catapult my career.

In early 1977, things blew up at North Texas Doctor's Radio, and Wayne left the company. Chuck and John had split up their partner-

---

"Maybe that's the way it is; people with hidden, shameful pasts who collaborate in wrongful acts have to stick together. Maybe we know we are accepted with each other, that we are just as good as our cohorts."

---

ship by this time also. Harvey had introduced Wayne to Chuck earlier, and that gave Wayne the opening to talk with Chuck about going to work with him.

Wayne joined Chuck as his business manager and set up a new holding company for all of his businesses called Docta, Inc. By now, everyone at Physician's Supply Service was paranoid about Wayne; he had the reputation of being a "hit man" for corporations, a reputation which he spread himself, explaining, "Sometimes that's what it takes to get the job done."

When Chuck and John ended their partnership, Chuck retained ownership of the Ft. Worth abortion clinic and Physician's Supply Service. So Chuck went to work immediately to open an abortion clinic in Dallas.

Patty, Chuck's wife, set up the new Dallas clinic, and Chuck used his secretary, Joan, to help. I can remember Joan saying, "I wonder how many fingers and toes we put down the disposal today."

Patty began to change right before my eyes. She had always been so nice and genuine to everyone, but she became unfriendly and even paranoid, thinking "everyone" was after them. Chuck began to have excruciating headaches, and Patty developed other health problems.

Advisory Referral Centers

Chuck saw a real opportunity to capitalize on the sexual revolution taking place among women. He determined to do two things. First, he would open non-profit centers under the pretense of doing sexual counseling for women, but the real purpose was to do free pregnancy tests and set up abortion appointments for the clinics. Second, he would develop key relationships with the leaders and strong advocates of the women's movement in the area and use their influence to get abortion referrals.

Late in 1978 my financial situation demanded I make more money if I was going to honor my commitment to send my children to college. I felt I had already failed in not being able to buy Joe Bob his first car; there was no way I was going to fail him again. He had to have a degree, and a good one, preferably from the University of Texas, like his father.

My income from medical supply sales was not good enough. Chuck and I had to have a heart-to-heart talk. "Chuck, I can't make a good enough living selling medical supplies. With two children about to enter college, I have to start thinking about the future," I told him.

"Just work harder. You can make more money."

"No. As much as I love working for you, I am submitting my resignation. I have to find another job."

"How much money do you need to make?" he asked.

"My monthly expenses are currently $2,057."

"Well, some other opportunities exist within our corporate structure where we might be able to use you. It's related to the abortion clinics. We have a non-profit corporation already sanctioned by the IRS which will enable us to open Advisory Referral Centers, offering free sexual counseling and pregnancy tests. It will mean some travel, but only limited overnight stays. Could you leave the children overnight occasionally?"

"Yes, they are almost old enough to leave alone. I would love to travel some. Where would this business be located?" This sounded interesting.

"The main office will be here with the first branch office in Shreveport, Louisiana, then in Tyler, Irving, or the Mid-Cities, Abilene, Waco, and other areas where we see pockets of abortions coming into our clinics. This could be a great job for you, Carol. Give me some time to work it out for you. Don't make any rash decisions. Keep on working hard selling medical supplies, and come back in two weeks. I think we can work something out."

"What do you mean, Chuck?" I asked anxiously.

" 'Carol, Wayne and I have been talking, and I think I have a good offer for you. I want you to be the new director of our Advisory Referral Centers, and your job will be to open and operate Advisory Referral offices in key locations.' "

"Just trust me, Carol. Keep working, and we'll talk in two weeks. Thanks for coming by to talk about this."

The time came for the two-week meeting. With high anticipation, I went to the corporate offices. Chuck seemed excited as he spelled out the details for me.

"Carol, Wayne and I have been talking, and I think I have a good offer for you. I want you to be the new director of our Advisory Referral Centers, and your job will be to open and operate Advisory Referral offices in key locations. ARC will advertise that we offer sexual counseling and pregnancy tests—both free. Remember, we are only interested in the pregnancy tests because we can then counsel the pregnant women and funnel them into our abortion clinics in either Dallas or Fort Worth. We will pick up a lot of business that we would otherwise have missed." He paused, "You will be paid $2,057 per month plus your expenses. You'll love it."

"How much travel will be involved?"

"You will determine that. Basically, you need to be in each location once a week until the staff is hired, trained, and the referral base established. You will also need to make contact with all the 'do-gooders' in the

area to let them know we are there for sexual counseling and pregnancy tests.

"The fact that our services are free will attract high school counselors and social workers alike. The fact that abortions are not paid for
by the state or the national government anymore will mean that you
can get referrals from welfare agencies also. They will be glad to send
you their pregnancy tests, and we can counsel the pregnant women on
where to go for their abortion.

"We have developed some literature, a logo, and Bob Roth has
written some public service announcements which you can get on the
radio free in the areas where we are open. Because ARC is non-profit,
no one will ask questions, and we get free advertising for our pregnancy tests.

"Take these brochures and read about ARC. You are a good salesperson. You will have no trouble at all setting these up. We want to
have seven centers open as soon as possible. They will really build our
abortion business.

"We have already started the clinic in Shreveport, Louisiana. We
hired the wife of the Attorney General to help get the clinic open
without any red tape. You know how hard it can be to get things done
in Louisiana. She really pushed that thing right through. We are ready
for business.

"When can you go to Shreveport to work with the two part-time
employees? They have already been trained to do pregnancy tests and
counseling. You just need to meet them."

The more he talked, the more interested I became. This could be
just what I was looking for. "I have some things to wrap up with PSS. I
can get to Louisiana week after next," I promised, as I took my second
step toward becoming the leading lady in the abortion industry.

I went to work as director of the Advisory Referral Centers in
January 1979. The concept worked well, providing a lot of referrals to
Chuck's abortion clinics.

The business plan called for me to open centers in cities without
abortion clinics, usually in conservative areas that would not allow an
abortion clinic to open. It was not hard for me to step right in and
begin to use the feminist movement to help me build the network of

Advisory Referral Centers. Chuck was already using several big names in the movement.

Cindy, a social worker, was a counselor at Planned Parenthood in Ft. Worth. She constantly invited me to attend "self-discovery" meetings. "Carol, I think you would find our meeting very helpful," she

---

" 'The fact that our services are free will attract high school counselors and social workers alike. The fact that abortions are not paid for by the state or the national government anymore will mean that you can get referrals from welfare agencies also.' "

---

suggested. "There will be four, maybe five of us. We get together in a group, get in touch with ourselves, and examine each other's bodies so that we become comfortable with our body parts. It is a very liberating experience."

She even talked about "sensitizing yourself by masturbating using crackers." I thought she was a lesbian and wanted no part of that.

She wanted to be in control of her life, no man telling her what to do. But, I saw her as out of control, much weaker than I ever dreamed of being and certainly not liberated—but bound up within herself. All she had done was shift her need for love away from men to women.

I was enjoying using men too much to meet my needs to give them up. But I knew I had to be careful not to show my disgust in order to maximize my use of women like her.

Director of the North Dallas Women's Clinic

Chuck and I were very comfortable together, but I never trusted Wayne. And he didn't trust me, mainly because I didn't fear him and would go directly to Chuck with any problem I had. Chuck never advised me to go to Wayne, and I think that bothered him.

I set up the Shreveport, Tyler, and Irving ARC offices. The first week Irving was open for business, a call came from Wayne. "How are things going over there, Carol?"

"Fine. I am just settling in. I think we have a great location on Highway 183 near two high schools. We should see a lot of girls."

"Carol, I need you to come to North Dallas Women's Clinic," he requested. "The director is no longer with us, and I need you to run things until I can find another director. Can you come?"

"Yes. I'll be right over." I took my third step toward becoming the leading lady in the abortion industry.

Wayne had never been an ally. If he was going to work with Chuck, however, I wanted him to be neutral, if not my friend. I was excited to have the opportunity to gain Wayne's trust, since it was a temporary situation.

Temporary soon turned into permanent.

"Carol, how would you like to run the front of the clinic?" Wayne asked after a few weeks.

"I would love it, Wayne." I took my fourth step toward becoming the leading lady.

Wayne was overseeing the abortion business; my old friend, Harvey Johnson, was the medical director, and they wanted me to handle the marketing and run the front office. I did a quick survey of the situation and determined I was sitting on a potential gold mine.

Greed—the love of money and the things I could have with it—blinded me just as it did Harvey, Chuck, John, and Wayne. I was one of them now—an abortionist who used whatever means available to get a woman to have an abortion for the sake of money.

I would like to say I took the job with the abortion clinic to help women, but I can't. I did it for money, pure and simple.

Numbers were the name of the game from a sales perspective, and I quickly saw many ways the business could be increased. "Chuck, if we make just a few changes, we can really increase our business."

"What would you suggest, Carol?"

"First of all, we need to utilize the facility every day, with abortions being done continually. Harvey has to find some more doctors to help cover the clinic all day, every day. I will book in the patients. Second, we can make a few changes in our telephone techniques; putting more emphasis on our professionalism will increase our numbers."

"Go ahead and implement your changes." Chuck was all for it.

He called every day. "How are things going, Carol?"

"I would like to say I took the job with the abortion clinic to help women, but I can't. I did it for money, pure and simple."

"We're still not busy enough during the first part of the week. We need an abortionist all day Monday and Tuesday. We could do a lot more procedures with two more abortion days."

Weekly, I drove to the corporate office for a meeting with Chuck and Wayne. Chuck and I would talk; Wayne asked questions.

In one of the weekly meetings Chuck said, "Carol, we want to be the Neiman-Marcus of abortion clinics in this area. North Dallas Women's Clinic needs to be warm, nicely furnished, with caring people. The big difference between North Dallas Women's Clinic and the other abortion clinics in town is that we are in North Dallas, and that alone demands a higher quality environment. Go buy a lot of plants for the waiting room and even for the recovery room."

The business more than doubled. Chuck leased additional space and set up an office for himself at the clinic. He liked to be part of the action.

At lunch together one day, Chuck openly said, "You know, my income has gone from ten thousand to one hundred and twenty-five thousand dollars the first year in the abortion business. There is so much money to be made in this business. You have been quite an asset at the clinic as my eyes and ears. You have helped increase our business."

I went away from that lunch meeting knowing full well the abortion numbers had been under one hundred and fifty when I started. Even the first partial month I was in charge we had 168, the biggest month NDWC had ever had. We were now doing well over three hundred abortions a month, about to top four hundred. The growth in the business was a direct result of my hard work, six days a week. I deserved more that just a salary; I wanted part of the business. At the right time, I would ask for it.

Figure it out. Chuck had offered to pay me twenty-five dollars for every abortion I got referred to him when I was selling medical supplies. Now, I was running the clinic for $2,057 per month; his income was more than ten times that. He had made a good deal bringing me on to run his Dallas operation.

Kelly was barely fourteen when I brought her in to help me in the clinic. I wanted to teach her how to be aggressive, assertive, and hard working. She needed to learn women have to work harder than men to avoid being second-class citizens.

She wasn't allowed to be involved in extra-curricular activities at school; she had to learn how to get ahead in life. I taught her how to sell abortions and handle the girls when they came into the clinic. She was good, really good, right from the start.

But regardless of how well she did things, Joe Bob got the affirmations, not Kelly. He was doing well athletically, socially, financially, and scholastically. Kelly was just doing a girl's job, helping her mother. I even finally got Joe Bob a contract to clean the abortion clinic in January 1980.

The clinic in Ft. Worth was having some problems, and I was asked to go solve them. I even took old reliable Kelly with me to help me when she could.

Another abortion clinic in Ft. Worth burned and had no place to send its patients so I made a deal with the director to pay them twenty-five dollars for each abortion they referred to us until they could get back in business. Soon, the Ft. Worth clinic was doing over four hundred abortions a month. Chuck was delighted. He and Wayne were taking the credit for the success.

PR and Marketing Advances

At our weekly meeting, Chuck announced, "Carol, I want you to move up to public relations. You will be able to establish a broader base of referrals, and you can work for both the Dallas and Fort Worth clinics."

I put on my PR hat and became creative. Early in the clinic, I noticed that many girls said they were raped, but they had not reported the "rape" to police or gone to a hospital. I had an idea how we could build our business to another level.

In one of our weekly meetings I said, "Many of the women come in complaining they were raped, but they have neither reported it to the police nor gone to the hospital. I think we can get a lot of publicity if we have a press conference announcing that we will do abortions free for rape victims if they report it to the police and go to the hospital. You know the percentage of conception in an actual rape is very low, and with the conditions attached, I don't think we'll do many free abortions. But we will get a lot of free publicity!"

"Who will go on television to talk about it? I won't, and Wayne won't. I hate television cameras," Chuck protested.

"I'll go on television. We'll have the press conference right in the clinic with coffee and doughnuts. We'll give the news media a tour and get prime time news coverage," I pledged.

"Which doctor will do the free abortions?"

"I'll talk to Harvey; he'll do them."

"Okay. Sounds like a good idea. Do it, Carol."

We got prime time news coverage at 6:00 P.M. and 10:00 P.M. Also, several newspapers and radio stations picked it up. I personally called on all of the "do-gooder" organizations in town and let them know. Lots of good free publicity!

"Carol, that was great! We got thousands of dollars of free advertisements we could never have paid for! Great idea!" Chuck was ecstatic.

We never did one free abortion on a rape victim.

Chuck could see great value in my marketing abilities. Wayne did not think the Ft. Worth clinic was aggressive enough. So we designed a "central booking" plan that is now used by other abortion providers. The Ft. Worth staff could not sell abortions, but the Dallas staff could, supervised by me. All of our yellow page ads showed one "800" number to call. When the calls came into the Dallas clinic, the women were sold on our service and directed to the appropriate clinic.

Directing a clinic involves more than marketing and selling abortions. The back is the medical end, and the front is the booking and business end—the money end. I was responsible for the front.

Finding and training telemarketers who could call themselves "counselors" while "selling" abortions was always difficult. I had to remind them constantly, "We are helping women," but those who didn't buy my pitch quickly left.

I started to believe my own rhetoric. I had to be convincing to convince my telephone counselors. But each time I met with Chuck, I was quickly snapped back to reality that we were in the abortion business to make money—a lot of money.

Always, there were complications in the back end, but I was no stranger to complications having assisted Dr. Wisner in surgery.

Dr. Leggett, a first trimester abortionist, worked for us in the Dallas clinic on Thursday mornings. We had a beautiful, blonde twenty-year-old girl come in to have an abortion. She was deaf. Dr. Leggett did her procedure and sent her to recovery. She kept bleeding and her uterus did not contract as it should. The doctor checked her again and discovered, as he said, "She was having twins, and I only got one."

Another abortion procedure had to be done, but the young woman was scared and did not understand why she had to have another procedure. You never tell a woman she is pregnant with twins, because she might change her mind. Because of our problem in communicating with her, however, Dr. Leggett told her the truth, "You're having twins."

Honestly, I never believed Dr. Leggett. I thought he had missed the baby the first time.

I held her hand for the second procedure. I will never forget the fear in those big blue eyes as she underwent the second procedure in one day with only a very light tranquilizer since we were out of anesthesia. She remained very still and never screamed.

I was on a date one evening when my beeper sounded. Chuck informed me there was a complication in Ft. Worth. The doctor had perforated a fifteen-year-old girl's uterus and had pulled her colon through her vagina. She was in John Peter Smith Hospital having surgery when I got there.

The family was very calm and blamed themselves when I arrived. What an opening. I let the mother go on blaming herself for her daughter's problem and allowed the clinic to assume no responsibility as to fault. The doctor emerged and explained he repaired the uterus, and she might be able to have children in the future.

I left feeling very confident the family would not file a lawsuit, but rather carry the blame themselves.

This experience taught me a very valuable lesson for the future. A successful abortion clinic needs doctors willing to put their license on the line in the cover-up of botched abortions, in order to keep families from filing lawsuits. There is something almost god-like about a doctor coming out of the mysterious surgical unit with his scrub suit on giving his report to the family.

The abortionist and the abortion provider need good physician cover. In my mind this meant I needed to be good to Harvey if I was going on to stardom.

By the end of 1979 I was doing my job well and feeling smug about it. It was time to ask for an equity interest in the business. Wayne and Chuck really needed me, and Tom, my ex-husband/lover advised, "You have helped build the business. Look at the records you have on your calendar alone. I would ask for an equity interest."

I went to Chuck and said, "I have more than doubled your business. I want an equity interest."

He said, "No," without any hesitation. "My family owns all the stock in this corporation. That is not going to change."

"A successful abortion clinic needs doctors willing to put their license on the line in the cover-up of botched abortions, in order to keep families from filing lawsuits."

Well, I knew I had helped build his business and that I could do the same thing for myself. Chuck didn't know who he was rejecting; two could play that game. I also knew Harvey would go with me, and I knew he and Wayne wanted to get back into a working relationship together.

In May 1980, I placed my own half-page ad in the yellow pages for 1981. I would be in business for myself with a money partner by October 1, 1980. Using Chuck's health insurance, I underwent every medical procedure I needed, hysterectomy, and oral surgery. Now, it was a matter of learning everything I could and marking time until I was ready to leave.

In June, Chuck called me. "Carol, the Dallas *Times Herald* wants to do an interview. Will you do it? You can do it, Carol. Just be a 'do-gooder.'"

"Okay, Chuck."

I was interviewed in my office at the clinic.

"Why are you at the clinic?" The interviewer ran the gamut of typical questions.

"We are helping women have safe, legal abortions." I spouted the standard line.

"Isn't this a business?" the reporter persisted.

I was feeling so confident that I relaxed my guard and answered honestly. "Of course, it's a business. We want to be the Neiman-Marcus of abortion clinics." Immediately, I knew that was a fatal answer.

After the interview, I called Chuck and told him what I said. "Chuck, I want to refuse to let them publish my remarks," I insisted.

"Carol, don't worry. Everything will be all right," was his response.

The reporter printed my comments—quoting the exact words I had heard from Chuck. Publicly, they appeared crass when compared to how all the other abortion providers answered the same question, "We are only doing a service to help women." My honesty earned us top coverage.

The headline on the inside page read, "Director Says 'Yes, This is a Business.'" Chuck was horrified. My prideful but truthful answer got me fired two weeks after the news report came out. Did someone forget to tell Chuck I was the future leading lady of the abortion industry?

He gave me three months notice—July, August, September. That was perfect: my pre-placed ad in the yellow pages was to break in

October. All I needed was the money man to back me, and I would be the leading lady.

In my time with Chuck, I had added item #9 to my list of special qualities—a woman with experience in marketing, selling abortions, and running an abortion clinic. With this added dimension, I was ready for an even bigger stage. I was on my way to success, the big time! The leading lady was about to debut.

9

DRIVEN BY AMBITION

G reat performances require hard work but result in recognition and reward. Performers experience disappointment and endure pain to have their moment in the limelight.

At the age of thirty-five I still craved the attention from my daddy I knew as a little girl but lost as a budding pre-teen. If I worked hard now, just as Daddy always taught me, I was sure it would result in recognition and reward. Maybe I would even recapture my father's attention and win his affection back.

I was about to make the big push to become the leading lady in the abortion industry; I knew that meant I would face more disappointment and endure more pain. However, with my special qualities I felt well equipped to handle the task. The memories of being the little queen of the May Fete at age two and a princess at age sixteen were enough to make me willing to pay whatever price success required.

When Chuck gave me notice in July 1980, I had three months to find a financial backer so Harvey and I could open Abortion Advisory Clinic. The half-page ad with Southwestern Bell was scheduled for publication in their new edition of the yellow pages, which would be published in October 1980. Harvey helped me select the name for the new clinic so I knew he was committed to join me when the time was right.

Just as soon as I found someone who expressed interest in being the financial partner, I went straight to Harvey. "I have someone who may be willing to finance the opening of an abortion clinic. Do you want to meet with us?" I asked.

"Let me talk to Wayne about it and get back with you, Carol," was his reply.

I anxiously waited for Harvey to respond.

"Carol, Wayne and I would like to meet with you and Rhett. Can you set it up?"

"Very good, Harvey. I'll get back to you."

I set up the meeting in Wayne's office, and Wayne did the negotiating for us with Rhett. Negotiations broke down, and Rhett backed out. I was crushed things did not work out the way I had hoped.

October passed without any success in finding someone to finance me. My expectation of opening my own clinic with Harvey by the first of October crumbled.

When my job with Chuck ended, I swallowed my pride and went back to selling medical supplies for International Medical Sales, Inc. I was doing okay, but I must admit my heart was no longer in medical supply sales. I wanted to be back in the abortion business making a lot of money—more money than I could ever make selling medical supplies.

In November on a Saturday morning, Harvey called and laughingly said, "I saw Joe Bob's picture on the front page of the *Dallas Morning News* sports section. Looks like he missed a tackle!" Good ole Harvey, never one to let an opportunity for criticism go by.

He continued, "By the way, I took over the Mockingbird clinic from Dr. Robinson in August. He couldn't run it long distance. I helped him out of a potential lawsuit by admitting a patient for him. He made me an offer where all I did was assume his debt.

"Carol, several people you know are down here working with me on Saturday. I can't afford to pay you right now, but why don't you come on down and work for the fun of it? Get Kelly to come, too. It will be like old times."

Working with Harvey Johnson for free was not my idea of fun, but I did agree. "Kelly and I will be down one Saturday before too long, Harvey."

When I hung up the telephone, I really hurt inside. I could not believe what I heard! Then I got angry. Harvey had excluded Wayne and me from his deal. If I had had the opportunity, I would certainly have included him. How could he have the gall now to call me to work for him for free?

It was February 1981 before I worked up the courage to visit Harvey at his new clinic. Kelly and I did work one Saturday as I promised. It was very clear to me he wanted to use us as he was using others. He was barking up the wrong tree.

"October passed without any success in finding someone to finance me. My expectation of opening my own clinic with Harvey by the first of October crumbled."

Harvey was running the Dallas Medical Ladies Clinic himself and doing everything as cheaply as possible, using anyone he could get to help him, including his Garland office staff and nurses from his regular practice. He had no management staff and was doing no advertising. He was doing all the abortions himself on Wednesdays and Saturdays.

I went home that Saturday after working all day for free asking myself, *Why didn't Harvey invite me into the deal? I am shocked. Doesn't he realize how much I can help him? Harvey has abandoned me and left me out in the cold. The one abortionist I wanted most to work with doesn't need me after all.*

I was disappointed, sorely disappointed.

However, great performers prove their true grit by rising above disappointment. I was down but not out. Harvey Johnson had not heard the last from me.

Back in Business

On one of our dates Lonnie, my banker boyfriend, jokingly asked me, "Why don't you go to work for Dr. McPhearson and help him solve his problems in his abortion clinic? He is putting twenty-seven thousand dollars a month through our bank, but he cannot manage his money well enough to pay back his bank loan."

"I'd like to talk with Dr. McPhearson. Have him give me a call," I suggested.

In late March 1981 the call I was waiting for came. "Hi, Carol. This is Phil McPhearson. Did Lonnie tell you I was going to be getting in touch with you?"

"Yes, he did. He told me a little bit about you and your business."

"I'd like to sit down with you sometime and discuss a possible working relationship."

"When would you like to get together?"

"The sooner the better for me."

"Would tomorrow be soon enough?"

"What time?"

"What is best for you? I'm flexible."

"How about 3:00 P.M.? Could you come to the clinic?"

"Yes. I'll be there."

"Do you know how to get here?"

"I think so. I'll find it."

"Fine. I'll see you tomorrow, then. Goodbye."

"Goodbye, Dr. McPhearson."

The following day I was in Dr. McPhearson's office at 3:00 P.M. sharp. This could be the opportunity I was waiting for.

"Hello, Carol. It's so good to see you. Won't you please come into my office?" Dr. McPhearson and I talked generally for an hour about my experience and his clinic before he finally asked me, "What will it take for you to come to work for me, Carol?"

"Dr. McPhearson, I'll come to work for you and run your clinic for twenty-five dollars for each abortion we do." If Chuck could pay me twenty-five dollars for each referral, Dr. McPhearson could surely pay me the same thing to run his clinic. Then, I added, "And I'm looking for an equity opportunity as well."

"Carol, I'm not prepared to offer you twenty-five dollars per abortion or an equity position. However, I am willing to pay you two thousand dollars a month to run my clinic."

"Dr. McPhearson, I appreciate your offer. When would you want me to start?"

"Monday."

I had my ace in the hole. I was going to give Harvey Johnson one last chance to join forces. I couldn't wait to get to his clinic and tell him about the offer.

"Harvey, Dr. Phil McPhearson has offered me a tremendous opportunity to go to work for him. Looks like you and I are going to be in competition. I don't want that. Do you? If I'm going to work for someone, it might as well be you."

"Carol, you know I can't afford to pay you a salary because we are operating on a shoestring. I can pay you twenty-five dollars for each abortion we do. If you build the business, you can make a lot of money. We did forty abortions last month, but I know you can increase the number quickly. How do you feel about it?" His offer was what I'd hoped for.

It did not take me long to compute how much money I could make—forty times twenty-five dollars equaled one thousand dollars—not bad for a part-time job. But, four hundred times twenty-five dollars equaled ten thousand dollars—and that was not bad for a month's work.

I understood Harvey Johnson, and I knew I had to be careful in my dealing with him. He had to think he was coming out ahead. "Harvey, you know I can't live on a thousand dollars a month. I will have to keep my other job and just work here on Wednesdays and Saturdays. I may not even be able to be here every Wednesday, but I can be here every Saturday. Will that work out?"

"We'll make it work. You can really build the business quickly. What do you say, Carol?" he said as he slipped his arm around my shoulder.

"You've got a deal. I'll be here Saturday morning." I left Harvey's office ecstatic, but I realized Harvey only included me because he and his free help could not build the business as he wanted.

Carol, the strong one, was back in business, on track again toward becoming her goal—the leading lady in the abortion industry.

Although Harvey did not include Wayne in the clinic deal, he still used him as an advisor. Wayne told Harvey he was making a bad deal with me. His advice at the time was almost prophetic: "Don't get in bed with Carol; it will not work." Harvey didn't listen, of course, and we were partners once again.

Clinic ownership was not discussed when Harvey hired me, but he knew I wanted to be more than an employee. In our new working arrangement Harvey was the medical director and the only abortionist. I was in charge of marketing, running the front office, the laboratory, procedure and recovery area, and all-round general flunky.

I knew what it took to keep Harvey happy—I made him think he made every decision. He was my ticket to wealth and the security for my children's college education. "Eventually," I reasoned, "Harvey will help me become the leading lady in the abortion industry. It is only a matter of time until I have a part of this business. I need Harvey Johnson, and he needs me."

I began to make changes immediately. I trained our telephone counselors to use "sales techniques" instead of "counseling techniques."

I put Kelly on the telephone in the afternoon. She was thoroughly trained in how to sell an abortion. However, there was a line in the clinic Kelly would not cross, even for me: she wouldn't go to the back where the killing was done. Kelly, like the others, was not a "freeby." I paid her really well to bring in the clients. Our numbers began to go up right away.

An immediate problem concerned Barbara, Harvey's young medical assistant who did not like abortions. She actually had a fetal development book in the clinic and often showed women how developed their babies were at various stages inside the womb. I stopped that practice immediately. Although Barbara was a good employee, if she could not sell abortions, she had to go. She left.

In April, our first partial month together, we did forty-five abortions; my first month's income was $1,125. At the end of the second month the total was sixty-five abortions; my part-time income was $1,625. In June we did eighty-nine abortions; my paycheck was $2,225.

Things looked good. Fate was smiling on me and my old pal, Harvey. We were once again set to help women—to help the post-abortion women's society grow by leaps and bounds while we lined our pockets with pure gold.

Meanwhile, we were still poor grubstakers who had to get our clinic up to speed with the competition fast. Furnishing a growing clinic takes money—unless you are Harvey Johnson. All I had to do was make up a list of what I needed and give it to Harvey.

"Here is the list of supplies we need. We need the sterilization wrap before you come back on Saturday. Can you get it and send it over by Jan so I can have everything ready on Saturday?"

"I'm not on call before Saturday, and you know most of my supply trips are 'midnight requisition,' but I'll see what I can do. What about suture—do we have any?" he asked.

"Carol, the strong one, was back in business, on track again toward becoming her goal—the leading lady in the abortion industry.

"No, we don't. And we would be in big trouble if we needed it."

"I'll be sure we get some. I think we have been getting the pregnancy tests from my office, right?"

"Harvey, I don't know where you get them from. I only know I give you the list and you bring supplies back from somewhere," I said.

"Pretty soon we are going to have to start buying our supplies. Someone is going to catch me," he winked.

"I'll start doing some price checks then. I think I can find some deals. You know, we're only going to be paying twenty-one cents for each pregnancy test by buying them directly from Neal. Your clinic is probably paying about fifty cents for the same test."

Harvey brought me whatever I needed from Garland Memorial Hospital and from his Garland partnership and continued to do so until we reached two hundred abortions.

I had a very small advertising budget to work with because of limited funds. Dr. Robinson, the previous owner, had taken out a small yellow page ad, and not much business was coming in from it. I had to come up with some creative, though inexpensive, advertising methods.

I found some coupon advertisers who were willing to run abortion clinic ads. We placed ads offering a 10 percent discount if the woman brought the coupon with her. It worked.

We also placed discount coupon ads in the *Dallas Times Herald* and the *Dallas Morning News TV Guide* section. We used the coupons to track our results. The ads worked again. Harvey joked, "One day someone is going to gather up our coupons and bring them all in. We're going to have to pay her to do her abortion."

We were like one big happy family. Kelly, my daughter, and Jan, Harvey's daughter, handled the telephones. Both girls were still in high school but had been well trained to do telephone counseling. In addition, they did lab work, in-house counseling, manned the recovery room, as well as washed and sterilized instruments when necessary. Fredi, Harvey's live-in girlfriend, kept the books and helped work the front. We continued to use Harvey's office staff from Garland as back-up.

A Man Like Harvey

My confidence in Harvey was at an all-time high. Things were going fantastic both in the clinic and in my working relationship with him. He was sleeping with Fredi, but that was all right with me. I was working my own agenda with him.

Harvey was well established in the Dallas/Garland medical community and had no problem sharing our association with the world. His open attitude with his peers increased my confidence in our relationship.

With a sensual man like Harvey and a woman like me, the sexual overtones were there but not acted upon. Sexual energy was always an undercurrent in our relationship, at least on my part, but I managed to control it.

Harvey was my constant telephone companion; we talked at least three times a day. He checked in with me when he got to his Garland office in the morning. "Good morning, Carol. How many do you have scheduled for today?"

"Today is a pretty full day."

"That's good. Talk to you later. Love you."

"I love you, too."

Harvey was always telling me, "I love you, Carol." I could pour my love on him as long as Fredi was not around. He called again in the middle of the afternoon and about nine o'clock to say good night. I was addicted to his phone calls.

Harvey was a little help with my children, too. He was very jealous of Joe Bob (as Tom had been) and loved Kelly (as Tom had not). For her part, Kelly really responded to the attention he gave her.

Needless to say, as close as Harvey and I were, Fredi and I did not get along at all. In fact, we were on a collision course. I wanted Fredi to stay at home and out of the clinic, but Fredi knew what happened when Harvey's woman stayed out of his business. Fredi herself started dating Harvey even before his second marriage to Phyllis.

Jan Batson, Harvey's long-time office nurse, once told me, "Harvey spent the night before he married Phyllis with Fredi and went right back to her bed the night he got back from his honeymoon." They continued to have an affair throughout Harvey's marriage to Phyllis. Fredi had reason to be scared Harvey would be in another woman's bed if she let him out of her sight.

Now Fredi wanted to be the only woman in Harvey Johnson's life. She thought if she could work with him, she could control who he saw. But that old devil continued to slip around and see other women.

Rather than really getting to know Fredi, I allowed Jan Batson to tell me all about her. Jan hated Fredi but was as two-faced as they come; she was so nice to Fredi to her face but behind her back told me about all the dumb things Fredi did. "Carol, you'll never guess what Fredi did this time. She charged a hairpiece thinking it was $6.50 when it was $65.00!" And on and on.

I thought, *Harvey could do better—he could have me.* That thought scared me to death. For the first time I let myself think about my deepest feelings toward Harvey Johnson. Deep inside I wanted more than just a professional relationship with him. Jealousy, that old haunting jealousy inside me, was spreading its web to entangle my relationship with Fredi. Realizing the danger, I pulled myself back together and went back to work.

Fredi did not understand how the clinic worked, but she surely did understand me and how I worked. I asked her, "How many patients are in today?"

"Are you figuring how much money you are going to make today?" Fredi asked sarcastically.

Keeping my temper under control, I replied civilly, "I have to keep the instruments sterilized and the rooms ready. The patient count has a bearing on how I do that." On the inside I was thinking,

What an idiot. Yes, I am figuring how much money I am making, but I do have other responsibilities. All you have ever done is teach school; you just don't understand medical offices. Why do I have to have you as a thorn in my side?

It was just that Fredi and I were very much alike—both headstrong, independent, and controlling. It was a battle of the wills in every area.

I wasn't the only one who struggled with Fredi. Alma Jean, Harvey's maid, constantly called me, telling me what Fredi was "up to." She called one day very upset.

"What's wrong, Alma Jean?"

"Fredi got fifty thousand dollars from her grandmother, and she is going to let Doc use it for something. She thinks she can hook him that way."

"What do you mean, Alma Jean?"

"I think Fredi believes he will have to marry her if she lets him use her money."

"What is he going to do with it?"

"I don't know. I heard them talking about leases and equipment or something."

"Where is the money now?"

"In the bank. But she wants him to use it."

"Alma Jean, Harvey is a grown man. We can only hope that he sees what she is doing."

Harvey thrived on working all of us against each other, using Jan against me, Fredi against me, me against them all, and so on. He was a master at it and enjoyed it very much. Part of my fun was laughing with him about what he was doing with all of us.

Harvey didn't respect any of us. When Harvey operated on Fredi, one of our scrub techs who assisted him came to me very upset. "Carol, I hated being in there with him. He showed Fredi no respect at all. She asked Harvey to remove a mole from her vulva, and he just sliced it off without cauterizing it or anything. He made a joke about it."

To make matters worse, while Fredi was in the hospital recuperating from her hysterectomy, Harvey's first wife committed suicide on Harvey's birthday, June 2. On that same date their five-year-old daughter had died of brain cancer several years earlier.

Harvey asked Phyllis, his second and now ex-wife, to go with him to his first wife's funeral. He parked her car in the garage where he and Fredi lived, in the spot where Fredi usually parked. While Harvey and Phyllis were out of town for the funeral, Fredi tried to get a release from the hospital.

When Harvey called home to check with Alma Jean, she was frantic. "Doc, Fredi is trying to get out of the hospital. What am I going to do if she comes home and finds Phyllis's car in the garage?"

"Fredi did not understand how the clinic worked, but she surely did understand me and how I worked. I asked her, 'How many patients are in today?'
'Are you figuring how much money you are going to make today?' Fredi asked sarcastically."

"Don't worry, Alma Jean. I'll take care of it."

Alma Jean called me immediately and told me about her conversation with Harvey. We laughed and laughed saying, "Fredi would die if she knew he is sleeping with his second wife at his first wife's funeral while his future wife is in the hospital!"

Harvey must have called his partner to make sure Fredi wasn't released. I'm sure he lost five pounds over that episode; I nearly broke my ribs from laughing so hard with Alma Jean.

He kept us all involved in his scheming ways. Each of us felt special to him because of the secret events he involved us in.

Enough of the side show. Harvey Johnson was no dummy. He knew exactly how to work each one of us, especially me. He knew I wanted to make a lot of money and operate my own clinic.

A Promised Partnership—Finally

We were sitting in Harvey's office one day using a table for a desk, when he said, "Carol, we can run the abortion clinic without anybody else if we have to. Fredi can run the front; you can do the back and oversee everything. I can do the abortions. Our daughters can do lab and recovery. We don't need anybody else. We're a family; we can run this clinic ourselves if we have to. We are making good money already, and you are making a good living, too."

"But not as good as I want to make, Harvey. You know I want to make more money," I reminded him.

"All the corporate money goes right back into the clinic for expansion. No one is taking anything out except your fee and the abortion fee for me. I live on that."

"I want to be more than an employee, too, Harvey."

"You are more than an employee. You, Fredi, and I are in this together. We are going to build this business and then issue stock. We are a family."

"You keep saying I'm more than an employee, Harvey, but nothing has been done about it."

"I've been thinking about it, Carol, and I'm ready now to do something about it. The corporation papers have not been changed since I took over the clinic from Dr. Robinson. We need to get that taken care of. I've thought about it, and I've decided to be the president; you will be the vice president; Fredi will be the secretary-treasurer. Can you take the papers to Dr. Robinson's lawyer in Duncanville and have him draw up the necessary documents? And can you do it right away?"

"Yes. I'll call him this afternoon." I wanted to dance to the music he was making. I wanted to shout, but I contained myself.

Although I didn't say anything, Harvey knew I didn't want Fredi in the deal. I kept quiet. A promised one-third interest in the business was better than what I had. He continued, "I'm ready to move on. Let's get this done and get on with making this business grow." *And making me rich,* I thought to myself.

When the papers were prepared, the lawyers called. The new corporation was Dallas Medical Ladies Clinic, Inc. The papers were signed, and I proudly made out the incorporation checks to the State of Texas.

When the papers came back from the state, it was business as usual at the office, but it was celebration inside for me. I finally did it! Carol Nan Everett finally became the star of her own show—a small play with a lot of potential. My dream of becoming the leading lady in the abortion industry was very much alive! Now was the time to really get to work. No more part-time work for me.

I began to pour all of my time into the clinic. We had to increase our advertising. I went to Harvey and asked, "What do you think about our assuming the half-page ad I placed in the yellow pages before I left Chuck?"

"What do you mean, Carol?"

"We probably can take over that ad and pay a mileage fee."

"Okay. Check and see what it will cost."

I called Southwestern Bell and asked, "What will it cost us to assume the half-page ad under the name of Abortion Advisory Clinic?"

"Carol Nan Everett finally became the star of her own show—a small play with a lot of potential. My dream of becoming the leading lady in the abortion industry was very much alive!"

"Nineteen hundred dollars a month plus mileage for that number to be transferred to your area," was the answer. Mileage would run about two hundred and sixty dollars a month.

I went back to Harvey with the proposition. "I think it will be worth it."

"That's a lot of money."

"I know, Harvey, but I believe it will pay off."

"Okay. Do it. But we have to track the calls when they come in to prove it is effective," he reminded me.

"Okay."

In September, the first month, the ad paid for itself.

"How many abortions did we do, Harvey?" I smiled knowing it had been a good month.

"We did two hundred. I wonder if Chuck knows we are here now! I hope he's hurting."

"I'll bet he is. I wonder how many abortions we missed before that Chuck got from that yellow page ad?" I chimed in. (Our Abortion Advisory Clinic ad was the number just before Chuck's Abortion Advisory Services ad.) At the time, I never understood why Harvey was so interested in hurting Chuck, but if it made Harvey happy, I sure wanted to hurt Chuck, too. Every problem, every chance we had to discredit him, we made sure we placed the blame directly on our principal competitor and former associate—Chuck Osborn.

My personal goal when I started with Harvey in April 1981 was to reach two hundred abortions per month by December and five thousand dollars personal income per month. I hit my goal in just six months.

"Carol, you are really making good money."

"Not good enough yet, Harvey. I have some big goals. You know I am going to have two children in college soon, and you know how much that costs."

"Yes, I know how much it costs."

I already had my sights set on my next six-month goal—four hundred abortions and ten thousand dollars a month take-home pay by the end of March 1982—and I planned to reward myself with a new Toronado. In order to reach four hundred abortions, we had to increase the business.

I began to push Harvey in two ways. "Harvey, we need to increase our abortion days and hire some doctors to help you."

"Okay, Carol. I'll get someone to help me so we can do abortions six days a week."

"And we need to start doing second trimester abortions. We can really increase our business if we start doing bigger ones."

"Up to how many weeks, Carol?"

"At least up to twenty weeks, don't you think?"

"Let me think about it."

The next Wednesday when Harvey came in, he said, "Start scheduling up to twenty weeks."

Even though it was harder on the patient, Harvey started doing a one-day, traumatic dilation abortion up to twenty weeks. We were the only clinic I knew of doing that kind of procedure in one day. Within a few weeks Harvey found other abortionists to help us so we could expand to six days.

The business rolled in. My goal for March 1982 looked within reach. Harvey was doing just fine helping me get where I wanted to go. But I still wasn't satisfied. We had to do more abortions—bigger ones.

"Harvey, everything has gone really well with doing abortions up to twenty weeks. What do you think about going to twenty-four weeks? It will increase our business and our revenue a lot. What do you think?"

"Let's do it to twenty-three weeks, Carol. That will give us a week for a margin of error," he agreed.

The ambition inside me to be at the top in the entire abortion industry drove me to push Harvey into doing bigger and bigger abortions. The recognition and reward waiting for me at the top beckoned me to push on. The dream was almost in reach.

10

THE PRICE OF SUCCESS

T he scene of Sheryl Mason lying in a pool of blood in the recovery room became etched in my mind. Her blood could be washed off the privacy curtains, the wall, and the bedding; it could not be washed off me.

Sheryl Mason walked into our "clean" clinic, and we killed her. My soul languished, *I am as guilty as Harvey because I sold her the abortion, and I pushed him into doing big abortions. I am covered with Sheryl's blood. I am in truth the Scarlet Lady.*

Carrying the responsibility for Sheryl's death became another endurance test for me. I was becoming very disappointed in our performance as "professional" abortionists.

I forced myself to accept the fact that we weren't the perfect clinic I imagined we were and to accept Harvey's rationale, "Our number was just up; we can't worry about it." I concentrated on selling abortions and continued to push Harvey to do more big ones.

Less than a month after Sheryl's death, we transported Laura in my car—not to the closest hospital nor to the hospital that would take the best care of her—but to the hospital that would cover for us, Garland Memorial Hospital, where Dr. Johnson was chief of staff.

Laura, a twenty-five year old referred to us by a doctor in Garland, was admitted to Garland for a hysterectomy. She was diagnosed as having placenta previa—the placenta being presented in the mouth of the uterus. Harvey once again rationalized, "If she had gone full term, the results would have been the same."

Having gone through the ordeal of Sheryl's death, I was much stronger now. Laura's hysterectomy was a minor glitch.

The abortion business, like all other businesses, usually has its own up-and-down cycle. January is a good month; February is okay. March is great, April tops, May good, and the summer back to okay. At the end of August, just before school starts back, things really pick back up. September is dynamite, October shaky; November and December are good. In our case every month the business increased.

Our yellow page advertising, plus our discount coupon promotions, continued to pay big dividends. Our contacts with "do-gooder" agencies were yielding good referrals. The increased abortion days, using more abortionists, and doing "bigger" abortions kept our business growing. We started to get referrals from other abortion clinics because of our one-day, second trimester procedure.

And, of course, women were beginning to come back for repeat abortions. [Editor's note: At present, there is a 45 percent repeat rate.] They began to refer their friends and bring their sisters in because of the good job we did for them the first time.

By March we were back on track, and I felt my ten thousand dollars a month income was a safe bet. On March 2, 1982 I rewarded myself and bought my new Toronado as planned. Harvey gave the dealership a statement saying I had earned seventy thousand dollars in 1981.

Even Harvey seemed to be impressed with my new success. "Carol, you are really making good money."

"Not enough, Harvey," was always my answer. I'm sure Harvey was thrilled to hear that; it meant more money for him, too. I was driven by an insatiable desire to make more money.

Personal Costs

The new car smell was still fresh in my Toronado when Dr. Burney botched Lisa's abortion and Dr. Johnson botched the abortion of the twenty-seven year old from a small town in Arkansas.

I kept pushing to do more abortions and "bigger" ones. I was hooked by the love of money and what it could do for me next—remodeling my home. After remodeling my home, I planned to buy two new sports cars for the children. I was consumed with the thought of all the things I was going to do.

Ironically, I also tithed from the very beginning of my relationship with Harvey. God had answered my prayer to be able to work with him. Now I felt I was right where God wanted me, helping women.

"I kept pushing to do more abortions and "bigger" ones. I was hooked by the love of money and what it could do for me next. . . ."

I kept a Bible in my top right-hand drawer and pulled it out if someone said, "Abortion is a sin." My answer was emphatic: "I am helping women because God wants me to. I tithe on all the money I make. I pray every day." And I did, but I didn't tell them I prayed for no complications or deaths and for more abortions that particular day.

When I went to church in my hometown, San Saba, all the deacons were so nice to me. Many of them never noticed me before I started sending my tithe back to the church. The minister was always very nice, and when the new minister came, he immediately knew who I was. One of the deacons asked my father, "Does she tithe at a Dallas church, too?"

Daddy bragged, "Probably so."

Everyone in the church paid special attention when I visited. They knew I donated two pews, one in memory of my sister and the other in memory of my grandfather. My grandmother attended the church and was very proud of me. She moved from her regular seat to sit in the new pew I gave in my grandfather's honor.

Money can do a lot for you even in "God's house among God's people." I used it to buy approval.

I even believed God was blessing me in the abortion industry because of my tithe, and if I stopped tithing, God would stop blessing me financially. The first check I wrote after receiving my check was to the church, and I did it religiously. I was afraid to forget "His" check for the financial blessing surely would stop—the abortion numbers would drop. And I didn't want that to happen.

God was surely answering my prayers and honoring my tithe. More women were coming for abortions in spite of Sheryl's death and the botched abortions of Laura, Lisa, and the young lady from Arkansas.

I was successful in my new role as the Scarlet Lady until May 1982 when beautiful, tall, thin Jenni danced into the clinic. Why did she have to be so arrestingly easy to remember? Why did she have to be so close to Kelly's age? Jenni's botched abortion came to haunt me more than all the others.

Why did it bother me so much? Why was Jenni's botched abortion making me question if I could continue in the abortion industry?

It had to do with the look in Kelly's eyes—the way she looked at me when I saw her in the rearview mirror as we drove Jenni to the hospital; the way she looked at me at the hospital when she said, "I want to go; I want to go back to the office." She looked right through me. What was it about that look?

Suddenly, all of my efforts to convince Kelly we were helping women were revealed as lies—lies to justify myself, and Kelly knew it. Kelly saw more than she needed to see. I made a big mistake having her go with me to the hospital.

Fear of Kelly's rejection engulfed me. *My baby is going to reject me. I know she sees even more inside me. Can she even see I am in this business to make money? Can she see I am one of them—a member of this post-abortion society?*

Kelly sees me covering up botched abortions. She knows I am a hypocrite. She knows abortions hurt, especially botched ones. She knows the pain of a botched abortion vicariously, having suffered with Jenni and feeling her every anguishing scream.

Kelly is just two years younger than Jenni. She must be thinking, "That could be me." I'm sure she thinks, "My mother did this; she is in charge. This is my mother."

I am really scared. I'm going to lose Kelly, my baby. Who will I have when she is gone? Doesn't she realize how much I need her?

I came to the startling revelation, I was not so upset about what happened to Jenni. I was upset about how Kelly felt toward me.

I accepted the revelation and reasoned, *When you take the leading role, you have to be prepared to pay a high price. Nothing, not Harvey, not Sheryl's death, or my kids, is going to stop me from achieving my goals.*

Hell and pain are a part of success. So what if you walk over a few people to win, bend the rules a little. Kelly will be okay. I've just got to work harder to win her over. She'll come around. Somehow I'll make it up to her for what I put her through.

"The first check I wrote after receiving my check was to the church, and I did it religiously. I was afraid to forget 'His' check for the financial blessing surely would stop—the abortion numbers would drop."

After reflecting over more than thirty-seven years of my life, I concluded these facts about Carol Nan Everett.

First, I was an unscrupulous woman who craved being the leading lady in all the abortion industry so much that I would participate in the cover-up of botched abortions.

Second, I loved money and what it could do for me so much I would continue to sell abortions, including big ones, knowing some of them would be botched, and consequently some women would be maimed for life or die.

I concluded, *I am still in the abortion business. A lot of work needs to be done if we are going to get our second clinic open by September and reach six hundred abortions by the end of the year.*

Professional Consequences

My attention shifted to Harvey. My confidence in him was so shaken by Jenni's botched abortion I made the conscious decision to quit seeing him as my personal physician.

In addition I concluded, *Harvey's stupid mistakes could ruin my plans to make a million dollars, to be rich. The mistake with Jenni almost cost me my relationship with Kelly, too. It cannot happen again.*

I knew Harvey had a tremendous battle going on inside him with doing big abortions. Maybe I had pushed him too far. He once confided in me, "The doctors at Garland Memorial Hospital are beginning to question my work." Harvey needed my help, my loyalty, my protection, and not my pushing anymore. I decided it was best for him and the clinic to schedule him only for first trimester abortions in the future.

I immediately stopped scheduling Harvey for big abortions. I managed to minimize Harvey's mistakes by giving them to Dr. Burney and Dr. Mosely. Harvey and I also began to distance ourselves personally and the clinic from botched abortions, making the other doctors take responsibility for their own mistakes.

The botched abortions continued.

Dr. Burney did an abortion on a Mexican woman about thirty-two years old and approximately twenty weeks along. He perforated her uterus and the forceps severed her urinary tract. With her IV in place I transferred her to Methodist Hospital in my car. Dr. Burney met me and admitted her. Her urinary tract was repaired surgically, and we saw the woman one more time for a check-up.

Dr. Mosely did an abortion on an eighteen year old who was eleven weeks pregnant. She screamed and screamed during the abortion, which was not normal. Dr. Mosely became very upset because the young woman would not stop screaming.

Billie, the nurse, kept telling the young woman, "Please be quiet; you are disturbing the other patients. You will be fine."

She stopped screaming when the procedure was over and was discharged from recovery with no special care. Several days later, she called the clinic complaining. She was asked to come back in for a check-up, where we discovered that her uterus had been perforated and her bowel pulled inside her uterus with the suction.

Dr. Mosely hospitalized her and had a surgeon do a colostomy. We divorced ourselves from that case quickly. "That's Mosely's problem, not ours. That is why they are independent contractors and are not paid by check," Harvey justified.

Dr. Miller handled cases on Monday night. He did an abortion and pushed the head of her fifteen-week-old baby into the woman's abdomen. "Carol, call Dr. Johnson. I have to admit her. She has to have surgery tonight."

"I immediately stopped scheduling Harvey for big abortions. I managed to minimize Harvey's mistakes by giving them to Dr. Burney and Dr. Mosely. Harvey and I also began to distance ourselves personally and the clinic from botched abortions, making the other doctors take responsibility for their own mistakes."

I called Harvey and told him what Dr. Miller had done.

"Let me call Medical Arts to see if we can do the surgery there."

"Harvey will call back in a few minutes, Dr. Miller. Let's finish the other procedures."

Harvey called back. "Take her to Medical Arts, and we will do the surgery there. I'll help Miller."

The next morning as we walked out of the hospital, Harvey told me, "Miller was scared. I repaired her uterus and put the baby's head in a disposable sheet. I wrapped it tightly so no one would discover it. It was not a part of the specimen."

Still Harvey and I concentrated our efforts on getting the Mockingbird office better prepared to support our second clinic. We had to get the second clinic open and operating very quickly in order for us to be doing six hundred abortions (for me to be making fifteen thousand dollars) a month by the end of the year.

"Harvey, the central telephone bank is going to be the key to making us more successful than the other chains."

"I know, Carol. Get it set up."

I began to train our telephone counselors in preparation for future expansion and to place additional ads in the Southwestern Bell Yellow Pages with one "800" number covering all of Texas, plus much of Louisiana, Oklahoma, Arkansas, and New Mexico. In preparation for choosing our second location, we had been doing some concentrated advertising in several potential areas and monitoring the results. Our plan called for us to build up to two hundred referrals coming from a key area, select a prime location in that area, secure a lease in a suitable facility, and open a clinic.

"It looks like the best location for our first satellite clinic is Mesquite. We are getting about two hundred referrals from that area now," I told Harvey.

"Okay, Carol. Locate a site and get back with me."

"Harvey, I've found a location that is great for the Mesquite clinic right on the inside of the 635-Loop with great accessibility for all of East Texas and Louisiana. The location has good visibility and is easy to locate even for out-of-towners. We will cut our competition off at the pass; the women will not have to come all the way into Dallas for their abortion.

"You know, I have dated a site selection man for a fast-food restaurant, and he helped me with the location selection. It's a free-standing building right next door to the hospital. It will be difficult to picket because of the private property lines. I don't think picketers can get to the door. It is going to be a great location. We are going to pile up some numbers."

"See what kind of lease you can work out for us, Carol."

I met with the owner of the building and negotiated our lease agreement. I called Harvey. "I have worked out a turnkey lease with 100 percent finish-out even down to the industrial strength disposal, a double action one that chops forward, reverses itself, and chops again as it reverses."

"That's great, Carol. When can we occupy the space?"

"September first."

We "nickeled and dimed" the start-up with twelve thousand dollars taken out of the Mockingbird location and a ten-thousand-dollar loan from the bank. We bought used exam tables and recovered an old couch. Harvey put his slippery, sleight-of-hand routine to work for us again. He supplied stolen instruments, etc. from the hospital and his private practice just as he did when we built up the Mockingbird clinic.

We set up a separate corporation and named the clinic Women's Clinic of Mesquite. The officers were the same as in our other corporation; still we did not issue any stock.

" 'It's a free-standing building right next door to the hospital. It will be difficult to picket because of the private property lines. I don't think picketers can get to the door. It is going to be a great location. We are going to pile up some numbers.' "

Dr. Miller agreed to be our Mesquite doctor which meant we had a doctor on location all the time. We started out doing abortions six days a week in Mesquite and went to seven days in Dallas. Sunday was our best day percentage-wise because we were able to work a skeleton crew very effectively.

The first month the new clinic worked beautifully. We did over two hundred in Mesquite and more than three hundred in North Dallas. I made over twelve thousand five hundred dollars.

Our central telephone bank simply booked the appointments, called the Mesquite clinic each afternoon and gave them their schedule. They called during the day to add other appointments as necessary. If the Mesquite clinic had one that was too big for Dr. Miller, they sent her to Dallas.

"Harvey, I'm very excited about the success of the new clinic. Our concept is right. I know it," I congratulated our success.

Harvey and I planned to have five clinics and lead the abortion business in the metroplex. We would use one advertising budget to advertise for all five of them. We would publish one local telephone number and one "800" number for out-of-town customers. All would call the Mockingbird clinic, be booked, and told which of our abortion clinics to go to.

Harvey wanted to have a place to make money without all the stress of private practice—taking calls, delivering babies. He often commented, "Carol, you know, I don't like to get up in the middle of the night and deliver babies."

I wanted to make a million dollars. In order for both of us to have what we wanted, we needed to open five clinics so we could do forty thousand abortions annually.

With the second clinic open, our next goal was to hit the six-hundred-abortion-a-month mark by the end of the year. If we were going to have the five clinics open and established by the end of 1984, we still had a lot of work to do.

As the business continued to grow, my ex-husband, Tom, reminded me again, "Carol Nan, you'd better get everything in writing."

"That's not necessary, Tom. If I can't trust Harvey, who can I trust?" I trusted Harvey. I was an officer in the corporation. My unwritten agreement with Harvey, as I understood it, was for one-third interest in the clinics, as soon as he was ready to issue stock.

Increased Tensions

I felt very secure in my personal relationship with Harvey. There were no sexual ties, but I was very emotionally attached. I often pondered, *Harvey knows my every thought, and I think I know his. We love each other. I depend on Harvey. He will never hurt me. I will never hurt him, either. We are truly the family he says we are. We will grow old together. We have the perfect relationship. He will never leave me because he doesn't have to. Ours is a business relationship with so many other benefits. We are friends, very close friends.*

Only one thing could potentially come between us, and that was Fredi, his live-in lover. I wanted her to live with him while I worked with him. I was certain if I went to bed with Harvey, our relationship would be ruined. But Fredi wanted to run Harvey's business and be his sex partner, too. We were headed for some rough waters.

Most of our problems were subtle, never discussed, but the tension was always there between Fredi and me. One time Harvey asked me to come to his house and bring the checkbook.

"Why are the last six checks written to you, Carol?" he questioned.

"I don't know. Let's look at what they were written for. That is for reimbursement for lunch Friday and Saturday. Look, they are all reimbursements for lunches I paid for related to business. The places where we bought the lunches don't accept checks. We used my cash," I defended myself.

Fredi seemed very upset. It was obvious she had been going through the checkbook behind my back trying to find something I had done wrong.

Another time Harvey wanted to have a poolside party at his house for all of our clinic personnel. "Carol, let's invite some other clinics, their doctors, and staff to our party, too. Can you take care of it?"

"Sure, Harvey. I'll get the invitations out to them."

Fredi was in charge of food, and as usual, it was embarrassing because there was not enough to eat. Embarrassing to have to say, "Harvey, we are out of food."

"Fredi, didn't you know how many people were coming?" he asked her.

"I figured one piece of chicken for each one," she shrugged.

"You should have known some of them would eat more than one piece of chicken."

"I'm sorry, Harvey," she pouted.

"What do we feed them now?" I asked.

"Nothing, Carol." And they walked off, Harvey irritated with the whole situation.

I was the one embarrassed. I invited all of them to "our clinic party." I always thought Fredi was too tight. Jan Batson and I often joked, "Eat before you go to Harvey's tonight. Fredi is in charge of food. There will only be one hamburger for each person. Take your own drinks. She will only have one drink per person."

Tension turned into troubled waters when I started dating Ibrahim Oudeh, a Palestinian from Israel who graduated from medical school in Mexico and was now eligible for his residency.

Ibrahim and I met through Harvey and Fredi. Ibrahim had worked with Harvey, met Fredi, and the friendship between Ibrahim and Fredi deepened because Harvey was gone so much. The two of them, Ibrahim and Fredi, enjoyed the same things, such as cooking and shopping. They spent a lot of free time together.

Fredi was quite attracted to Ibrahim. I knew it, and so did everyone else at the clinic. Harvey did not seem to mind their friendship. As a matter of fact, it seemed to take some of the Fredi-pressure off him. He was quite confident Ibrahim could not compete with him for Fredi.

For some reason Ibrahim started spending more time at the clinic and more time taking me out. I really didn't think much about it then. Kelly had just gone off to North Texas State University for her first semester, and Joe Bob was back at the University of Texas. I was alone for the first time in my life and planned to devote myself to getting the business better established in preparation for expansion.

I was open for a relationship with a man. I was lonely and wanted someone who would adjust to my schedule; Ibrahim fit that bill. He was living with another woman which didn't bother me at the beginning. He was available on demand and interesting when I chose to be with him. Besides, our relationship made Fredi do a slow burn inside, and I knew it.

One evening right after Ibrahim and I started dating, Ibrahim was quite upset. "One of Harvey's friends told him about a jewelry store going out of business. He went to the sale and bought Fredi a wedding ring. I saw Fredi wearing it at his house last night."

I just listened.

Finally the announcement came; Harvey called me at the office. "Fredi and I are going to get married. We are going on a two-week trip for our honeymoon. Get the calendar, and mark me out."

"When are you going to be gone?" I asked.

"Two weeks in February."

I marked him out, sat back in my chair, and cried. I hurt so badly.

Then the jealousy inside me exploded. *I hate Fredi. I hate everything Fredi stands for. She is sleeping with the man I love. She is sleeping with the man I would like to be sleeping with.* Yes, deep in my heart I finally admitted that I wanted Harvey.

I just had to strike back. Since Harvey and Fredi were planning a big honeymoon trip, Ibrahim and I needed to take a trip, too—January before their trip. "Ibrahim, let's go on a little trip. Harvey is going to be gone in February. It's so hard on me when he goes off. I'd like to rest up before he leaves. Where would you like to go?"

"Mexico."

"Set it up, and I'll pay for it." I made sure everyone knew we were going on a trip in January, especially Fredi.

"Tension turned into troubled waters when I started dating Ibrahim Oudeh, a Palestinian from Israel who graduated from medical school in Mexico and was now eligible for his residency."

Ibrahim was no dummy; he knew how to turn my jealousy to his benefit. He approached me one day. "Carol, I have been looking for someone I can trust to buy some rental houses with."

"So have I. I know of a rental house in Oak Cliff that a friend of mine is selling that is a pretty good deal. It is a seven-unit apartment house and is supposedly a 'cash cow.' I would like to buy it."

"Let's look at it together, Carol."

I made the appointment. We looked at it, and the owners gave us the financial information; they wanted 10 percent down, and they would carry the note.

"Let's do it, Ibrahim."

"Can you get the down payment?"

"Yes. I will get my father to co-sign a loan for ten thousand dollars at the San Saba Bank." (Little did I know that by the time this loan came due, I would be out of the abortion business and have to ask my father to pay it.)

"Sounds good to me." Of course it would.

I made the application for a loan in late November, and we signed the contract on January 5, 1983.

Fredi came into my office one day, saw Ibrahim standing next to me, turned and ran out of the clinic. I mused, *I am not supposed to have this much fun at Fredi's expense.*

Ibrahim followed her. They stood outside in the parking lot for over half an hour with Ibrahim at times holding Fredi while she cried. Several employees reporting to work saw what was happening in the parking lot and came into my office and told me.

Later I asked, "Ibrahim, what happened in the parking lot?"

"We just talked. Fredi was really upset."

"About what?"

"Fredi asked me why I'm involved with you. I told her we are going to buy real estate together; we are going to be partners. She said, 'If you want a partner, why don't you ask me? You know I want to buy rental property.' I told her I've already made a commitment to you."

Of course, the fact was he knew he could work me and get more money out of me than he could out of "tightwad Fredi."

A new brand of hatred and anger filled my relationship with Fredi. In my mind we were no longer just competing for Harvey but for Ibrahim, too. Fredi's jealousy only fueled my fire.

"Let's buy another house, Ibrahim," I offered.

"What about Jan Batson's house in Garland? I think I'll live in it myself."

"If that's what you want to do, let's do it."

We began the process to purchase Jan Batson's house around December. I made sure Fredi knew.

Whenever Fredi was around, I was careful to use terms of endearment with Ibrahim just to set her off. If Harvey were there, however, she couldn't do much more than steam.

"Darling, would you hold this tray for me?" I beamed.

Fredi could barely contain herself as she sarcastically said, "Ibrahim, darling?"

I took great pleasure in her mockery. Even Ibrahim noticed the way Fredi mocked me.

I was so glad when the time came for Ibrahim and me to take our trip to Mexico. With Harvey and Fredi's wedding getting very close, things were tense for both of us. We needed a breather.

"Ibrahim, I'm really excited about leaving on our trip tomorrow."

"So am I, Carol. I have something for you." He took my hand and slipped a pearl ring on my ring finger and said, "I love you, Carol."

"I love you, too."

What Ibrahim actually loved was my credit card I furnished him, and I knew it.

When we got back from Mexico, we seemed closer, but that was because Ibrahim was hurting over the pending marriage. He needed me to help him through the ordeal. That was okay because I needed him, too.

"I was very concerned before the marriage, so I took Harvey to lunch and forthrightly said, 'Harvey, you have to protect me from Fredi in case something were to happen to you.'"

I was very concerned before the marriage, so I took Harvey to lunch and forthrightly said, "Harvey, you have to protect me from Fredi in case something were to happen to you."

"I know, Carol. Give me some time to think about it, and I will get back to you."

Harvey got back to me in a couple of weeks. "Carol, we will take out a one million five hundred thousand dollar insurance policy on me and pay for it out of the clinic. You will be the beneficiary, and in case of my death use the money to buy the clinics from Fredi free and clear."

Needless to say, I was elated with the agreement. Cathy Byles, Wayne's wife, wrote the insurance policy, and the check for the first premium was written. I felt very secure.

Harvey's and Fredi's wedding day finally arrived. Ibrahim, Kelly, and I went together. After the wedding we went to the reception which turned out to be pretty embarrassing. I saw Harvey drunk for the first time. He came up to me and kissed me in front of everyone and said, "I love you, Carol."

"I love you, too, Harvey." Inside I thought, *But I am not your new bride.*

The whole scene was out of place. We left early. I cried privately.

After they were married, Fredi assumed her new title of Mrs. Harvey Johnson with great zeal. She walked into the clinic and introduced herself to a new employee. "I am Fredi Johnson, Dr. Johnson's wife."

When I overheard her introduction, I came off the floor where I was working. "Don't come in here acting as if you are someone special because you are Mrs. Harvey Johnson."

"I didn't," she smirked.

"You most certainly did," I shot back. "You said you are Dr. Johnson's wife, and that has no bearing on the bookkeeping job you do. Just don't come in here acting as if we are supposed to treat you differently. Your job has not changed just because you got married."

She left.

My jealousy was out of control. I guess the marriage took a greater toll on me than I realized.

Ibrahim found a condominium deal he wanted to buy in Houston, just about the time the bottom was starting to fall out of the market there. Even though all the signs were bad, I agreed to buy it because Ibrahim wanted it. I thought, *I can just take the write-off; the deal will pester Fredi.*

Fredi and I kept everyone torn up all the time at the clinic. Things were so bad between us we could not concentrate on expanding the business. Suddenly, my dream of becoming the leading lady in the abortion industry was in jeopardy; I had enough sense to know we had to resolve our differences some way. I tried to work it out myself with Fredi, but it was no use. We were entrenched enemies.

Finally, in late spring as a last resort, I turned to Wayne Byles, Harvey's old friend and confidant. "Wayne, I know the Carol/Fredi problem is hindering the advancement of our business. We need some help."

"Carol, I would like to bring in a business counselor I know. Maybe he will be able to help straighten things out."

"I'll talk to anyone who can get us back on the road to expansion."

"I'll talk with Harvey and Fredi about it and see if we can't bring him in to help."

I was relieved because I felt certain almost anyone we talked to would try to get Fredi to move her activities out of the business and into the bedroom.

I felt better after talking to Wayne. I knew Harvey was enjoying his old game pitting me and Fredi against each other.

With the pending help on the way from Wayne, Harvey and I settled down and began to plan for the future.

"Where do you think we should go next, Carol?" he asked.

"I think we should look at the Waco/central Texas area closely. We are seeing so many women from that area, and there are no abortion clinics that do big abortions in central Texas."

"Carol, I would like to go to the mid-cities area. We can cut Chuck off at the pass by being on I-20 or I-30. We can really affect his Ft. Worth clinic."

Things seemed to be moving in the right direction again. Harvey started to get his business affairs in order so we could issue stock. He had Cathy Byles talk to me. "Carol, since you are going to be a stockholder, we will have to set up a corporation for you or start withholding from your check."

"It doesn't matter to me, Cathy. Whatever is best."

I knew Harvey was a man of his word. I couldn't wait to tell Tom. I knew he would be surprised.

Within a short time Wayne called to say, "I've made arrangements for you and Fredi to meet with the business counselor, Jack Shaw. His office will be in touch with you to set up a time."

Fredi and I each met with the counselor one time. Jack Shaw was a strange man, like none other in my world. I could not figure him out. I felt I had to understand him in order to be able to manipulate him, but he didn't cooperate at all.

"Carol, why are you involved in the abortion business?" he asked.

"The bottom line is money. I can't make this kind of money anywhere else."

I kept waiting for the counselor to tell me what he and Fredi were discussing, but he never would. That made me mad.

After Fredi and I met with him separately, he asked for a joint meeting with Harvey, Wayne, Fredi, and me. We met at the corporate attorney's office where he presented us with his initial findings. What I essentially heard the counselor say was, "Fredi, you should be happy; Harvey wants you to stay at home and be his wife."

I was jealous. I would like to have that opportunity—to stay at home and be Harvey's wife—but that was not going to happen. I had to be satisfied Fredi would be moving out of the clinic. I could certainly run the clinics without her nose in our business; however, I knew there would still be fireworks with Fredi.

The counselor concluded, "I want to visit separately with Carol and Fredi four more times and then have another meeting with the group."

Of course I agreed. I can talk to a guy anytime who is on my side.

During my next meeting with the counselor, he said, "Carol, within thirty days something is going to happen."

"What do you mean?"

"I'm not sure. But within thirty days, someone will be leaving the clinic," he repeated enigmatically.

I left his office with those words ringing in my ears. I just knew he was referring to Fredi.

11

LIGHTS, CAMERA, ACTION

H arvey called and informed me about a phone call from an ex-employee. "Carol, Dana called and Channel 4 has been sending their reporters into abortion clinics to see if any will do abortions on women who are not pregnant."

"Uh oh, we've had a rash of negative pregnancy tests recently," I remarked.

"How many?"

"I'll have to look. How does Dana know?"

"Her husband has coffee regularly with someone in Sachse who works for Channel 4 who told him." He paused. "Where do you keep the negative pregnancy tests?"

"In a separate file up front."

"Go up there and count how many have been in recently."

I went to the front and counted six negative pregnancy tests from the past couple of weeks and reported to Harvey.

"Did we tell them they were pregnant?"

"Ibrahim did sonograms."

"Well, you know Ibrahim finds almost everyone pregnant." He went on to say, "Can you stay at the clinic late tonight? Fredi and I will come there. Ask Jan and Ibrahim to stay, too. We'll go through the negative pregnancy tests to see what is going on."

"I'll be here, Harvey."

We've Been Set Up!

When I hung up the telephone, my mind raced back a few days. Janet, one of the laboratory technicians, had come to me and reported, "Carol, we just had another negative pregnancy test, the sixth in the last few days. Something is going on."

"Where is she?"

"Dr. Oudeh is doing a sonogram."

I joined Ibrahim Oudeh in the sonogram room. "How does it look?"

"She's pregnant. See there." He pointed to a shadow on the sonogram screen. Ibrahim patted the girl and said, "Baby, you are pregnant, but it is very early. That is why the pregnancy test you took was negative. Please get dressed and come to the office so we can talk."

I left the room knowing that Ibrahim would do everything he could to get that woman to have the "procedure today."

Harvey had approached me back in December and asked, "What do you think about sending Ibrahim to sonogram school in Houston?"

"That would be great, Harvey. We need a sonogram technician. Have you talked to him?"

"No, but I will. Do you think he will do it?" he asked.

"I know he needs an income." I thought a minute, then said, "I'm sure he will. He needs to do something while he is applying to residency programs."

Ibrahim happily agreed, attended the school, and returned eager to do sonograms and make money. His function was to routinely perform a sonogram on any patient over twelve weeks pregnant as well as on women whose pregnancy tests were negative to see if we could prove they were in fact pregnant. Ibrahim was being paid fifty dollars per sonogram, and some of the doctors individually paid him extra to assist them in doing abortions.

"After all, it costs as much to get a non-pregnant one in as a pregnant one," Harvey reasoned.

"That's right, Harvey," I chimed in. "Let's see if we can prove she is pregnant so we can sell another abortion." It was a good sales technique.

About six o'clock in the evening Harvey and Fredi arrived to review the negative pregnancy tests. I saw a new side of him—the angry, vindictive, paranoid side. Harvey was scared.

We had dinner across the street at a local restaurant then returned to the clinic to do our research. As we walked into the front office, Harvey said, "Let's look at those negative pregnancy tests."

I went to the drop file and pulled out the records. "Here they are. Some of them did not even fill out forms. They were probably walk-in

---

"Janet, one of the laboratory technicians, had come to me and reported, 'Carol, we just had another negative pregnancy test, the sixth in the last few days. Something is going on.' "

---

pregnancy tests that came in during procedure hours, and no one had time to spend with them."

"Here is one that filled out the forms. Pull the schedule for Wednesday. Was Linda Wells scheduled for a procedure?"

"Linda Wells, six weeks pregnant, scheduled at 8:30 A.M. We have an address and everything."

"What's the name of the reporter Dana said is doing the report?"

"Laura Randle."

"Get the telephone directory. Look up Laura Randle to see if she is listed."

"Here is a listing for Laura Randle! The address is 1416 Meadow Lane, 555–0579."

"That is the same address on this chart! She only changed her name. Laura Randle was in our clinic? We did a pregnancy test on her that was negative, and then we did a sonogram? What do you remember about her, Ibrahim?"

"Let me see the chart. Just from looking at the chart, I don't remember anything. My normal routine is to do a sonogram and then tell her if she is pregnant or not."

"Do you remember if you told Laura Randle she was pregnant?"

"No. I don't remember anything specific about her."

Deep in my heart I felt that Ibrahim found every woman pregnant, that he tried to get every woman that came in to have an abortion. I knew we were caught. We had been doing abortions on women who were not pregnant for some time, and I had not been willing to admit it or stop it. I had turned my eyes the other way. *After all, I am not the doctor. The doctor is responsible for the medical procedure,* was my rationale.

But do you think an abortionist who works on a straight commission is going to tell a woman who has signed her consent form and has already paid in full that she is not pregnant? I closed my eyes and collected my twenty-five dollars.

Later in recalling this event, I would remember that Laura Randle had been in our clinic as a gynecology patient several months before she did the report. Harvey and I personally gave her special attention because she was with Channel 4. It's hard to imagine now that we were so rattled the night we reviewed the files, we did not piece it all together then. Actually, Laura Randle had been working on setting us up for months, and we never realized it.

I rejoined the conversation. "Harvey, what do we do now?"

"Let me think about it. I need to talk to our attorney because I really don't know what to do. Wait until we are contacted, I guess. I think they will contact us before they air it," he theorized.

He turned to me then. "Be very careful when a pregnancy test turns up negative. Tell Janet that you want to see every one of them as soon as that test is negative. Question each one carefully and tell them the pregnacy test we use is not the most sensitive. They still could be pregnant. We would like for them to wait two weeks and come back for another pregnancy test at that time. We can beat Laura Randle at this game!"

I thought to myself, *Laura Randle has already beaten us.*

Actually, Laura Randle did not come into the clinic for a pregnancy test herself. She sent in three different women over several days.

The first girl came in with a urine sample known to be negative before she entered the clinic. The lab did a pregnancy test and Janet told her, "Your urine test shows to be negative, but you could still be pregnant. The test we ran is not sensitive enough to pick up an early pregnancy. Would you like for us to do a sonogram and an examination so you will know and not have to worry?"

"Yes, I would," the girl agreed.

Ibrahim did the sonogram and when he finished, he said, "Yeah, babe, you're pregnant. Do you have your money? Want to do it today?"

"Not today," she responded.

"Actually, Laura Randle had been working on setting us up for months, and we never realized it."

After the girl left the clinic, she was once again tested by a doctor hired by the television station to be sure she wasn't pregnant.

In our research that evening we must have discovered the first girl Channel 4 sent in. By the time the second and third girl came in, we had our new system in place. They were each told a different story; we weren't about to get trapped again.

Why Now?

Channel 4's investigation of our clinic could not have happened at a busier time. Wayne and Cathy Byles were busy installing a new book-keeping system. Harvey was getting his business affairs in order so we could finally issue the clinic stock. Fredi and I were in the process of trying to make peace with each other with the counselor's help.

Dana's call regarding Laura Randle came right after my second visit with the counselor, the one when he told me within thirty days someone would be leaving the clinic. So I was also looking forward to Fredi's soon departure.

Business was booming. Our advertising was kicking in all over a five-state area, and each month our business continued to grow. In my mind, we were getting ready to really take off. Soon we would be ready to open our third, fourth, and fifth clinics. I would finally be a millionaire! I could hardly wait.

I had been promising each of the kids a new car. While they were home from school for the summer, we looked around.

"What kind of car do you want, Joe Bob?"

"A new pick-up."

But my dream was for him to have a new sports car.

"What kind of car do you want, Kelly?"

"A Mazda."

I wanted them both to have sports cars just alike except for the color—Kelly's pink and Joe Bob's brown.

"But, I want a black one if I'm going to get a sports car," Joe Bob insisted.

I had to compromise with him, but Kelly always tried to please me. On July 2 I bought two 280 ZX Datsuns—one pink and one black—both with no miles on them. Kelly sold her Oldsmobile, but Joe Bob kept his pick-up.

My business dealings with Ibrahim were beginning to go sour and consumed all of my "spare" time. Back in April Ibrahim had come to me with the final deal we would do together. He suggested, "My family are all butchers in Israel. I'd like to buy a butcher shop in Richardson. We can make about eight thousand dollars a month clear profit."

Wow! That stirred up old memories of Daddy and me when he worked in the butcher shop.

"How will we run a butcher shop?"

"I have a friend who is a butcher. He will run it for us for one-third interest in the business."

I co-signed a note at the bank for fifty thousand dollars, and we became the proud owners of Promenade Meat Center in Richardson, Texas on May 2. One month after it opened, the butcher shop owed twelve thousand dollars to suppliers, and I had fed it two thousand five hundred dollars. I had to fire Randy, our one-third owner. With two employees I began a self-designed crash course to learn the butcher business in my "spare" time; somehow, I managed to keep Harvey from knowing about my side business.

While I was preoccupied with my other business interest, Harvey was consumed with fear about Laura Randle. He was paranoid because we had not heard from her. I had never seen him acting so strangely. "Harvey, why are you so worried?" I asked.

"This could ruin the clinic, and we are just beginning to make headway."

Secretly, I believed Harvey was afraid Sheryl's death at his hands would come to light along with all the other botched abortions he had covered up. His medical reputation would be ruined. I realized it was a possibility, but I always considered fear as our greatest enemy.

I had an uncanny sense of peace that everything would be all right and tried to reassure Harvey. "Harvey, we just have to let this crisis pass and then move on. Everything is going to be all right." But my attempted reassurances only seemed to convince him I was crazy.

It wasn't long before Laura Randle called the clinic. "Is Dr. Johnson in? This is Laura Randle with Channel 4 News."

The call was transferred to me. "May I help you?"

"This is Laura Randle with Channel 4 News. May I speak with Dr. Johnson?"

"He is not in at the moment. May I take a message?"

"Yes. Ask him to call me at the station." And she gave me the phone number. "When do you think he will call?"

"I am not certain, but I would think this afternoon," I hedged.

"Thank you."

I quickly called Harvey's private practice office. "Harvey, Laura Randle just called for you. She wants you to call her back."

"What did she say?"

"Nothing. She wanted to talk to you."

"I don't want to call her, but I have to . . . don't I?"

"Yes, you do. We really don't have anything to worry about. I've seen this happen to other clinics, and it only helped their business."

What seemed like an eternity passed before Harvey called me back. "She wants to interview me on camera."

"Did she say what the interview was about?"

"No, she was elusive but wants the interview. I can't do it. It can't come out that I am the medical director for an abortion clinic."

Fine time to figure that out, I thought.

"Carol, you will have to do the interview."

When the going gets rough . . . just throw Carol to the lions! "I don't think she will interview me. She wants the medical director."

"I am going to talk to the attorney, but I think you are the one to do the interview. We'll talk later tonight," he promised.

I was aware of how those interviews go from my experience with Chuck. Anything I said would be twisted and used against me. I reasoned with myself, *I do not want to do that interview. I want no part of it. But how can I tell Harvey 'No'?*

Harvey called that evening at his regular time. "Carol, you've got to do the interview with Laura Randle next week. You know I can't do it."

"I know, Harvey."

"You'll do just fine. I'll see you at the clinic tomorrow. Good night, Carol. I love you."

"I love you, too, Harvey."

Saturday night I was cleaning up the back area, angry that Harvey, Fredi, and Ibrahim were up front talking. I hit the cabinet with one of the hoses from the suction machine, and it bounced off and hit me in the eye. It cut my eyelid, and I just knew my eye was going to be black. Crying and bleeding, I rushed into Harvey's office where Fredi, Ibrahim, and Harvey were. "I cut my eye. I can't do the interview."

Harvey was crushed but sensed he had pushed me too far. He consoled me, reassured me, "Everything is going to be all right, Carol." It was the first time in a long time he had consoled me.

Thank heaven, that solved it. I didn't have to do the interview.

Fredi came in my office early the next week and said, "You don't have a black eye."

"It's the marvels of make-up, Fredi." She thought she had caught me. She was right. I didn't have a black eye. But I was not going to hang myself to cover for Harvey again.

We sent a letter rather than do the interview. I signed the letter; I set myself up again.

On Wednesday afternoon Harvey, Jan Batson, his former nurse, and I were in my office visiting when an employee burst in. "A patient just came in and said there is a someone outside the clinic filming something for the news."

Harvey's face contorted. I stood up. "Don't leave, Carol," he screamed as he reached for me.

"Harvey, I was only going to lower the thermostat." I turned to the employee. "Thanks for telling us." I closed the door.

I could see the fear coming over Harvey in waves. He turned to me. "Don't move. Stay right there. Jan, you go out the back door, come up between the buildings and see what is happening."

"Okay." Jan walked out.

Harvey's face was red, full of anger directed at me. He had never talked to me in that manner before. I was scared of Harvey for the

---

"It cut my eyelid, and I just knew my eye was going to be black. Crying and bleeding, I rushed into Harvey's office where Fredi, Ibrahim, and Harvey were. 'I cut my eye. I can't do the interview.' "

---

first time in my life. I had seen him angry with Fredi, and Alma Jean had told me about his violent rages, but this was a first for me.

More than the cameras, I was concerned with what was happening in my office. For the first time in our relationship I feared Harvey might strike me. I had experienced that as a little child and knew what to do—be very quiet. I did not say a word. I was very still.

A relationship of years was being destroyed before my eyes like a nuclear bomb, destroying that bond in such a way it could never be rebuilt. I started to see that Harvey abused me, abused Fredi, abused everyone. I had never seen that before.

I would never knowingly hurt Harvey, but I now realized he would hurt me if it served his purposes. Our relationship did not matter as much to him as it did to me.

"Harvey, I need to go to the front to see what is going on in the office," I delicately suggested.

"Sure, sure." He dismissed me.

The front office was abuzz, everyone looking out the window to see what was going on. I spoke in a reassuring tone of voice, "Don't be concerned. If they are filming us, we don't want to be filmed staring at them. Let's get back to work."

Nervous laughter followed, and we started back to work.

Jan came in through the front door. "They are gone. They were filming what looked like a news segment. They were zeroing in on the clinic while the reporter talked."

Harvey uttered an expletive, something he never did.

What was going on with this man? We had killed a woman, maimed several other women, yet I had never seen Harvey Johnson so upset before. He was angry at me almost as if he blamed me for the whole thing. I didn't understand.

"They will investigate the clinic."

"Who will?"

"The National Abortion Federation."

"I don't think they have ever investigated any abortion clinic. When The Women's Center had a death at their clinic a few years ago, cameras from Channel 8 burst into their staff meeting, and the story aired right after the death. It helped their business, remember? No one investigated them. No one is going to investigate us over a news report. Don't be so paranoid."

Who'll Be the Scapegoat?

I started to dread being around Harvey. I dreaded the days he worked in the clinic. I had no choice; I had to be there. He needed me, especially now.

The week before the exposé aired for the first time, Harvey made a request. "Carol, I know you want to go to your twenty-five-year class reunion this weekend, but with all this going on, I wish you wouldn't."

"I won't go if you don't want me to, Harvey. I'll stay here."

"I would just feel better if you were here."

Another sacrifice made for Harvey.

Everything was crumbling around me, but I was calm. I could not understand the peace I felt. I missed my next appointment with the counselor as well and didn't even call to cancel.

A new chasm developed between Harvey and me. I didn't understand his uncanny fear. I tried to reassure him, but he didn't understand why I was so calm. He kept telling me how upset he was. I kept reassuring him, "Everything is going to be all right. Harvey, any publicity—bad or good—is good for business. They will at least know where to find us."

Harvey had lost his sense of humor and was starting to lose weight. "This Laura Randle diet has taken off over ten pounds already," he said attempting to be light-hearted over something that was really bothering him.

During the weekend, Channel 4 started to air a teaser hourly saying they would be revealing something about abortion clinics in Dallas on the 10:00 P.M. news the following Wednesday. We knew it would be us.

On Monday in the middle of the night, my father called. "Carol, your Grandmother Taylor just passed away. We'll call you about the funeral arrangements in the morning."

I was very sad when I hung up the telephone. One of my goals was to buy my grandmother a new car. She had been driving a wreck. I had already been looking at a car for her. I wanted her to have a nice new car like my children.

Tuesday morning at 8:00 A.M. I had breakfast with Cathy Byles to go over how I was to be compensated as a stockholder. She explained how my checks would be written in the future. I finished the meeting and rushed to work.

"During the weekend, Channel 4 started to air a teaser hourly saying they would be revealing something about abortion clinics in Dallas on the 10:00 P.M. news the following Wednesday. We knew it would be us."

Later in the day Mother called about the funeral arrangements. "Carol Nan, the funeral is going to be Wednesday afternoon."

"Mother, can you postpone the funeral to Thursday? I need to be at the clinic tomorrow. We will work tomorrow and be in San Saba tomorrow night." Even as I asked, I realized it was a lot to ask of my mother, but I couldn't have Harvey freaking out on me while I was off at my grandmother's funeral.

Mother was upset but agreed to postpone the funeral. With the news story breaking Wednesday night at 10:00 and it being Harvey's day to work at the clinic, I just couldn't leave him alone. He needed me more than ever before.

Wednesday was a tense day with Harvey in the clinic and my leaving in the afternoon for my grandmother's funeral. Somehow we got through it. I was relieved to go to San Saba with Kelly. Joe Bob and his girlfriend drove down in his car. For a short period of time I could be away from the pressure seeping out of Harvey's every pore.

We arrived at my parents' home in time for the 10:00 P.M. news. It was terrible. The exposé showed the non-pregnant reporter walking into our clinic as well as a shot of Ibrahim and me walking across the parking lot into the clinic. They aired sketches of how we sold abortions to women who were not pregnant, and in the background played Ibrahim's voice the reporter had recorded with a hidden microphone saying, "Yeah, babe, you're pregnant. Do you have your money? Want to do it today?"

My stomach turned. I was physically ill. I called Harvey. He was quiet, dejected. He could hardly talk.

"It was terrible, Carol."

"It will be all right, Harvey. You'll see."

"No, it won't. How soon can you get back to Dallas?"

"I'll be at your home tomorrow night in time to watch the next segment."

"See you then."

I called Ibrahim. "Did you see it?"

"Yes. Harvey is going to blame me for everything."

"No. Harvey wouldn't do something like that. He will be loyal. He will defend you, Ibrahim."

"No. Just watch, Carol. It will all be my fault."

"I don't think so. We'll talk about it tomorrow. See you then."

Ibrahim joined me Thursday morning for the funeral. "Carol, I am going to take the blame for this. I just know it."

"Harvey wouldn't do that to you. You were following directions. He will protect you. Just watch," I promised, believing it would be true.

The funeral seemed endless. Something inside me went on cruise control. I still had this strange peace inside, but there was so much turmoil around me. I felt as if I needed to let the dust settle down, and then Harvey would be his old self.

"They aired sketches of how we sold abortions to women who were not pregnant, and in the background played Ibrahim's voice the reporter had recorded with a hidden microphone saying, 'Yeah, babe, you're pregnant. Do you have your money? Want to do it today?' "

Suddenly, a new thought sped across the surface of my mind. *Maybe I'm going to be the scapegoat, not Ibrahim.* I pushed that idea aside quickly. *It will be all right. Harvey will not do that to me.*

Finally, we were on our way back to Dallas. We didn't arrive in time to go to Harvey's before the news, so we went straight home to my house and watched the broadcast.

I called Harvey. "Sorry, Harvey. We were late. I just got back in town and stopped at home to watch the news. I am on my way to your house."

"Don't come over, Carol. The attorneys are here. I'll talk to you later." Harvey's voice was different. Something was really wrong.

"Harvey, are you all right?"

"Yes, I'm fine. Wayne wants to meet you for breakfast with Billie at the Executive Inn. Can you be there at eight o'clock?"

"I can be there."

During breakfast Wayne kept asking me, "Carol, why are you out of control?" It was as if he wanted me to lose control. I could hardly keep from laughing at the manipulative game I knew he was playing. But why was he doing it?

We repeatedly went over my daily activities. I finally concluded Wayne was going to have Billie, the director of our Women's Clinic of Mesquite, take my place temporarily to take some of the pressure off me. He seemed to be nervous about what my reaction to that was going to be.

When I got to the clinic, I received roses from the staff and a bouquet from Billie. The employees really rallied behind me and supported me with many hugs and much love, trying to comfort me in the aftermath of the negative exposé.

But Harvey did not call at his regular times which was very strange. I tried to call him, but each time his response was, "Carol, I can't talk now."

At the end of the day Harvey told Ibrahim not to come back to the clinic. I was really surprised. Ibrahim was right and I was wrong. Harvey did use him!

I drove home Friday evening, thinking Ibrahim was right after all. I remembered thinking earlier, *Maybe I'm going to be the scapegoat for what happened at the clinic.* Then I reasoned, *I am the most likely candidate to be sacrificed next. Harvey's actions for the last few days make sense. I am going to be the scapegoat. Harvey is going to use me after all. We aren't family.*

Harvey is the one who hired Ibrahim. He is the medical director, not me. I am going to be blamed for the things he trained Ibrahim to do. They are going to use my personal relationship with Ibrahim to try to prove we were working together.

I also remembered Tom admonishing me to get everything on paper. "Cover yourself, Carol Nan. You are wide open."

"Tom, this man will not hurt me. I trust him."

That conversation rang in my ears.

Kelly and Joe Bob, with their dates, and I went to dinner that night. Not much was said about the news. I went to bed early. Saturday was always a big day. If I had only known how big!

Dressed in my scrub suit, I arrived early, as usual, and went to work. Harvey came in at nine o'clock, depressed, dejected, withdrawn.

Wayne and Harvey met most of the day. Jack Shaw, the counselor, joined them about mid-morning. I went through the motions of working, but my very inquisitive mind was on the job with me. Why was

Jack meeting with Wayne and Harvey? I already knew I was going to be replaced temporarily, but what else were they discussing? I knew they were discussing me. I wanted to be a fly on the wall in that meeting.

About noon, a telephone call came from a young woman who had been in for an abortion at six weeks but did not come back for her two week check-up. Her complaint now was, "I can feel a foot in my vagina."

I looked at her chart and found her abortion had been done some fourteen weeks earlier. If her fetus had been missed, she was now at least twenty weeks pregnant. Dr. Leggett was her doctor, and he did occassionally miss one. I told the receptionist, "Ask her to come in right now."

Personal terror. The only big baby abortionist who could do one free—because it was originally missed—was Harvey. I swore he would never do another big baby abortion. What could I do?

Later in the day the young woman came in for her examination. Dr. Johnson checked her. After Harvey examined her, Harvey, Billie, and I discussed the situation.

"Leggett missed it. She is right—the baby's foot is dangling in her vagina."

"Harvey, it's twenty weeks along. That baby has been growing for fourteen more weeks."

"I know."

Harvey was in no shape to do a "big" abortion. To make matters worse, he didn't want to put her to sleep because of the extra cost.

I looked at Billie and said, "Let me out of here before you start this one." I could just see him botching the abortion and pulling the bowel through the vagina again.

"Okay, Carol."

Wayne met me in the hall. "Carol, can you join Jack and me in Harvey's office?"

Wayne started, "Carol, it might be better if you keep a low profile for a while. Perhaps you can go to Oklahoma and set up an operation up there."

"What do you mean, Wayne?"

"With all the negative publicity you need to stay out of this clinic. You will be taken care of. We just need to find somewhere else for you to go for now. You don't need to come in tomorrow. Billie will handle everything."

I was relieved to hear Wayne say I would be taken care of. They only wanted me to go to Oklahoma.

I left Harvey's office and went to the back to gather my things. As I passed by the room where Harvey and Billie were preparing to do the missed abortion, something unusual happened. The smell of death in the back part of the clinic made me nauseous for the first time.

At the same time, a part of me wanted to go in that room and help Harvey, comfort him.

Billie saw me and came out to talk with me. "They want me to do your job, but your friendship is more important to me than this job. I won't do it if you don't want me to."

I looked her in the eyes and knew it wouldn't matter how I responded to her. I said, "Do the job, Billie. I'll feel better knowing you are taking care of it." I thought, *After all, it's only temporary.*

I went to my office and wrote myself a check and met Jack in the hallway. Together we started walking out of the clinic.

"What is going to happen next, Jack?"

"I'm not sure, Carol, but everything will work out for the best."

I walked out of the clinic with Jack Shaw, the strange counselor I had known for only twenty-five days. As we walked away from the clinic, I thought to myself, *I hope I can trust Jack. I have not been a good judge of character in the past, yet there is something different about him. Besides, I have no one else to turn to. I have to trust him.* Inside I sensed the forces in control could be trusted. It was as though an enormous weight was being lifted off my shoulders.

I felt peaceful.

12

THE DIFFERENCE AFTER ONE PRAYER

K elly, I'm going to church in the morning. Will you go with me?"
The silence at the dinner table was arresting, to say the least.

"Church? Yes, Mom, I'll go with you." Kelly's quick assent was just what I needed to hear.

Sunday morning, Kelly and I went to a little church meeting in a portable building in Plano, the place where my new counselor Jack ministered. I entered the church carrying the weight of 35,001 abortions, one mother's death, and multiple botched abortions. Yes, 35,001—the babies of 35,000 other mothers and my baby. Six years of involvement in the abortion industry cost a lot. The price was much higher than I ever imagined.

I left church feeling the sermon had been prepared just for me.

Kelly and I picked up Joe Bob and his girlfriend for lunch. It was wonderful just spending time with my family and not running off to work.

After lunch I found myself alone and took the opportunity to review the events of the past twenty-five days, especially the meetings with Jack. In our first meeting together with Wayne, Harvey, and Fredi, he seemed to be on my side; the second time I met with him, I wasn't so sure. That time he seemed to be able to see inside me; I knew I had to turn the tables on him and get in control of the interview.

I started asking him questions. To this day I don't know why I asked him, "Are you a preacher?"

"Yes, I am, Carol."

"Well, I want you to know I am a Christian, too. I pray every day." (I meant about the business—that we'd have a lot of patients, no complications, and no deaths.) "I keep a Bible in the right-hand drawer of my desk, and I tithe on all the money I make."

"That's good, Carol, but those things don't make you a Christian."

My Fateful Meeting with Jack—and God

It surprised me that he wasn't impressed with my tithing. I regrouped quickly and asked, "What in the world are you doing in this situation?"

"God sent me."

This man was crazy! I shot back, "I believe God has me in the clinics, too, helping women. We counsel every woman who comes into our clinic."

When I stopped telling him about how good I was, he said, "I've been praying with some others about this, and I believe God has given me thirty days to get my job done. Something is going to happen within thirty days. Someone is going to be leaving the clinic."

"What do you mean something is going to happen?"

"I'm not sure, Carol."

Someone will be leaving the clinic all right, but it won't be me. It will be Fredi. I changed the topic. "Jack, how did you and Wayne get acquainted? I'm really curious as to why Wayne chose you to be the counselor to help us with our problem."

"It's a long story, but I'll make it as brief as I can. About five years ago a man I helped worked with Wayne and set up an appointment for us to visit with him. We went to see Wayne at his office in Garland. I shared Christ with him, and it made him quite upset at the time. I had not heard from Wayne again until just recently. He related his story to me at that time.

"Wayne told me he had been driving down North Central Expressway in all the heavy traffic with a very heavy heart. He began to turn to God for help. At that time he began to remember everything I had shared with him five years earlier in his office. It all came back to him so clearly while on that expressway. He prayed to receive Jesus

Christ as his Lord and Savior right then. He wanted me to be the first to know.

"I told him it was wonderful and how thrilled I was for him. I encouraged him to visit with me soon. Carol, since that time Wayne and I have met together several times, and I have helped him in some

---

"When I stopped telling him about how good I was, he said, 'I've been praying with some others about this, and I believe God has given me thirty days to get my job done. Something is going to happen within thirty days. Someone is going to be leaving the clinic.' "

---

other areas. He is very interested in helping you, Harvey, and Fredi make peace with God, too. God and Wayne are the reason why I am here today with you.

"I know Wayne has tried to share with you in his own way, but he doesn't believe he is able to say what needs to be said to help you now. Isn't it true Wayne has spoken to you?"

"Yes, I guess he has." It was all well and good Wayne wanted to help us. I could endure whatever he thought would help if it would get Fredi out of the clinic.

"Carol, everyone is searching for attention, recognition, security, acceptance, and identity. Call it what you will. Everyone is searching for the same thing—love. And we search for it in all the wrong places. The greatest need we have in life is to be loved. It is like we go around screaming inside, 'For God's sake, won't someone pay attention to me, recognize me, accept me, love me?'

"Although the love we search for is genuine, most of the love we find is counterfeit. Every outreach we make, every person we turn to, they fail us or we fail them sooner or later. We walk away from relationship after relationship beat up and hurt. We carry a lot of pain inside over damaged relationships.

"You see, Carol, most of our relationships are based on performance. We think or feel we are loved when people do to us and for us what we think or feel should be done to us and for us. Do you know what I mean?"

"Yes, I'm afraid I do."

"Carol, the moment we were born we started reaching out to our family, to our parents to love us. If they are following God's plan, we receive genuine love, but if they are doing the best they know how apart from God's plan, their love is counterfeit.

"We reach out to family, friends, the opposite sex, material possessions, education, sports, accomplishments, social status, work, profession, and other sources to give us the recognition and attention we crave. Can you identify with what I am saying?"

"Yes." Something was beginning to disturb me big time.

"Carol, in our first meeting you said you are in the job you are in because of money. Am I correct?"

"Yes, I did say that."

"I'd like for you to read this passage," and he handed me his Bible.

And protracted wrangling and wearing discussion and perpetual friction among men who are corrupted in mind and bereft of the truth, who imagine that godliness or righteousness is a source of profit—a money-making business, a means of livelihood. From such withdraw.

[And it is, indeed, a source of immense profit, for] godliness accompanied with contentment—that contentment which is a sense of inward sufficiency—is great and abundant gain.

For we brought nothing into the world, and obviously we cannot take anything out of the world;

But if we have food and clothing, with these we shall be content (satisfied).

But those who crave to be rich fall into temptation and a snare, and into many foolish (useless, godless) and hurtful desires that plunge men into ruin and destruction and miserable perishing.

For the love of money is a root of all evils; it is through this craving that some have been led astray, and have wandered from the faith and pierced themselves through with many acute [mental] pangs.

" 'Money will not satisfy you. It, too, will be used to destroy relationships because you can't buy people. You can use money to try to buy love, but true love cannot be bought. Counterfeit love can be. Do you think you have ever tried to buy love?' "

But as for you, O man of God, flee from all these things; aim at and pursue righteousness—that is, right standing with God and true goodness; godliness (which is the loving fear of God and Christlikeness), faith, love, steadfastness (patience) and gentle-heartedness.

Fight the good fight of the faith; lay hold of the eternal life to which you were summoned, and confess the good confession [of faith] before many witnesses.

In the presence of God Who preserves alive all living things, and of Christ Jesus Who in His testimony before Pontius Pilate made the good confession, I [solemnly] charge you

To keep all His precepts unsullied and flawless, irreproachable until the appearing of our Lord Jesus Christ, the Anointed One.

Which will be shown forth in His own proper time by the blessed, only Sovereign, the King of kings and the Lord of lords. (1 Timothy 6:5–15)

"Carol, is it possible you are in the business you are in because of the love of money—greed?" he said when I finished reading.

"Yes, I suppose it is." *I am really in trouble now. Everything in me is going crazy. He is hitting me right where I am living.*

"Guess what, Carol? Money will not satisfy you. It, too, will be used to destroy relationships because you can't buy people. You can use money to try to buy love, but true love cannot be bought. Counterfeit love can be. Do you think you have ever tried to buy love?"

"Yes, of course." *What's with this guy, anyway? I'm not here to work on me, I'm here to work on Fredi.*

"You see, Carol, even when we use money to express our love, most of the time it has a string attached to it. We want something in return. When we get it, we feel loved; when we do not get what we want, we feel unloved.

"Carol, the Bible says, 'God is love.' He alone is the source of real love. God is the only one who can love unconditionally. When we try to love God's way because we are supposed to, we fail. The Bible says to 'Love your enemies; do good to those who would despitefully use you.' God requires you to love Fredi. Have you tried?"

"Yes, but it hasn't worked."

"Thank God it hasn't, Carol."

"Why do you say that?"

"Because your inability to solve the problem with Fredi has brought you to the place where you can make the greatest discovery of your life."

"What do you mean?"

"You can discover the love you have been searching for all your life and begin to love Fredi as God wants you to. Not just Fredi, but anyone else you may have a problem loving. Do you know why you fight with Fredi and can't love her?"

"No, I guess not."

"Let's look at another passage." Again, he handed me his Bible to read.

> What leads to strife (discord and feuds) and how do conflicts (quarrels and fightings) originate among you? Do they not arise from your sensual desires that are ever warring in your bodily members?
>
> You are jealous and covet [what others have] and your desires go unfulfilled; [so] you become murderers. [To hate is to murder as far as your hearts are concerned.] You burn with envy and anger and are not able to obtain [the gratification, the contentment and the happiness that you seek], so you fight and war. (James 4:1–2)

When I finished reading, he asked, "Carol, are you jealous of Fredi?"

"Yes, I am." There, I admitted it.

"God wants you to love her and to be happy for her. He wants you to care for her just as He does."

That sounds good, but this guy doesn't know Fredi or the people I've been dealing with all my life. He lives in a fantasy world. Besides, is he telling Fredi the same things?

"You see, Carol, if God is the only one who can love unconditionally, then God has to be inside us loving as only He can through us."

I can sure give him a list God would have trouble loving. "How does that happen?" I asked.

"The Bible says, 'God's love is shed abroad in our hearts by the Holy Spirit who is given unto us.' Let's read 1 John 4:7–15."

> Beloved, let us love one another; for love is [springs] from God; and he who loves [his fellowmen] is begotten (born) of God and is coming [progressively] to know and understand God [to perceive and recognize and get a better and clearer knowledge of Him].
>
> He who does not love has not become acquainted with God [does not and never did know Him] for God is love.
>
> In this the love of God was made manifest (displayed), where we are concerned: in that God sent His Son, the only begotten or unique [Son], into the world so we might live through Him.
>
> In this is love: not that we loved God, but that He loved us and sent His Son to be the propitiation (the atoning sacrifice) for our sins.
>
> Beloved, if God loved us so [very much], we also ought to love one another.
>
> No man has at any time [yet] seen God. But if we love one another, God abides (lives and remains) in us and His love [that love which is esentially His] is brought to completion (to its full maturity, runs its full course, is perfected) in us!
>
> By this we come to know (perceive, recognize and understand) that we abide (live and remain) in Him and He in us: because He has given (imparted) to us of His [Holy] Spirit.
>
> And [besides] we ourselves have seen (have deliberately and steadfastly contemplated) and bear witness that the Father has sent the Son [as the] Savior of the world.
>
> Anyone who confesses (acknowledges, owns) that Jesus is the Son of God, God abides (lives, makes His home) in him, and he (abides, lives, makes his home) in God.

"Carol, the word *confess* includes acknowledging Jesus Christ as Lord over our life. For Him to be the Lord of our life means He begins to reign in our heart, ruling our life in every way, loving as only He can, through us, even the Fredi's of our life."

He is certainly beginning to make sense, but I didn't come to the counselor to be "preached" to. I came to make peace with Fredi. Can he be right?

"Now, if Christ Jesus isn't living as Lord of our life, then we are in control ourselves, missing the mark God intends for us to hit, living where we should not be living, doing what is displeasing to God. We are loving the best we know how, but it is not good enough. We are living in sin as far as God is concerned. In confession we acknowledge we have been running our own life.

"Carol, would you like to make peace with Fredi and begin to love her God's way?"

"You're asking a lot."

"I'm not. God is."

Great. Now he's got God right in the middle between Fredi and me. If I'm going to please God, I'm going to have to love Fredi and want what is best for her over what is best for me. No way!

"Carol, I wouldn't be much of a salesman if I didn't offer to close the deal. Would you like for me to pray with you?"

"Yes, I guess so. I will pray with you."

I had listened, but I have to say honestly there were still a lot of unanswered questions in my mind.

"Here is the prayer we are going to pray, Carol: God, I have been running my own life and have missed the mark you have for me to hit. Father, thank You for sending Your Son, Jesus Christ, to die for my sins. Thank You for raising Him from the dead and making Him living Lord over all. Come into my heart Lord Jesus and begin to reign over my life. Begin to love through me as only You can and make me a worker in Your vineyard. Amen.

"Would you like to pray that prayer with me, now?"

"Yes, I would. Do I pray out loud?"

"Please repeat after me."

I prayed with the counselor/preacher and left his office without believing the prayer would make any difference. I had prayed before, and there wasn't any difference afterward. I did not really expect that prayer to change me either.

"I prayed with the counselor/preacher and left his office without believing the prayer would make any difference. I had prayed before, and there wasn't any difference afterward. I did not really expect that prayer to change me either."

I drove back to the clinic excited because I only had to meet with that counselor two more times. On the way back, however, I wondered for the first time how I would make a living for me and the children if I were to leave the clinic. Let me tell you, I quickly suppressed that thought!

Hit with a 2 x 4

Upon my return to the clinic, I noticed something was different. When I left, it had seemed all the women were dancing in through the front door singing, "I'm pregnant. Do my abortion." But when I got back, all the women were coming in the front door crying. I had never noticed that before.

I went up to the receptionist and the counselors on duty and asked, "What happened while I was gone?"

"Nothing that I know of." The answer was unanimous.

For some reason I was not comfortable in my normal working environment.

I was saved by the bell—Bell Telephone that is. Harvey called. "How are things going, Carol?"

"Everything's great, Harvey. We're having a great day." It was business as usual with him. I could never share with Harvey what was really happening inside me; I was a bundle of confusion.

I hung up the telephone and continued to stumble around in a daze. In my confusion Wayne called.

"Wayne, I prayed a prayer with Jack today," I found myself saying. "I suppose I have to leave the clinic, but I don't know what to do." Now where had that come from?

"When I find myself in a seemingly impossible situation, I just ask God to hit me over the head with a 2 x 4," Wayne gently guided me.

I closed the door to my office and prayed from the floor of that abortion clinic, "Lord, if there is a Lord, if this is not where you want me, hit me over the head with a 2 x 4."

I walked out of my office with a peace I cannot explain. I returned to work thinking, *Perhaps I am to stay in the clinic until I can lead Harvey out of the business. Yes. That is what I must do. I am supposed to help Harvey get out of this business, too.*

I love Harvey. Jan loved him and left him. Two wives loved him but left him. Alma Jean loves him, and now she is leaving him, going to prison for her daughter's hot checks. I can't leave Harvey. No, I have to stay. I have to be loyal to Harvey. Harvey would be loyal to me. I have to lead Harvey out of the abortion business with me.

We can move to opening surgicenters now. We can sell these abortion clinics and use the money to start our surgicenters. We just have to let this crisis pass. We can move on as soon as things calm down. Harvey will see the reasoning in this move.

Yes, God wants me to help Harvey leave the abortion business. I will join Wayne in working to help Harvey (not Fredi, though) make peace with God.

I also started taking the women into my office, closing the door, and asking, "Why are you crying?"

One woman in particular said, "My parents would kill me if they knew I was pregnant."

"No, they would not kill you," I heard myself say. (I knew how to sell abortions—take the fear, amplify it, get their money, push them through.) But instead I said, "Your parents love you. They will be disappointed, but they will stand by you. Would you like for me to go home with you to tell your parents?"

How strange. I was actually looking at the women differently. I wanted to draw close to them and love them.

I thought, *If I don't watch out, I'll be the one leaving the clinic, not Fredi. Or worse, there won't be any women having abortions if I keep helping them by encouraging them to tell their parents, talk to husbands or boyfriends.* I rationalized, *If I'm talking people out of abortions, how am I going to make a living? I just lost seventy-five dollars. How will I keep those two children in college with one thousand dollar monthly allowances, new cars, money-money.*

It was business as usual all around me but not business as usual inside me. There was a song in my heart, a joyous song that was not there before. It was a song more joyous than I had known with Tom, more joyous than I experienced as I emotionally bonded with my third child within my womb—the songs that were ripped from my being when I aborted life growing inside me. The French meaning of my name Carol, "joyous song," was coming out again but this time with a new dimension of love.

I have since learned we must be careful what we ask for from God. Laura Randle was God's 2 x 4. And I got hit with it.

After reflecting on the events of the previous twenty-five days, I concluded the exposé wasn't the problem at all. My relationship with Harvey was the problem. Or was it my relationship with God? I had to make a decision about staying with Harvey or getting out. Wayne had

---

"It was business as usual all around me but not business as usual inside me. There was a song in my heart, a joyous song that was not there before."

---

offered me the opportunity to go to Oklahoma and open an abortion clinic; that was no longer an option. Harvey wanted to do surgicenters, but would he see the value in selling the clinics to open the surgicenters? Maybe we could open a surgicenter, and I'd run it while he stayed with the abortion clinics.

As I wrestled with my future, Harvey called. "Where were you this morning?"

"I went to church." Then I found myself explaining. "Wayne told me Billie was going to take care of the clinic."

"I expected you to be there today."

Inside me something clicked. Harvey was demanding and using guilt to motivate me. Well, I wanted no part of that! "Harvey, when I left yesterday, Wayne told me not to come in, not to worry about it. I took the day off."

"It's okay, Carol. Did Wayne talk to you about going to Oklahoma and opening a clinic for us?"

"Yes, he did, Harvey. But I need to sit down with you to talk first."

"Baby, I'm too tired. This is too much. We'll talk later in the week after the exposé finishes running."

This was to be my last conversation with Harvey as "family" and partners. Harvey and I were finished in my mind. I began to focus on the future.

What Do I Do Now?

I was scared. Fear gripped me unmercifully. *When I walk through this door, what will be on the other side? How am I going to make a living? pay for the cars? the house? the investments? Maybe I'll lose everything, maybe even the children, because the money will be gone. What if all that love they supposedly feel for me is tied to money because I've tried to buy their love?*

Wayne promised in front of Jack I would be taken care of. Financially it would be difficult, but I would have some time to readjust. After all, I was a promised one-third partner in a thriving business worth one million five hundred thousand dollars—that was five hundred thousand dollars to me in some form. Surely the settlement between us would be no less than two hundred and fifty thousand.

Joe Bob only had two more years in college; Kelly had three, but Harvey said, "Tell Kelly I still want her to work for me. And, tell her no matter what I will help her get through school."

I had trusted Harvey Johnson with my dearest secrets and with one of my dearest treasures, my daughter. I let him get close to Kelly and trusted him not to violate her or her feelings. Now I hoped he would honor his word.

The emotional divorce between Harvey and me started. *I won't have to protect him from anyone or anything anymore.* I even thought, *I disdain abortion. I hate it. I hate Harvey and everything about abortion.*

I made arrangements to see my counselor Monday morning at 9:00 A.M.

"Jack, I've made the decision not to go to Oklahoma. I've also decided I don't want to work with Harvey anymore. I need to regroup in my life and start all over. I want to reach a settlement with Harvey. The minimum I want to settle for is two hundred and fifty thousand dollars for my one-third interest."

"Carol, let me talk to Wayne and see what their position is. I am quite sure we haven't heard the last about what they will try to do," Jack remarked honestly.

"It looks that way, Jack. Harvey is really acting strange. Last night he wouldn't meet with me. I bet he is going to protect himself from me by using Wayne as his shield."

"I suspect you are right, Carol," Jack said honestly.

"What do you think I should do?"

"What about the Promenade Meat Center?" he asked.

"It's in a mess right now."

"Does it have the potential to provide you with a living?"

"I'm not sure right now." I had to honestly respond.

"Carol, you just concentrate on getting the butcher shop in order while I work things out with Wayne."

"I'm going to go to the clinic and clean out my desk, tell everyone good-bye and close that door in my life."

"I know that won't be easy for you to do."

"I'll call you later and let you know how the day went."

I got to the clinic about eleven o'clock and stumbled around like I was lost. Billie and I went to lunch as usual on Monday. "Billie, this is my last day."

"What do you mean, Carol?"

"I've decided I'm getting out of the abortion business."

"What are you going to do?"

"Run my butcher shop, I guess. I don't know."

When we got back to the clinic, I pulled my car to the back and started to slowly clear my desk. I felt really strange being there. The employees kept asking me operational questions even though Billie was in charge. I wanted to get out of there and go home.

About four in the afternoon I bade farewell to all the employees through many tears.

They kept asking, "Why are you leaving, Carol?"

"With no fanfare or applause, the Scarlet Lady, who dreamed of becoming the leading lady in the abortion industry, walked out of the clinic twenty-seven days after her strange counselor told her, 'Someone is going to be leaving the clinic.' "

Quite frankly, my only answer was, "Because I am supposed to."

With no fanfare or applause, the Scarlet Lady, who dreamed of becoming the leading lady in the abortion industry, walked out of the clinic twenty-seven days after her strange counselor told her, "Someone is going to be leaving the clinic."

I always thought it would be Fredi, but it was me.

Monday evening the exposé aired for the fourth night. I watched as Channel 4 interviewed women who had problems with the clinic. I had problems with it too, but problems of a different kind. I hated to see myself aligned with abortions; it seemed like another time and place.

The deep peace I felt inside was still overriding the storm surrounding me. The children seemed to share my calm as if they were relieved, too.

On Tuesday morning Kelly went to work at the clinic. About ten o'clock she called. "Mom, I can't stand this place. Do I have to stay here? Do I have to keep working here?"

"No, baby. Quit and come on home. I'll call Harvey and tell him you aren't going to work there anymore." Kelly was relieved and so was I.

I thought, *There will be no ties—no ties at all with the abortion industry as soon as I call Harvey.* I dialed his office. "This is Carol. I'd like to speak to Harvey."

"He isn't in. He's out for the day."

I called his home and Fredi answered.

"Is Harvey in?"

"Carol, he can't talk to you now."

"Fredi, could he—or could both of you—meet me for lunch?"

"Harvey is too upset today, Carol. He will call you."

The corporate attorney called instead. "Can you come over to my office to go over a few things about four o'clock this afternoon?"

"I'll be there."

At 4:00 P.M. I walked into the corporate attorney's office. Two attorneys questioned me about the "complications" (botched abortions) I was involved in and what I knew about them. I knew they were checking me to see how much I knew—how much damage I could do if Harvey and I didn't resolve things.

I related the names and details of fourteen botched abortions, mostly abortions performed by J. Harvey Johnson, M.D.

A few minutes after I got home, the telephone rang. "Carol, this is Billie. I wanted to tell you I just wrote a letter firing you. Harvey called me and told me what to say and told me to sign it. I'm sorry. I wanted you to hear it from me."

"Fired? You can't fire a partner. Is this how he is going to do it?"

"I'm sorry, Carol."

"Thanks, Billie. I'll talk to you later."

I called Harvey at home again and demanded that Fredi let me talk to him. When he came on the line he said, "I'm sorry, Carol." Not "Hello"—just "I'm sorry, Carol."

"So this is the way you intend to treat me after all we've been through together? This is how you treat your own family? Well, we'll see about that. Good-bye," and I slammed the receiver down.

I was disgusted at myself for trusting such a man, but I was also relieved. He had abandoned me; in the end I had not deserted him. It was truly over. Now, how was I going to make a living?

I quickly called Jack Shaw and told him all that had transpired throughout the day.

"Carol, meet me and Gwen at 9:00 tonight at Denny's at 635 and Preston."

"Thanks, Jack. I'll see you at nine." The last segment of the exposé was airing at ten, but I didn't care. I had to get my agreement worked out fast and get on with my life.

I met Jack and his wife Gwen at Denny's on schedule. I had briefly met Gwen at church. She seemed like such a lovely woman. I tried really hard not to cuss too much around her, but under the circumstances it was very hard not to.

"Jack, did you talk to Wayne today?"

"Yes, I did. But, he's not saying much."

"Well, I'm not going to settle for one penny less than two hundred and fifty thousand dollars. The appraisal on the two clinics came back at one million five hundred thousand dollars."

"Yes, but those were done for insurance purposes. Wayne had it done; that is just a rough estimate. And it was done for you to be able to buy Fredi out."

"Even exaggerated, Jack, one-third interest in the business should bring two hundred and fifty thousand dollars," I emphasized.

"Carol, you will be lucky to get one hundred and twenty-five thousand. There has been no stock issued. Do you have anything in writing?"

"No. Nothing. I trusted Harvey completely. He was redoing his will and getting his business affairs in order before he issued the stock. But what about the insurance policy? I know it was issued. I signed the check myself."

"Wayne told me the insurance policy was never issued because of all the problems between you and Fredi."

For the first time since the meeting with Jack when we prayed together, I was scared and depressed. Everything seemed out of control. I had lost and had no money.

"Jack, what am I going to do?" I whispered.

"Just go out to the butcher shop and work. I'll get with Wayne and put this to bed. Don't worry. It will be all right." I don't know why I believed this man was any different, but I took comfort in his hope.

The butcher shop was really in a mess, more than I could have imagined. I called Ibrahim to confront him. "Are you going to help me with this mess and come up with your part of the money?"

All I could get him to agree to do was take the Garland house we had bought together. Thank God for small favors. Ibrahim was out of my life.

Joe Bob called Fredi. "I won't be mowing your lawn anymore."

"Why, Joe Bob? Keeping our lawn has nothing to do with your mother's situation," she whined.

"For the first time since the meeting with Jack when we prayed together, I was scared and depressed. Everything seemed out of control. I had lost and had no money."

"It does to me. I will not do business with anyone who treats my mother like Harvey has."

On Friday Wayne called. "Carol, some of the employees are quitting. Would you come out for a few minutes Saturday to calm things down?"

"Yes, Wayne. I'll be there."

My presence was all Wayne wanted.

The employees kept wanting to know, "Why did you leave, Carol? What happened is not your fault."

Wayne didn't want me to answer any questions. I listened as Jan, Harvey's daughter, kept telling everyone what happened from her father's perspective. I actually didn't have to say anything. The employees knew better than anyone what was going on in the clinic after the exposé.

But they didn't know what was going on inside me, and I couldn't tell them.

After the meeting Wayne took me back to the office and handed me the checkbook. "Write yourself a check for twelve thousand dollars."

I wrote the check and left. I went to the bank Monday morning to turn that check into a cashier's check just to be sure Wayne didn't stop payment on it. Was I ever paranoid.

Jack called Tuesday morning. "Carol, can you meet with me, Wayne, and Harvey tonight at the Regency Hotel at eight?"

"What is going on?"

"Hopefully, we can get everything ironed out tonight."

"I'll be there."

I had been waiting to see Harvey Johnson face to face. Originally, I wanted to tell him why I left the clinic, about what was going on in my life with the Lord. Now I was too hurt and angry to talk about that. He was going to get the full load. I figured Harvey would be super sweet and try to get me to back down on my threats to "sue him and tell it all."

Instead Harvey was direct and angry. "Why didn't you tell me about the butcher shop?"

"I didn't want you to think it would take away from the clinic."

Quite honestly, I was surprised at Harvey's anger over my not telling him about the butcher shop. What did he think—that he owned me?

Throughout the meeting Harvey wouldn't look me in the eye. So, he knew I was angry, very angry.

"Harvey, I have trusted you completely. You know one-third of the business is mine. Tom told me to get it in writing, but I said, 'No. Harvey will never abuse me.' You know I've worked like a dog to build our business, and now you say it wasn't our business. How can you live with yourself?"

He still didn't say anything. He was just like all the rest of the men in my life—weak. And when it came to fullfilling his part of the bargain, forget it!

"And what about your promise to Kelly? I guess you have forgotten what you promised her, too? I helped you build the clinic business. Now, you can help me build the butcher shop. Don't you think that's fair, Harvey?"

"Yes, Carol. I guess it is."

Things were so tense between Harvey and me, Jack suggested, "We need to stop this meeting and let Wayne and me work out something between you. Let's call it a night."

I left the meeting pleased to some extent. At least Harvey knew how angry I was at him. I was beginning to hate him—or was I beginning to hate myself for loving him and for trusting him?

As I drove home that evening, I thought, *One thing is clear to me: not sleeping with a man is no assurance you will not get hurt either. I guess I can never have a relationship without being hurt.*

Jack met with Wayne to work out a settlement. After several days he called. "Carol, I believe I have a settlement we can live with."

We met and discussed the details.

"Carol, they are willing to pay you a total of seventy-two thousand dollars. You wrote yourself a twelve-thousand dollar check at the office. The remaining sixty thousand will be paid five thousand dollars a month for twelve months."

"How do I know they'll pay me in full?" I questioned.

"I will have them draw up a personal note and have Harvey sign it. Everything will be in writing," he promised.

"That is not nearly as much as I hoped I would get. Maybe we should sue them and let everything come out in the open."

"Honestly, Carol, that would be very expensive and time-consuming. I think you need to get on with your life," he advised.

"Jack, five thousand dollars is not nearly enough to meet my needs with two kids in college. I could lose everything."

"I know, Carol. I can't promise that you won't. You are going to have to make some big adjustments in your life."

I'm going to have to make some big adjustments in my life? What does he think I have been doing ever since that first prayer? "I understand, Jack. I guess if you think this is the best we can do, then I will accept it. They'd better pay like they've promised."

"I'll call Wayne and tell him to draw up the necessary papers. Everything will work out for the best. You will see in time," were his final words.

13

JOURNEY THROUGH THE WILDERNESS

W hat happened next in my life was bizarre but beautiful, wild yet wonderful. My journey out of the abortion industry led me through my wilderness, and then into the beginning of a joyous, fulfilling life. You see, the real Carol Nan came out of her cocoon in the next eighteen months. The transformation was painful but necessary. Today, I am a joyful woman; my life is filled with grace and beauty because of everyone who touches it.

When I left the abortion industry, I was really nervous. I did not feel Harvey could be trusted to pay the sixty-thousand-dollar balance even if he signed a note. But Jack said, "You have to trust that it will all work out for the best."

The words Jack spoke to me when he said, "Carol, you are going to have to make some big adjustments in your life," were so prophetic.

I walked out of the abortion industry carrying a lot more baggage than I had when I entered. But, I had new strength to help carry the baggage and new friends to help me get rid of the baggage I did not need to be burdened with anymore.

I carried a lot of debt from foolish spending and a budget requirement that far exceeded five thousand dollars a month. I had a taste for the power of money and for "the good life." I had added the guilt of the 35,000 abortions I had sold plus my own. But, also in my baggage was the knowledge of the prayers I had prayed—with Jack and alone on the floor of the abortion clinic, and I had firsthand knowledge of the swiftness of God's 2 x 4.

I walked into my wilderness unequipped for all I ran into. I must admit, with my personality, I can always find a lot of adventure in exploring a wilderness. I will be one of the first, if not the first, to find a big pit to fall into if there is one. I found adventure and pits. When Jack said adjustments, he was not kidding!

I had a lot of old tapes playing from my past that beckoned me to return to my old life, especially as I faced new challenges without the tools I thought I needed. And the new people I became involved with were nothing like the people I had been around all my life. It was as if one day I died and woke up living somewhere else.

And did you know there are wild animals lurking in the wilderness? Some of them are wolves in sheep's clothing. I was like Little Red Riding Hood except I didn't know where I was going or the way to get there—wherever *there* was. I appeared to be lost, but I know now that I was right where I was supposed to be.

I call it my wilderness because it represents the time I wandered around aimlessly (or so it seemed to me) and saw little rationale for why I had to go through all I went through. I did not understand the changes that had to take place in me—thoughts, attitudes, actions, desires, values, motives, motivations—in order for the real me to emerge.

I want to assure you I still am not anywhere near who I intend to be, but I am experiencing a lot of tolerance from others as I evolve into the new me. I wish everyone could experience the understanding I have received from those around me who love me for who I am—not what I do. In fact, when I do fall into my old habit patterns of jealousy, assertiveness, and competitiveness, they look inside my heart and see I don't mean to be hurtful even when I am.

The Transformation Process

A butcher shop of all places was God's first place for me to visit in my wilderness journey. I find that very ironic. My father introduced me to a butcher shop and the slaughtering of animals when I was only two.

The abortion clinic was the butcher shop I chose in my other life. Of course, we didn't butcher animals; we butchered women and babies.

At least The Promenade Meat Center was a butcher shop to sustain life rather than to snuff out life. I spent six years of my life with abortionists, not physicians. They did not preserve life. They destroyed it—sometimes the mother, every time the baby. The abortionist is not

---

"I want to assure you I still am not anywhere near who I intend to be, but I am experiencing a lot of tolerance from others as I evolve into the new me."

---

just a practitioner practicing his/her trade but a practitioner trained to do good and using the training to do evil. I was one of them—evil to the core.

When we finished the violent act of killing the baby, we took it to the central supply room, reassembled and counted the parts, put them down the commercial, heavy-duty garbage disposal and turned it on. We listened as the blades shredded the head, body, arms, legs, hands and feet. It was much like grinding the meat scraps to make hamburger meat in the meat market.

We were evil. I was evil—evil enough to be involved in 35,001 mutilations—evil enough to push those body parts into the commercial disposal and grind them to bits.

God had his places of refuge and refreshment in my wilderness journey. The spiritual baggage I carried from being in the abortion industry weighed heavily on me. I was out of the abortion industry but not out from under the weight of guilt of 35,001 abortions. I felt as though a big, conspicuous "A" was emblazoned on my forehead, especially when I walked into church.

Somehow, although I felt awkward, I got involved in the church as much as I possibly could. The people were warm and loving just like my pastor, Jack Shaw.

I couldn't figure it out. What was their angle? Sooner or later I knew it would surface. I was much more suspicious of them than they ever thought of being judgmental toward me.

I began to like using the Bible to live by. I started a devotional time the day I walked out of the abortion clinic, reading two chapters of the Bible every morning. Prayer became more and more a part of my daily life. I screamed out in desperation several times a day. The answers were always there; sometimes it took me a while to see them.

Since the time Jack first told me he was a preacher, I was very defensive with him about abortion. But as we spent more time together, I began to say to him, "I am not certain abortion is wrong."

Rather than argue with me he always replied, "Carol, take one day at a time and pray, 'Lord, whatever is in my life You want to take out or change, help me to recognize it and cooperate with You.'" He always prayed, "Lord, show Carol the truth. Let her see any deception in her life You want her to be free from." He never condemned me.

I should have known after our first prayer together not to pray with Jack unless I expected an answer. It was just a matter of time until God would reveal His Word on the subject. Deep inside I longed to know the truth about abortion and its effect on my life. I longed to be free from the weight of my own secret abortion. I wanted to tell Jack about my secret so many times, but I couldn't.

Nelson and Stephanie Cook were God's special gifts to me, helping me come to grips with facing little children, little babies, and their parents. They would invite me into their home for dinner and let me babysit with their only child at the time.

Stephanie shared about the difficult time she had getting pregnant. Of course, with my abortion history I could have felt terrible, but the atmosphere was so full of love, no condemnation, only trust. I really needed that at the time. I also needed to be entrusted with the care of their daughter to know that they did trust me and love me unconditionally.

Stephanie was a committed Christian and discipled me in many ways. I began to feel like a woman again and even had feelings of motherhood without condemnation. And their little girl, Kimberly, was so beautiful and loving. She couldn't see inside me. God was breaking down walls within me.

As a part of my discipleship time with Jack, he encouraged me to write my testimony and prayerfully look for an opportunity to share it. I really got into the project, eager to see what would happen. I wondered if God could use me to help someone else.

In the butcher shop, I watched for the opportunity to tell someone about my newfound faith. One day a young man came in and intro-

---

"As a part of my discipleship time with Jack, he encouraged me to write my testimony and prayerfully look for an opportunity to share it."

---

duced himself. "Hi. I'm Ron Henderson. I own the company that washes your windows. It's time to collect for the month."

"How much do I owe you?" I asked.

"Ten dollars."

"Here you go. I haven't seen you around washing our windows."

"No. I'm a seminary student, and I don't have time to wash the windows. I do the administrative work."

"A seminary student! I've just become a Christian," I exclaimed.

"Good for you."

"I'd like to share what happened to me with you. I'm learning how to give my testimony. Do you have five minutes?"

"No, I'm in a hurry today. Maybe next month."

I thought little about Ron Henderson until about a month later when he came by to collect another ten dollars for the month's window washing. "Carol, do you have time to share that testimony with me?"

"Yes. I surely do." I related the story of my involvement in the abortion industry, about Jesus Christ finding me there, and my asking Him to be my Lord and Savior. I talked about God having a sense of humor, too. "Just look where He put me—in a different kind of butcher shop!"

"Carol, I thought you were going to tell me another dry conversion story, but this is truly a miracle. Thanks for sharing with me."

I visited with Ron from month to month after that when he came to collect his money. In God's time my eagerness to share with Ron and his faithfulness to follow up with me proved to be very significant in my future.

When I was involved with church activities and my new friends, things went great. But sometimes, my old friends from the abortion clinic dropped by the butcher shop. I didn't know what to say. I didn't want to talk about the clinic and did not feel I could really share my new situation with them. How could they understand if I didn't?

When they left, I really struggled with my thoughts and emotions. It was like I flipped a switch, and the old me started reciting old stuff. *The life I so carefully planned and built is gone. The hurt is still here. The pain is unbearable.*

Why wasn't I happy with two clinics? Why couldn't I be satisfied? But, no. I wanted to be a millionaire. None of this would be happening if I had not wanted to work things out with Fredi so we could expand.

The counselor was supposed to solve the problem, work out the problem between Fredi and me. He said someone would be leaving the clinic within thirty days. I never dreamed it would be me.

Then the old stuff would switch off and new stuff would play in my mind again. *The prayer did make some kind of difference in my life. I do feel some kind of peace that I can't really explain. I really don't want to go back to the abortion business. I really don't want to be involved with someone like Harvey, anymore.*

Poor, poor Harvey. I really worked him over in my mind when the old tapes played. *Harvey emotionally raped me. Harvey helped me kill my baby. Harvey was the authority figure I turned to expecting him to say, "Carol, you don't want an abortion." But, he didn't. He helped me kill my baby when he was the only one that could help me.*

I hate him. I hate him because he didn't act like a good physician. I hate him because he helped me with the "easy" way out. He helped ruin my life and my marriage. He killed my baby!

I hate Harvey for what he did to me with the clinics. But, it's not the first time Harvey Johnson has cheated his partners, and it probably won't be the last. It will be the last time it happens to me though.

My mind would wander down the "old life" trail for a while. Then it would shift to the "new life" as I wandered along.

My life is changed now, and I will never go back to that life. As tough as things are—and there are times when I don't think I'm going to survive—even the worst on this side is better than the best on the abortion side.

"The life I so carefully planned and built is gone. The hurt is still here. The pain is unbearable."

Just being able to sleep at night knowing I didn't kill any babies today is a relief. I don't have to worry about the baby that was too big to go down the disposal being found in the trash can I had to dump it into. I don't have that cold feeling anymore.

The changes in my life were good in spite of the emotional turmoil. I worked all day, went home, cooked a steak from the butcher shop, made a salad, watched television, and dropped into bed exhausted from the day's work. I remember resting like I never had before. I started to feel better than I had in many years.

My father tried to help. "Sister, you'd better get married while you can. You're getting too old to wait much longer."

Gee, thanks, Daddy! Bless his heart, he was concerned.

I turned to Tom, my ex-husband, frequent advisor, and former sex partner. He came by the butcher shop one time, and that was it. I should have known Tom could not provide any emotional stability to my wilderness.

Adventures in the Pits

In November my personal financial picture really took a turn for the worse. Harvey cut off his payments as I knew he would. He made the first twelve-thousand-dollar payment and two five-thousand-dollar payments and then quit. I called Jack. "Just as I suspected, Harvey isn't going to honor his agreement."

"Yes, he will, Carol. He will honor the note payment or we will seek legal remedy. I'll call Wayne and get back with you."

"I've seen Wayne work before," I warned. "He is going to blame me because the business is down. He will claim I'm the cause of the poor cash flow, but his management style will be the cause. Just be prepared."

"You may be right, Carol."

Sure enough Wayne filled Jack's ears with my failures as a business manager and what I had cost the clinic. Jack kept telling me, "Carol, it will work out. We will get you the money."

I will never forget standing next to those coolers in the butcher shop, screaming at God, kicking the coolers. No one was there except God and me. Yes, I could feel Him try to comfort me, but that was not something I could understand at the time. I just kept screaming for weeks and weeks. Harvey's latest action really hurt me deeply.

Now, at the lowest point in my life, abortionists started calling me asking me to go to work with them.

Our abortionist/psychiatrist, Dr. Miller, came by the butcher shop to talk to me about setting up a new clinic near Prestonwood Mall. His idea was for the patients to shop while they waited for their abortion. The clinic would give them a beeper and beep them when it was time for their abortion. I thought it was a novel idea, especially coming from him.

Another abortionist from New York wined and dined me in a similar move. He offered me an arrangement like the one I had with Harvey. Dr. Stein thought the way to get me to work with him was to have an affair with me. That made me sick. He only thought of me as a weak woman—not a potential partner. I almost laughed in his face.

From a strictly financial point of view, the timing was perfect for me to go back into the abortion business. I was about to go crazy over the financial crisis I was in. I was at the end of myself, viewing all my past mistakes and how brutally they had affected my life and my children. I desperately needed money.

Dr. Stein suggested I convert to the Jewish faith. He explained, "Jews believe that life begins at birth. You can do abortions with no qualms with my religion."

"The more pressure I came under financially, the more I was tempted to go back into the abortion business. I chose to tighten my belt and hold on."

I liked my new faith, however, and hated the killing business. It was a difficult decision to turn down each effort of the abortionists to re-enlist me. Somehow, I managed to avoid falling into those pits.

Financially, I was "in a pickle," as they say. Without the five thousand dollars coming in from Harvey, things really got bleak. I called Jack continuously. "Have you heard anything from Wayne?"

"Yes. He tells me he is trying to resolve everything. It is evident to me he signed the note against Harvey's lawyer's advice. We will get it worked out," he always assured me.

"I hope so. I don't know how much longer I can hold out at the butcher shop. Harvey agreed to help me during this time."

"I know, Carol. It will get resolved."

At the butcher shop we went from one daily crisis to another. I was constantly screaming, *God, why? Where is the money going to come from this time?* The more pressure I came under financially, the more I was tempted to go back into the abortion business. I chose to tighten my belt and hold on.

The first thing to go of those things I bought with the "blood" money from the abortion industry was my Toronado. I really got angry at first with God. I sold it to help take care of some of the immediate bills and to relieve the monthly outgo the first month Harvey failed to pay me.

I cried out to God. I didn't understand why old things hurt when they fall away. I felt very alone, downtrodden, as if I had no friends in the world. My old tapes assured me I had self-destructed out of a situation that was perfect. I had a good working relationship with Harvey, no sex. I could support my children and pay their way through college. Everything was going perfectly. Then I'd hit another brick wall, but this time there was nowhere to go. I was stuck in the butcher shop.

The emotional and spiritual struggle intensified. Jack was there every step of the way either talking to me on the telephone or spending a few minutes with me daily discipling me, feeding me Scripture. He constantly showed me how to live the Christian life.

I didn't trust myself with anything. I called Jack or Gwen constantly with the crisis of the day because I needed help from someone competent. They answered my questions with "paraphrased Scripture," teaching me how to use my new Christian principles in my everyday life. I didn't understand that they were using Scripture at the time, but the answer always made sense.

"Jack, what am I going to do about all of the bills? The vendors are calling me constantly wanting to be paid."

"Carol, you have to be honest with them and tell them where you are and what you intend to do. Offer to return their merchandise if they want you to. You are operating under grace with them," he reminded me patiently.

"Try to see things from their point of view, but don't take responsibility for their business decisions. You didn't sell you the merchandise. They did. They are trying to pressure you because of their own mistakes. They should have known that you'd be a 'slow pay' account. You were not a choice account to begin with. Relax and put your marketing skills to work."

"What about the lease payment?"

"Call the landlord and be honest with him. Tell him what you found when you came in, how far behind you are. See if you can defer the rent payments for ninety days, moving them to the end of the lease. If the location is not good, time will prove it up. Look at the empty space around you. Find out how the other tenants are doing. Go to the center merchant's association meeting. Get on top of the facts about the traffic. Market, Carol. Get creative with ways to package your merchandise."

"What about the bank loan interest payment?"

"Go see them, too. But get a handle on the accounts payable first. Then go to the bank and update them. Ask them to work with you."

"Thanks, Jack. I'll get those things done and get back to you."

And always, "Keep your chin up, Carol."

As the financial pressure mounted, I discovered there is a difference between "needs" and "wants." All of my "needs" were met—yes, later than I would have wanted—but they were met. I prayed for pa-

---

"The emotional and spiritual struggle intensified. Jack was there every step of the way either talking to me on the telephone or spending a few minutes with me daily discipling me, feeding me Scripture. He constantly showed me how to live the Christian life."

---

tience one time, and an older Christian cautioned me, "Oh, don't pray for patience because you will get it. It's just the way it comes will be painful."

I was starting to learn about waiting on the Lord.

On one occasion when things were really bad, Kelly was with me in the butcher shop. The electricity was scheduled to be cut off at 5:00 P.M. I prayed about the need and was at peace with the situation.

Kelly didn't understand the change in me. She just knew we would be out of business if the electricity was cut off, and she was watching me. Finally she asked, "Why aren't you going crazy?"

I had the opportunity to tell her, "The Lord will meet our need."

What an example when a man Kelly didn't know, but a new Christian friend of mine, walked in and tried to give me more money than we needed! Now, I'm not suggesting it happened that way every time; however, it seemed to when I really needed it.

Each need was met in God's timing—not mine. Yes, I was tested, and after a few months I realized I was starting to trust God to meet my needs. Sometimes the need was met by a new Christian friend who would call to say, "I have something for you, Carol. I will be by shortly." Then they came by with cash or a check in hand.

I just thought I needed a tax shelter. The condominium in Houston was the next "blood money" thing to go. They started foreclosure proceedings in November which finally concluded in foreclosure in January. One by one I watched each of the possessions the "blood money" bought slip away. Not all at once, but gradually, the Lord purged my life of all the "blood money" things.

In time my financial problem became clear to me—how do I manage this monster I have created rather than blame God for not letting me hold on to it?

The children could live on less than a thousand dollars a month in college. Somehow I could pay for the two sports cars. The apartment in Oak Cliff was manageable. God would help me take care of my living expenses. The butcher shop would either make it, or it wouldn't.

Christmas was slim at our house, but it was very warm in my heart. We actually celebrated the true meaning of Christmas for the first time. Even the "recycled" gifts were given gratefully to the people I loved.

I thought my wilderness journey was over, but it had only entered into phase two. There was a lot more to come. But the pitfalls were different, just the opposite of what I expected.

Beware Lest You Fall

In January 1984 Jack introduced me to a shopping center developer who hired me to work in his restaurant division. Suddenly I was introduced to a true "high roller" lifestyle with all the trimmings.

I agreed to go on salary for five thousand dollars a month, which was an adjustment. My first assignment was to get a job with a major sandwich shop, to learn the way they operated their business. I went to a store near the butcher shop so it would be easy to run back and forth. I shall never forget applying for that job. I don't know who was more shocked: the girl behind the counter or her young black manager.

We walked through the kitchen to his office. "Why do you want to work here?" he asked.

I explained, "I have just gone through an experience of losing my income, and quite frankly, I can use the money. I would like to work the noon shift so I can have evenings off."

"That is the shift I have trouble filling. I can only pay you $4.25 per hour," he apologized.

"That's fine."

"Can you start at eleven o'clock tomorrow?"

"I'll be here. Thank you."

The relationship between the young manager and me was very close. He sensed something different in me—the smell of something he had not been around—and he wanted that something. Little did he know I was just getting to know the Lord myself.

I had been working at the sandwich shop a couple of weeks when my boss, the developer, called. "Carol, I've just finished the lease on our first restaurant site. Can you come by the office late this afternoon to celebrate?"

"Sure, I'll be there."

The environment, the champagne, the attention he turned on me was awesome. Part of me desperately wanted it all—the powerful corporate man with a plane that could whisk me away. Part of me knew that it was wrong. I was scared. I had to find a way to say no. I had done it before; I could do it again.

I failed the test. I fell into an awful pit.

I continued to work at the sandwich shop until May. I went to the corporate offices just before the ICSC (International Convention of Shopping Centers) convention held in Las Vegas. From Las Vegas it was off to Chicago, the Florida Keys, Santa Fe—all on his private plane. I watched as tens of thousands of dollars were spent on frivolous things.

It reminded me of myself, but I was a rank amateur compared to the crowd I was now traveling with. Even Harvey couldn't compare. It was all too much for a little ole country girl to understand. Here this man could talk the Christian lingo, but he did not live it. He was a wolf in sheep's clothing, and he even wore a specially designed ring, a wolf head with big stones for the eyes.

I began to understand there are two kinds of Christians—those who talk it (including me, now) and even use Christianity, and those who have a real heart desire to please the Lord. Finally, I began to be able to separate the two.

What an awesome dilemma. I had heard about "hypocrites," but now I felt like one. Every time I got around Jack or was in church, I felt awful. Thank God, I did not run from that place of refuge and refreshment, though. I continued my church activities and daily Bible study, looking for a way out.

In the midst of my dilemma, God did not abandon me. One Sunday morning Gordon Werner, a deacon at the church, shared from Psalm 139. In my devotional time I turned to it and read for the first time, "For You did form my inward parts, You did knit me together in my mother's womb" (verse 13). I was convinced I had been killing babies. The words that really got me were "Your eyes saw my unformed substance, and in Your book all the days of my life were written, before they ever took shape, when as yet there was none of them (verse 16).

I remembered holding those little babies' bodies in my hand as I cleaned the instruments. I specifically remembered that each of them had intestines—yes, some threadlike—but, they all had intestines. I remembered wondering why God gave them intestines if He knew they were going to be aborted.

I knew now God intended for each of the 35,001 babies to live, each one that I had helped abort.

The weight of my sin became very heavy, but I remembered 1 John 1:9, "If we [freely] admit that we have sinned and confess our sins, He is faithful and just [true to His own nature and promises] and will forgive us our sins (dismiss our lawlessness)." And now the part I love, "and continuously cleanse us from all unrighteousness—everything not in conformity to His will in purpose, thought and action."

It took a little while, but Jack's prayer finally worked. I knew abortion was not only wrong, but a terrible sin against God. The sin could be forgiven and I could be cleansed, however. I began to feel like the big "A" I thought was emblazoned on my forehead was beginning to be dissolved.

At that time I became pro-life. I asked God, "What am I going to do?" I was in a stew. I wasn't spiritually in a position to reach out with my newfound truth because of my hypocrisy. And besides, I was afraid of becoming a pro-lifer because I had viewed pro-lifers as angry, vio-

> ## "I began to understand there are two kinds of Christians—those who talk it (including me, now) and even use Christianity, and those who have a real heart desire to please the Lord."

lent people—not because I knew any of them but because of the press. They certainly were not portrayed as kind, loving people.

Emerging from the Wilderness

I continued to wander through my wilderness but not alone. Now I prayed, *God, please help me out of this situation.* (Notice, I did not say this time, "Hit me over the head with a 2 x 4.") Gradually, inside I began to feel stronger. The time came when I refused to play the game any longer with my boss.

At the same time God hit the developer over the head with a 2 x 4. He must have prayed with someone, too. In September I was one of fifty-one people released from his company.

During my time with the developer, I was offered all the things of the world that I thought would make me happy. I could and did try it all, but it left me so empty. Nothing can fill that emptiness when you know you have strayed from the Lord, when you experience utter darkness, blackness without end, and emptiness that you cannot describe.

I went back to the butcher shop again. Just when I thought it couldn't get any worse, Jack announced, "Carol, you are going to have to file suit against Harvey. Let's put it into the legal courts to collect the note."

"Okay, Jack. I knew it would come down to this sooner or later. I haven't been paid anything in a year. Why should I expect anything now?"

I called my lawyer and told him to proceed with filing the suit on Harvey Johnson and the clinic. I was prepared to tell everything in the courtroom if I had to. I surprised myself by being able to leave the battle with Harvey to the legal system.

The butcher shop was a losing proposition; I prayed to get out. A buyer came along in November, and we made arrangements with the bank for him to assume the note with me remaining as a guarantor. The buyer agreed to pay me five thousand dollars for my equity.

On the day we were to close the deal, the health department came in and threatened to shut us down if the floor wasn't redone. The purchasers backed out because of the added expense. In a panic I called the office where Jack was supposed to be.

"He's out of the office. I don't know when he'll be back. Is this Carol?"

"Yes," I tearfully replied.

"This is Jerry. Are you all right?"

"As good as I can be. The deal to sell the butcher shop just fell through, and the health department is about to close the place. Ask Jack to call if you talk to him."

"I will."

In what seemed like just a few minutes, I looked up and Jerry Green and Richard Bowles, two men from my church, walked in the front door. I rushed out to meet them. Each gave me a big hug.

We talked the situation over. Then they prayed with me. I called the buyers and offered to forego the five-thousand-dollar equity payment if they would go ahead and close the deal. They agreed.

"What are you going to do when you get out of here?" Richard asked.

"I don't know."

"Call me as soon as you are finished here."

"I will. Thank you both for everything."

As soon as I knew when I would be finished at the butcher shop, I called Richard. "What do you have in mind?"

"We need someone to handle our leasing. Are you interested?"

"I sure am."

The day I walked out of the butcher shop and went to work for Jerry and Richard, at Bowles/Green, a real estate development company, I walked out of my wilderness. These two men were a breath of fresh air. The day I went to work with them Richard said, "Carol, you are only with us until God moves you into full-time work."

"Full-time work? What do you mean?"

"For God."

I thought, *He is crazy.* I should have known better. I felt good; I was out of my wilderness and on my way into a new, fulfilling life. My wilderness journey was rough at times. But I felt so protected and very loved—even in my pitfalls. I felt so special to the Lord. He cared enough for me to take care of me while I learned to walk with Him, even when I stumbled.

I was to discover that I was only beginning to experience my walk with the Lord.

14

PLAYING FOR THE OTHER TEAM

I had been working for Jerry and Richard a few months when Ron Henderson called. "Carol? This is Ron—Ron Henderson. My company washed your windows at the butcher shop."

"Yes, Ron. I remember you."

"I am now on staff at the Right to Life office, and we have been praying for God to send someone to help us who has firsthand experience in the abortion industry. Would you be willing to talk with someone from Right to Life?" he asked.

"Yes, I'll talk to them, but Jack Shaw, the man who led me to Christ, will have to be in the meeting."

"That won't be a problem. Bill Price will be calling you to set up the meeting."

"Let me give you my work number. You already have my home number. I'll be expecting his call."

"Thanks, Carol."

I hung up the telephone and thought, *God doesn't miss a trick! He uses the weakest attempts on our part to do His work.* My first five minute testimony to a seminary student was about to bear God's fruit.

The next day Bill Price called. "Carol, this is Bill Price with Greater Dallas Right to Life. Ron Henderson told you I would be calling, didn't he?"

"Yes," I agreed.

"We are working on pro-life legislation for Texas and would like to meet with you to see if you could help us in Austin this year." I couldn't believe it!

We set up an early morning appointment the next week. I contacted Jack to make sure he could be at the meeting. "Jack, I'm scared of what they will do, the pro-choicers and even the pro-lifers. And I'm scared of what might happen if I tell the whole truth. I'm not worried about being sued by Harvey. But what about Sheryl's death and other botched abortions?"

"Who are you going to trust, Carol—God or man?" That was Jack—he always makes it sound so simple.

"God."

It was time for prayer, prayer, and more prayer. *God, is this what you want me to do? What will happen to my children? to me? This could be dangerous.* I kept quoting the Scripture to myself, "For God did not give us a spirit of timidity—of cowardice, of craven and cringing and fawning fear—but [He has given us a spirit] of power and of love and of calm and well-balanced mind and discipline and self-control (2 Timothy 1:7).

Our first meeting was cancelled due to snow and ice. We rescheduled, and I prayed some more. When the ice and snow melted, Bill Price, Curtis Brown—the attorney who had drawn up the legislative bill—Jack, and I had our meeting. After formal introductions we proceeded to evaluate the possibility of my helping them.

"Bill, Jack will help me make my final decision about working with you and Curtis. I know how important the bill is to you, but I have a lot of hesitancy to get involved right now," I said as we got started.

"I'm sure you do, Carol. Let me explain what we are trying to do."

When Bill and Curtis finished Jack said, "Bill, you cannot sensationalize Carol."

"We will not do that."

Curtis continued, "We need to do an affidavit, Carol. Would you tell me everything you can about your experience in the abortion industry?"

I kept it pretty shallow, but they were very excited.

When we finished the meeting three hours later, Curtis said, "I'll go back and finish your affidavit and send it back to you for you and Jack to review. If you are satisfied with it, please sign it and return it to me."

After the meeting I was numb, but very joyful inside. *So this is what I am to do with my life. Maybe Richard is right.* His words, "You are only with us until God moves you into full-time work," rang in my ears.

"'Who are you going to trust, Carol— God or man?' That was Jack—he always makes it sound so simple."

I tried to keep my mind on my work until the affidavit came. When it was delivered, Jack read it and I read it. Then we sent it to Ed Blackstone, my attorney. All three of us made a few changes, and I sent it back to Curtis Brown. He made the changes and sent it back for my signature.

Fear Not

I remember standing in front of that notary public thinking, *How can this be me? I am going to Austin to testify for a pro-life bill as a pro-lifer, not as a pro-choicer.*

Somehow the pro-life community heard about me and began to ask me to speak, but Right to Life wanted me to be a surprise witness in Austin. They asked me not to do any pro-life speaking engagements before the legislative hearings.

I anxiously awaited a phone call concerning when the hearings would be. It finally came; the hearings were set for Monday, April 15th.

I immediately informed the prayer chain at the church and my home Bible study group that I met with in North Dallas. They began to pray that God would use me as His instrument.

On Sunday night, April 14, I spoke as a pro-lifer for the first time at my home church. The attendance was unbelievable (and we did not even serve food); they came to hear me and pray for me.

I stumbled through my testimony as best I could, fighting my tears and fears. When I finished, Jack asked me to remain in front while the church leaders and members joined around me at the altar to pray with me. It was a very special time.

I don't know what I expected, but when I left the church, my spirit was soaring. I felt very strong inside.

The next morning I flew to Austin. When I entered the Capitol building, I walked right into my old friends, the pro-choicers—"the hairy-legged women," as I call them now. I felt the anger and oppression I had not been around since the day I left the abortion clinic. I heard their angry argument, "Who is going to speak first?" I rushed by them to the pro-lifers.

We went inside the room where the hearing was to take place and ran into more very loud pro-choicers. I could feel the oppression even stronger. I grabbed my things and rushed outside to talk to God for a while.

I sat down on a big rock near the Reagan building in the morning sun. The strength I felt the night before was already sapped. I wasn't nearly as prepared to fight in God's battle as I thought I was. I began to cry out to God for help.

Lord, I know You can zap those abortion clinics. I've read about Your power in the Bible, and I've felt your 2 x 4. Why don't you zap those abortion clinics, and let me go on with my life?

At that point in my Christian walk, I did not read the Old Testament. I didn't like the law or legalism. I loved the grace of the New Testament. I even had my personal Bible trained. All the Old Testament pages were stuck together, and the Book just opened to the New Testament.

But my Bible had been chewed on by my dog. I had Kelly's new, untrained, Amplified Bible with me. It didn't know it wasn't supposed to open to the Old Testament. It opened to the book of Isaiah:

You whom I [the Lord] have taken from the ends of the earth and have called from the corners of it, and said to you, You are My servant—I have chosen you and not cast you off [even though you are exiled].

Fear not [there is nothing to fear], for I am with you; do not look around you in terror and be dismayed, for I am your God. I will strengthen and harden you to difficulties; yes, I will help you; yes, I will hold you up and retain you with My [victorious] right hand of rightness and justice.

Behold, all they who are enraged and inflamed against you shall be put to shame and confounded; they who strive against you shall be as nothing and shall perish.

You shall seek those who contend with you, but shall not find them; they who war against you shall be as nothing, as nothing at all.

For I the Lord your God hold your right hand; I am the Lord, Who says to you, Fear not; I will help you!

Fear not, you worm Jacob, you men of Israel! I will help you, says the Lord; your Redeemer is the Holy One of Israel.

Behold, I will make you to be a new, sharp, threshing instrument which has teeth; you shall thresh the mountains and beat them small and shall make the hills like chaff.

You shall winnow them and the wind shall carry them away, and the tempest or whirlwind shall scatter them. And you shall rejoice in the Lord, you shall glory in the Holy One of Israel. (Isaiah 41:9–16)

After reading the passage, I felt reassured. *God has called me. He is going to protect me. He will give me the tools, the words, and use me and people like me to cut the abortion clinics out of our society.* Now I use this passage to say that verse 15 means when we unite together—all pro-life groups—He will use us as a threshing instrument to cut abortion clinics out of our society. Each of us is a tooth in that threshing sledge to be used in His battle.

I felt as if the Lord had written the passage just for me. I understood the Lord wanted to take the very worst things in my life and use them for good. I had prayed that He would. My prayer had been, *Use them for Your glory—every filthy thing I have done—please, use it for Your glory, Your way, not mine.* Testifying in Austin before the legislature was God's way of using them, I concluded.

Yes, I felt the Lord with me on that rock in Austin, Texas. When I read those words from the Amplified Bible, I knew God had a plan for me—Carol Everett—sinner extraordinaire—even me. I sat on that rock crying in amazement that God would use me.

I began to focus on what I would say in the hearing. *I can tell the truth about what I have seen behind those words—"rights" and "choice"—the murdering of babies and maiming of women and the murder of women. I have witnessed it first hand. I can tell about*

*botched abortions and their cover-up that goes on behind closed doors of
abortion clinics across the nation. I can tell about 35,000 babies murdered and ground up like hamburger meat in commercial disposals.*

I marched back into the hearing room and testified absent of the
fear I had felt earlier. Yes, I could hear the insults. Yes, I could feel
the hatred. No, I did not enjoy the attack on me personally before the
legislative committee that day.

But, for the first time in my life I was part of a purpose bigger
than making money. I was involved in a goal—a worthy goal—not my
goal, but God's goal.

Sometimes now, when I hear people say they don't get anything
out of the Bible, I remember how clearly the Bible spoke to me April
15, 1985. God's Word in Isaiah 41:9–16 challenged me and gave me
the courage to serve God as never before in my life. And I know the
Bible is alive today.

After I finished testifying, I left the Texas State Capitol excited
that God had used me. I felt strong inside. Yes, the Lord could use me
in this cause, and I was ready.

Unresolved Guilt

But, my enthusiasm quickly returned to reality back in Dallas. I still
had bills to pay. I was asked to speak and give media interviews, but
speaking engagements and interviews did not pay the bills. I tried
once more to make a deal with God. *God, I can dedicate one day a
week, maybe two sometimes, to help fight abortion. But, love offerings
won't take care of my needs.*

As time went on, Jerry and Richard were very understanding and
supportive of my pro-life activities. The church prayed for me faith-
fully. I thought maybe God was going to let me be successful in real
estate leasing and fight abortion on a limited basis.

Things seemed to be working out just fine—except the more I got
involved with pro-life activity, the more often my own abortion surfaced. The more I talked about how things work inside an abortion
clinic, the more my insides churned with memories of my abortion.

My private struggle only heightened when Kay Thorogood gave
me a gift—a little "precious feet" pin to wear—the international pro-
life symbol. I struggled with wearing it except to pro-life functions

because it reminded me of my own abortion. I could not admit that I had been bad enough to kill my own child. To me, that was an unforgivable sin. I did not want to tell anyone.

Finally, I tested Jack. "I've got to tell you something. I hope you won't hate me after I tell you. I had an abortion, and Tom White is the father."

> **"For the first time in my life I was part of a purpose bigger than making money. I was involved in a goal— a worthy goal—not my goal, but God's goal."**

Jack had previously met Tom when Tom visited the church at my invitation and had visited with Tom privately. Now he said, "Carol, that makes some things fit together. I can see how you were so open to get involved in the abortion industry. That explains why you are still so angry at Tom."

He did not condemn me. He took it matter-of-factly and continued right on treating me just like he always had.

In November 1985 my best friend from the church, Barbara, called. "Carol, I need to go to Corpus Christi. I bought the antiques out of an estate for the store. I need a truck driver! Could you fly down with me Tuesday night and drive back home with me on Wednesday?"

"Yes. I can do that. Let's go." Barbara is such a neat, interesting lady. I enjoy her.

We flew to Corpus Christi where her cousins met us at the airport, fed us dinner, and put us up for the night. Early the next morning we picked up our truck, loaded the furniture, and started our ten-hour journey back to Dallas.

Barbara and I had enjoyed another "adventure in moving" a couple of years earlier when she moved closer to our church. I was her truck driver in that first venture; this time Barbara wanted to drive. I looked forward to having a really fun trip home.

We started off having a great time, talking about anything and everything. During our conversation we talked about the pro-life movement and about a post-abortive woman I had recently met.

There was a pause in the conversation. Here was my opening. "Barbara, I know how she feels. I had an abortion, too. Tom was the father." I exposed my private membership in the post-abortion women's society to another woman, a Christian friend, for the first time.

Silence. I had heard that silence before.

Why doesn't she say something? I never should have told her. I thought I could trust her, but obviously my trust is misplaced.

I felt rejected. Inside I thought, *If I can't tell Barbara about my abortion, I can't tell anyone. So, I will have to continue to keep it to myself.*

The rest of the trip seemed to take forever. We had very little conversation the rest of the way home. We delivered the furniture to the shop, and I went home determined to stop seeing Barbara. *She isn't the friend I thought she was.* My case against her began to build, my old rejection pattern working all over again.

After our trip together, I saw Barbara on Sunday but made sure I was too busy to see her during the week. Things got really tense between us even to the point of conflict with her oldest son. I was angry at her and felt she truly rejected me. Our relationship remained strained until Barbara finally brought Jack into our struggle. He got us together and helped us resolve it.

"Barbara, I thought you were rejecting me when I told you about my abortion on the way back from Corpus Christi," I said.

"Carol, I didn't know what to say to you. I didn't say anything for fear of saying the wrong thing."

"I am so sorry, Barbara, for the way I have treated you."

It was wonderful to receive her forgiveness. But, I still believed most people would not love me or even like me if they knew I had an abortion.

It will stay my secret. No one knows except Jack, Barbara, Tom, Harvey, and me. None of them will tell. My secret is safe. I will never tell anyone else.

A few weeks later Ron Urban, one of our ministers, asked me, "Carol, will you give a five-minute testimony in our evening service on Sunday?"

"Sure, Ron. I would love to."

No problem, I thought. *I do that all the time.*

That Sunday afternoon I visited with Barbara, her boys, and some other church family members. I spent very little time in prayer or preparation.

Facing My Own Abortion

Sunday night I stood before my church—the people I loved the most outside of my family and the people who loved me.

"I had an abortion."

Where did that come from? The words just slipped out. I told the whole church my secret. I could not believe I told them. There must be something about the environment of love and acceptance that allows for releasing old baggage that weights us down.

I was scared but I proceeded. "I haven't said that before in my testimony. I didn't want to say that." And I started crying.

As I stood there in front of my Christian family, it was as though the spotlight was shining directly on my forehead. The big "A" I always imagined was emblazoned there seemed to be really magnified. Although it had begun to diminish when I confessed to God my sin of killing 35,000 babies, at that moment it seemed bigger and brighter than ever before.

My guilt and shame rushed to the surface. "Yes. I had an abortion in 1973. I killed my baby. I have been a member of the secret society of post-abortive women since that time."

Somehow, I got through the rest of my testimony. Inside I thought they would all reject me. They could never love a woman who had killed her baby. It was over. I would have to leave this church and never come back.

But when I stepped down from behind the pulpit, something entirely different happened. They reached out to me in love—as if they still loved me no matter what I had done. Person after person, and sometimes two at a time, hugged me and cried with me. Standing there in the midst of God's people with love being poured out on me through my Christian family, the big "A" was washed off my forehead forever.

God forgave me of all my sin when I prayed with Jack the first time, but I was not able to accept it all at once. Acceptance came for me a little at a time.

I must tell you, heart to heart, I really felt like God washed me in His love, in His unconditional love, that night through the acceptance of His people. I knew that night the blood Jesus Christ shed for me on the cross covered me completely—all my sin. Before God's people, I stood there—the Scarlet Lady—covered in Christ's blood—not Sheryl's blood, not the blood of 35,000 abortions, and most of all, not covered by my own child's blood any longer.

> Come now, and let us reason together, says the Lord. Though your sins are like scarlet, they shall be as white as snow; though they are red like crimson, they shall be like wool. (Isaiah 1:18)

On the night I openly confessed to my church, my healing as a post-abortive mother started. I began to cry uncontrollably. Tears flowed non-stop for five months.

When my sister died, there was grief, but it was not like the painful grief that surfaced this time. This pain was a deeper grief, and I mean that literally—a gutteral grief from the depth of my soul—a crying out that would not stop. It started with a tightness, a knot in my throat that would not allow me to talk without pain.

At pro-life functions I would hear over and over, "I just don't understand how a woman could have an abortion. What kind of woman has an abortion? Why does a woman have an abortion? How could any woman have an abortion?"

Secretly, I wondered, "Where is their understanding?" Privately, I was that woman.

Now people asked me those same questions, and I had to provide answers. I desperately wanted to defend post-abortive women, but I had no defense. I even wondered myself, "How? Why?"

After each meeting I struggled. *I am a murderer. I killed my child, my helpless little baby. If I had only waited, something would have worked out.*

The painful question kept tormenting me. *How could I have done it? I give off the impression I'm a good mother, but that is a lie. I killed my own baby. Why did I do it? I played God in my life. I chose not to take the gift He gave me.*

I thought about what my life would be like if my third child were alive. I imagined my child with me even though his brother and sister were grown and on their own. We would be living together. I would still have at least one child at home to share my life with.

"On the night I openly confessed to my church, my healing as a post-abortive mother started. I began to cry uncontrollably. Tears flowed non-stop for five months."

At the depth of my grieving, life did not seem worth living. No, I didn't consider suicide this time, but there seemed to be no reason to go on. Life was just a pointless, worthless effort.

Those close to me tried to console me. Even George, a dear friend, suggested, "Carol, maybe you need to have a funeral for the baby. I'll go with you. Jack and Gwen will go."

"Thank you, George. That is very kind of you to offer. I don't think that is necessary."

Work and church became escapes. Pro-life work was payment for my sin of aborting my child. Finally, it dawned on me what I was doing. *Why am I punishing myself so?* I prayed and asked God for the answer.

I came to the realization that I was punishing myself because I had rejected my own flesh and blood, the gift of love God had given to me. My pattern has always been to punish those who reject me until they admit to me their mistreatment of me. Subconsciously, I was punishing myself.

God was freeing me from an old habit pattern that Satan was using to try to destroy me and my relationships.

I prayed for God to help me stop punishing myself and others and to help me stop grieving. I discovered part of the healing process was to deal with each person involved in my abortion.

I tried to talk to Tom, but he kept saying, "We made the best choice we could at that time. It's behind us now. We have to go on with our lives." Every time I saw him or talked to him on the phone, I brought up the abortion. His answer was always the same. He just couldn't hear my heart.

I struggled with telling Joe Bob and Kelly. *They will hate me. I swore I would never tell them. But God I've told you to use everything from my past life to help others. If this will help Joe Bob and Kelly, I'll tell them.*

I could just hear their questions. Why did you do it? Did you ever think about aborting us? How could you do it? How old would the baby be today?

Joe Bob graduated from the University of Texas on December 18 and married Carol, his longtime sweetheart December 21. There are two Carol Everetts in the world now, Jr. and Sr. I did the best I could to be happy for them, but his leaving home only added to my grieving.

After his graduation I announced, "You will have to take over your car payment now that you are out of school." It was really hard on my pride to admit to him I couldn't continue to make the payments.

"I can't afford to, Mom. You know things are going to be tight for Carol and me. She has a car, so I will just drive my pick up. I'll give the Z back to you to sell." I took his car and began to drive it, but I was not happy with myself.

After a lot of inner turmoil I finally resolved I had to tell the children about the abortion.

In March 1986 both of them were home on the same weekend I was scheduled to speak at the Texas Right to Life Convention in Denton. They agreed to go with me. I tried to tell them the night before but couldn't. The next morning things were not right to talk to them. I didn't tell them on the ride to Denton.

Before we went into the meeting, I asked them to pray with me because I knew what I had to do.

When I got up to speak, the knot in my throat was so large I could not talk. I finally managed to start. "In 1973 I had an abortion." The lump got smaller. I could not look at my children. I was sure they would hate me.

Tears flooded my eyes. I had to stop to ask the audience to pray with me before I could continue. My children finally knew the deepest, darkest secret about their mother. It was a relief to finally tell them.

I was shocked they didn't want to talk about it. All they asked me was, "Why didn't you tell us?"

And all I could say was, "How does a mother tell an eight and ten year old, 'I just murdered your sibling'?"

They let me off the hook, which I regretted. I wanted to hear, "You made a mistake. You screwed up." But they were silent, like Tom.

"Tears flooded my eyes. I had to stop to ask the audience to pray with me before I could continue. My children finally knew the deepest, darkest secret about their mother. It was a relief to finally tell them."

When we left Denton that day, the knot in my throat was gone forever. And the "precious feet" I wore only to pro-life meetings—they are now worn daily to remind me of my other child—my third child everyone would now know about.

Little did I know that three major bridges were crossed that day. I told my children about my abortion. I stopped grieving and punishing myself. I also met Jack Wilke, M.D., the president of National Right to Life.

Actively Pro-Life

In the lobby afterward Dr. Wilke asked for my card and said, "I wondered what changed a woman like you."

How I have grown to love and respect Dr. Wilke and his lovely wife, Barbara. They have given unselfishly of themselves to the pro-life movement. The Lord has used the two of them mightily to do His work and to encourage others like me in so many ways.

In June 1986 Dr. Wilke was responsible for my being invited to speak at the National Right to Life Convention in New Orleans. I was well received in Texas among pro-lifers, but I was nervous about facing the National Convention. I arrived at the convention very early and found my workshop room.

There was a man sitting in the room when I walked in. We struck up a conversation.

"I'm Carol Everett. I am doing the next workshop, and I'm scared no one will come."

"What is the title of the workshop?" Ed from North Carolina asked.

"Ex-Abortion Provider Turns Pro-Life." I watched closely for his reaction.

"Oh, your workshop will be well attended. But don't worry; I'll stay just in case no one else comes."

I liked this man. We talked until others started arriving. More and more convention attendees packed the room until it was standing room only. During the meeting Ed stood up and declared, "This is the best attended meeting of the convention!" He made me feel so welcome and accepted.

After my appearance at the NRTL Convention, calls started coming in from all over the nation for speaking engagements. I began to be too busy working with pro-life to continue my job with Richard and Jerry. Richard's prophecy was about to be fulfilled.

Jack and I had to have a heart-to-heart talk. "What do you think about me going to work in the pro-life movement full-time?"

"Carol, re-read the Book of Esther prayerfully," was his advice. I had read it earlier at Jack's direction, but it didn't mean much to me. This time, however, it really spoke to me. Esther was chosen to be queen for her beauty, but God placed her in the palace "for such a time as this." Esther was used of God to deliver her people, declaring, "If I perish, I perish." Oh, how I identified with "for such a time as this"!

I was reminded of the passage in Isaiah and about my time with God on the Capitol steps. I went back to Jack and reported, "I know

God means for me to use my life, at this time, to fight abortion. I want to help the world hear the cry of the unborn saying, 'Let me live.' I know I am to go to work as a pro-lifer full-time."

"It's a matter of God's timing, Carol. Let's see what God does next."

Would you believe it? In May we reached a settlement with Harvey Johnson. Jack arranged for the church to receive my part of the monthly settlement. The abortion "blood money" became God's money put into God's house. The church set up a fund to help fight abortion.

What would God do next?

Another surprise. It was time to trim my household budget to prepare to live on less income. I got rid of the final items purchased with the "blood money"—the two 280 ZX's. I sold both cars and signed an unsecured note for more than eleven thousand dollars with the bank. The butcher shop closed again, leaving me a note for fifty-three thousand dollars at the bank.

At one time my total unsecured debt was more than one hundred and fifty-four thousand dollars. Somehow with the Lord's blessing, in less than three years, my debt was reduced to sixty-four thousand dollars. [At the time of this writing, my debt has been reduced to three thousand six hundred dollars.]

I had learned to work through my trials and not run from them. I knew God had a job for me to do. Somehow, I knew the remaining sixty-four thousand dollars would be taken care of. I marched ahead with my plan.

In August 1987 I talked to Jill, Bill Price's assistant, and mentioned, "I want to go into pro-life work full-time."

She seemed surprised but said, "Carol, I'll mention it to Bill."

In October Bill Price called. "Could you meet me for lunch, Carol? I would like to talk to you about coming on staff."

At lunch Bill said, "I think I can raise the money for you to come on staff, but I can't offer you a position until I can raise the money."

"Is that the way it will be year after year?" I asked.

"The money has always come in for everyone to stay on after a year, and I am sure it would come in to keep an ex-abortion provider on the staff of a pro-life group."

After discussing the monetary issue, Bill said, "Carol, there will be times that you will not be able to share your Christian testimony."

"I understand that legislatures do not respect Christian testimony. What would I be doing?"

"Pretty much the same thing you are doing now. You would continue your speaking and educating. Your title would be public relations director. You would also help me with fund-raising."

"Sounds good to me. Let's see what happens."

In February 1988 when I went to work with Dallas Right to Life full-time, the Ft. Worth Star Telegram did a feature article on me. Tom's mother was still living in Ft. Worth. I called Tom and told him what was going to be released, including my acknowledging our abortion. I did not want him or his mother to be surprised by the release. Tom really reacted in anger when I told him.

God richly rewarded me throughout the year with many wonderful experiences and with many new friends.

On December 20 I was preparing for a video to be filmed in our office for D. James Kennedy's ministry when Bill came in. "Carol, I need to talk to you. I told you that the funds had always come in to keep everyone on staff after their first year. I am sorry, but the funds have not come in to keep you on staff for another year."

I was stunned by his news.

"Carol, you can stay on and do your own fund-raising. You know it costs an amount equal to your salary for support personnel, office space, and other expenses. You can have 10 percent of anything you raise over the seventy-two thousand dollars."

My initial reaction was, *If I have to raise my own funds, I might as well do it for myself. This is clearly the Lord closing this door.* Aloud, I said, "Bill, I am pretty busy right now with the video being filmed. Can we talk about this later?" I was visibly upset.

"Certainly. I am sorry I had such bad news just before the filming."

In a later meeting I told Bill, "I want to pray about this over the holidays. I want to be certain where God wants me."

When I returned after the holidays, we met again.

"Bill, I believe I am supposed to resign."

"Carol, if that's what you want to do, I'll pay you for the month of January and you can keep all of your honorariums."

" 'Carol, I need to talk to you. I told you that the funds had always come in to keep everyone on staff after their first year. I am sorry, but the funds have not come in to keep you on staff for another year.' "

"Thank you, Bill. I really appreciate it."

Where was I to go next?

I set up an appointment with Jack to discuss my situation. "I've decided to leave Dallas Right to Life, and I need some advice."

"Carol, I will help you set up your own organization if you want to. I have extra office space here and will be glad to help you get organized. If you would like, we could also talk about your joining with Marketplace Christian Network."

"I would rather come under your umbrella, if possible, Jack. I believe that is the best place for me."

Jack and I worked out our agreement which included Charlotte, my assistant at DRTL, joining the MCN staff. In January 1989 I went to work with Jack as the director of MCN-ProLife.

15

RESTORATION

S ome say the day of miracles is passed. But, I am living proof
   miracles still happen.

In January 1989 when I went to work with MCN, I was very excited. I kept telling Jack, "I think something really great is about to
happen."

"Don't be surprised when it does, Carol."

Jack gave me a minute to try and figure out what he meant. "The
surprise will be what happens, Carol. And the way it happens might
even surprise you. Sometimes the surprise is the messenger and sometimes it's the circumstances surrounding the event. You're right,
though, Carol, something fantastic is about to happen."

Jack was right. The next two and a half years held many surprises—joyful, peaceful, loving surprises. Fantastic things began to
happen in the business, but the real surprises came in the area of
relationship enrichment.

The Process Begins

On February 16, 1989, I called Tom. "I need to meet with you this
morning. I will just take a minute."

"Okay, Carol. Be here at eight o'clock."

"Thanks a lot, Tom. I'll be right over."

I was at Tom's front door at 8:00 A.M. sharp.

"What is so important, Carol Nan?"

"USA Today is coming to the office this morning to interview me
about being a post-abortive woman. It's going to be on national television. I wanted to tell you so you would not be surprised."

"You could have told me that over the telephone. What else is
going on?"

"Our abortion just about destroyed my life."

"Well, I guess you think it hasn't affected me. It bothers me, too."
Tom began to cry along with me; it was the first time I saw Tom hurting over our abortion. For the first time I felt Tom gave my feelings
some validity. But what about his? I ignored them. I was still struggling
too much with my own feelings to be able to reach out to help him.

"Tom, I've got to be free to tell my story. In the future I am going
to tell it and not hold anything back. I hope you can accept it. I want
you to release me to do it."

"Okay, Carol. Go ahead."

When I left Tom's house I felt a lot of relief.

I went to the office and did the interview. A couple of weeks later
Tom called and asked me to do him a favor. "Carol, my car is in the
shop. Could you take me to pick it up?"

"Sure, Tom. I'll be happy to."

On the way to pick up his car, I said, "Tom, USA Today is showing
the interview tonight. I wanted you to know. Will you watch it so we
can talk about it later? I really want your input on how it comes
across."

"Okay, Carol Nan."

When I let Tom out of the car, he just stood there. I knew he
wanted me to respond to him, but I just drove away. Why didn't I turn
around and go back? I just kept driving.

That evening as soon as USA Today was over, I called Tom. "Did
you watch USA Today?"

"I didn't get to see all of it. Right in the middle of the show
Mother called. She was not happy."

Needless to say, it was not the right time for Tom and me to talk.
At least I didn't think so. But, in actuality it would have been the
perfect time. He had to be struggling with the same rejection I was
struggling with. We just could not help each other then.

A short time later Tom started dating Sandy. He and Sandy began to visit with Jack at our office. Jack had been helping Tom for some time on how to build better relationships. It really bothered me to see Tom and Sandy come in together.

I set up a meeting with Jack to discuss my feelings. "Why does Tom have to parade Sandy into this office? I think he's doing it just to hurt me."

"Carol, I think you are jealous. Do you still love Tom?" he asked directly. "I think you would like to be married to Tom. What do you think?"

"Tom began to cry along with me; it was the first time I saw Tom hurting over our abortion."

"I don't know."

"Why don't we pray about it and find out what the truth is."

We prayed another one of those killer prayers. Sure enough, I had to admit in my private heart, the door remained open for Tom to enter in again. My emotions took off on the same roller coaster ride they had been on throughout our past marriage.

And on the emotional roller coaster ride, I watched my invisible black slate resurface. It had been buried in my memory for years. All four of the items were still on it, too:

1. Tom's belief that children are liabilities rather than assets had to change.

2. Tom had to accept responsibility for his part in the abortion.

3. Tom had to admit he was insensitive to my needs demonstrated by his never asking me if I wanted the child. He had to apologize for that.

4. Tom had to admit that our marriage was only a business deal
with selfish pleasure thrown in, that he was not a husband to
me—just a sex partner and good negotiator.

Not a single one had been checked off. All of my subconscious
thoughts and emotions from our past relationship came out in the
open. I had to admit to myself I was still waiting for Tom to realize I
was the only woman who ever truly loved him. I didn't fall into a heap
like his first wife; I honored my agreement and aborted our child. It
was time we resolved our relationship problems. I felt it could only be
done by Tom admitting his wrongs, his mistakes.

I began to realize I was operating on the assumption that God was
pleased with the list on my black slate. I had actually been praying for
Tom to meet my subconscious demands. I was playing "God" in my
life and Tom's life. I was angry because I didn't see Tom turning back
to me; he still wasn't cooperating.

I also discovered that I subconsciously believed Tom and I would
get back together after the children left home. It would just be Tom
and me. The children would be less of a liability. I was jealous of
Sandy because I thought I should be with Tom. I asked God, "How
many more deep roots are there that still bind me to Tom?"

First, I acknowledged to God that Tom was an idol in my life.
Then, I asked God to free both of us from my need to punish Tom.

My prayer continued, *God, if You can forgive me for all I've done,
You can forgive Tom for all he has done, too. If You can forgive Tom,
so can I and so do I. Help me to remember this prayer and Your love
for both of us.*

Things began to improve between Tom and me. Finally, in August
I called Tom. "I need to ask you to forgive me, Tom."

"What for, Carol?"

"Tom, I've blamed you for a lot of things—especially the abortion.
I've been punishing you for a long time. I'm sorry. Will you forgive me?"

"Yes, Carol. I forgive you. Will you forgive me for my part in the
abortion?"

Did I hear Tom correctly? Did he admit his part in the abortion?
"Yes, Tom. But it's interesting you only asked me after I asked you to
forgive me. Are you sure you mean it? You never called and asked me
to forgive you first."

> **"But the only change I know I can do is to let the Lord use my experience to show others how destructive abortion really is. Maybe I can help others see abortion is a sin. The destruction is against the family unit, not just the baby and the mother, but the entire family."**

"Hang up the phone, Carol."

"Why, Tom?"

"So I can call you."

I hung up the telephone and waited for it to ring.

"Carol Nan, will you forgive me for my part in the abortion?"

"Yes, Tom. I will. Thank you, Tom."

"I love you, Carol."

"I love you, too, Tom."

"Carol, I will always love you, as long as I live."

"I know, Tom. Good-bye."

"Good-bye, Carol."

I sat in the office thinking my whole life had not been the same since my abortion on February 16, 1973. Tom's life had been altered, too. Kelly had really been affected; so had Joe Bob. In many ways we were all victims of that act of murder.

It is a shame that others have suffered for my sin. It really hurts me that my other children are victims also. They were certainly innocent. Yes, I am sorry that Tom was hurt by the abortion, but oh, how I wish he had wanted our child. There are so many things I would like to change if I could.

But the only change I know I can do is to let the Lord use my experience to show others how destructive abortion really is. Maybe I can help others see abortion is a sin. The destruction is against the family unit, not just the baby and the mother, but the entire family.

By November I felt in my heart Tom was very serious about Sandy. I even called Jack and asked, "Is Tom going to marry Sandy?"

"It looks very serious to me, Carol."

When I hung up the telephone, I was crushed. I thought Tom still loved me. He said he would love me forever. Deep inside, my invisible black slate still wasn't clean. I knew there was more to be dealt with, but I wasn't willing to pursue the matter further at that time. A short time later Tom and Sandy were married.

Acceptance of Family

Things were relatively quiet in my life for about three months. At one of our regular meetings in May 1991, Jack asked, "Carol, is it possible the baby you aborted was a little girl instead of a boy?"

In all of my thoughts, I always had imagined my child was a boy. There had never been a doubt. "Why in the world did you ask that?" I questioned.

"I've just been wondering. Why do you feel it was a boy?"

"I've never thought about it being a girl. I've always assumed it was a boy."

I left Jack's office really disturbed. *What are you trying to do now, God?* (Don't ask unless you want to know.)

A few days later I went back to visit with Jack. "You are exactly right. Today I believe my baby was a little girl, not a boy. It ties back to how I had wished I was a boy because I felt my father wanted a son so badly. Daddy was my idol, you know. I wanted a boy especially for Tom because I idolized Tom, too. I thought the baby boy would be just like his father.

"I have begun to think of my aborted child as a girl instead of a boy. I've even given her a name—Heidi. Her name means "noble or kind" in German. To me, her name means "hidden one." She was hidden from me for seventeen years, and she is hidden from the world, but she lives in my heart."

Somehow, tied to the acceptance of my third child being a little girl was a new-found appreciation of myself as a woman. It was as though being a woman took on a much greater significance to me.

I don't believe any of us really think about how abortion touches every relationship in our lives until encouraged to do so.

At my urging, Kelly spent time with Jack, trying to deal with the effects my abortion had on her life, as well as what happened to her while she was in the abortion clinics. Kelly was uniquely affected be-

> ## "It was the perfect time for God to help us as a family deal with some deep scars caused by my life of destruction. I prayed for God to open the opportunity for us to be able to talk about our hurts."

cause I dragged her into the abortion clinics with me; I knew she needed to talk about her time spent in them.

Kelly shared with Jack,

> I wish I had never worked in an abortion clinic. I was fourteen years old when Mom went to work in the first clinic. I went to work there with her. I did filing, general office work, and answered the telephone.
>
> From the beginning I believed I was helping the women. But I wasn't. I was so blind about the real issues I was involved with. I believed it was just a fetus—not a baby.
>
> It was hard to walk out in the front of the clinic and see my friends from school there to have an abortion. They really reacted when they saw me.
>
> Mom was in charge, but Dr. Johnson is the one I performed for. I worked in the clinics for five years and saw a lot. There is no denial anymore about what I saw—I saw body parts in there. Sometimes I think I've had millions of abortions, although I've never personally had one.
>
> I remember a woman who drove a BMW. She had four abortions. She said it was her way of birth control.

One of the things that bothered me the most was the women who were injured. Some of them were retarded women who didn't even realize how they got pregnant. And there were young children who came in who were forced by their parents to have abortions.

I especially remember one "big baby" abortion that was botched [Jenni]. I helped Mother take her to the hospital. Her bowel was pulled through her uterus. She just kept screaming. It scared me to death.

I thank God I never got pregnant. If I had, I would have had an abortion, too, because in my mind it wasn't a baby. But, not today. No, I wouldn't have an abortion today. My opinion has changed drastically. I feel strongly today God chooses for life to begin—He gives life. I am strongly opposed to abortion.

(I thank God, too, Kelly never had an abortion. Also, I am so grateful to God to see that Kelly never really bought into the abortion business even though I tried to push her into it. She was stronger than her mother.)

Jack also asked Kelly, "Tell me your impressions of your mother today."

When I think about my mother today, I can't help but cry. She is a fighter. She has worked so hard. When we were growing up, she held down two jobs to see that we were taken care of. She would take us home after finishing one job, feed us, and be off to the next job. She is the most dynamic person I know. She's dynamite. I have so much admiration for her.

She thinks she hurt Joe Bob and me—abused us in our childhood. That is not true. She is my very best friend today. Sometimes I tell her things she doesn't like to hear, but I still tell her.

Today, she takes a lot of abuse from the family because of her pro-life work, which is unfortunate. I think she is the greatest.

When I read what Kelly said about me, it just broke my heart. She is probably the person I have hurt the most. That she can see me the way she does overwhelms me. I messed up so badly, but God has been gracious to me through my daughter's love for me.

The focus of Kelly's time with Jack changed when he asked, "Kelly, why do you think there wasn't enough room in your home for a little sister?"

There was always enough room as far as I was concerned. Joe Bob and I were told something went wrong with the pregnancy. I never thought Mom had an abortion. When she told me a few years ago that she had an abortion, my reaction was, "No, she had a D and C." I still haven't accepted the fact that it was a sibling. I know it is hurting Mom, now. I need to address it. I don't know why she had an abortion. I don't know why!

Kelly is still trying to figure out how her mother, the person she loves and admires so much, could have aborted her sister. That's okay with me because sometimes I still try to figure it out, too.

Jack and Kelly's time together intensified when Jack asked, "Kelly, if you could change anything today, what would you change?"

I would like to see more emphasis on the family. I wish families cared for one another again like they once did.

Abortion would be illegal.

I would want my aborted sister to come be with us. I hate to say it, but I've never thought about that before. Recently, a baby in our family was put up for adoption. I wanted to know about that baby. Sitting here talking to you now, my heart is just breaking for the sibling that was aborted. This is new to me . . . to think about her being aborted is awful, terrible. Recently, a close friend got pregnant. It made me stop and think. Our aborted sibling never had a chance. It doesn't make much sense.

My entire family would be supportive of my mother.

Gangi would be well.

Jack asked Kelly one final question. "Have you ever thought about joining your mother in her crusade?"

Yes. One time she left a message on my answering machine, "I'm scheduled to be on the Capitol lawn at twelve o'clock—Can't make it—Will have your speech ready." Mom was teasing, of course, but I didn't think it was funny at the time.

I can't handle the attacks on me right now. I'm not strong enough to handle them. I hear their lies—I know better.

Probably, I'm a little bit scared too. But it's something we all need to do. I'm scared of standing up there and taking all that abuse.

I can't think of anyone who would be better to help me. She has seen it all, too. I'm waiting for the day we stand beside each other in this fight. Come to think of it—we are right now!

Letting Go

Dreams only come true in fairy tales. I joined Kelly in wishing Daddy would get well, but his condition worsened. The cancer had increased over 50 percent by early January. He was put back in the hospital for three more chemotherapy treatments which did not work. The last treatment affected his brain, heart, and liver.

At that time I told him, "Daddy, I have just one thing I need to talk to you about."

"I'm ready to meet my Maker." But I wasn't so sure he really believed it.

On February 4 the doctor cautioned, "If you want to see your father while he still knows you, I suggest you get here fast."

I flew to Austin that afternoon and spent the night with my father. My prayer this time was, *God, tell me when the time is right to talk to Daddy.* God had not used anyone else to reach my father. Maybe he would use me.

The next day about half past two Mother left for a while. Daddy and I were alone. I shared with him about Jesus Christ and how I prayed to receive Him in my heart. When I finished, I asked, "Would you like to pray a prayer and ask Jesus Christ to come into your heart and be your Lord and Savior?"

"Yes."

I jumped out of the recliner and got on my knees beside his bed. I grabbed Daddy's hand and through tears prayed, "God, I am a sinner. Please forgive me of my sins. Thank you for sending your Son, Jesus Christ, to die for my sins. Reign on the throne of my heart as Lord and Savior. Use my life for your glory. Amen."

When Daddy said, "Amen," I was overjoyed.

Daddy turned his head away from me so I wouldn't see him crying. I knew with all my heart that my father was at the end of himself and that he really wanted to be in heaven.

"The next day about half past two Mother left for a while. Daddy and I were alone. I shared with him about Jesus Christ and how I prayed to receive Him in my heart."

A peace filled the room. Daddy and I shed tears of joy; I felt Daddy was at peace. He did not voice another angry word while I was there.

I had to leave on the 8:30 P.M. plane. I touched my father, and I told him I loved him and that I would see him later. Somehow I knew though, it would be the last time I would see Daddy alive.

Right before I left, his kidneys stopped functioning. I shall never forget that look on his face. He knew he was dying. He didn't fight it. He accepted it. Peace ruled in his heart—and mine.

Mother sat on the family bed and said, "I wish you didn't have to go. Is there any way you can stay?"

Oh, how I wanted to stay. "No, Mother. I'll be back Sunday. I have three speaking engagements that we can't cancel. I love you. Kelly and Joe Bob will be here. I am sorry I can't stay. Everything is going to be all right." And it was all right!

It was my last time to see Daddy alive.

I returned home to Dallas very glad and peaceful inside because I knew Daddy was really ready to meet his Maker.

I was in the office the next day when Tom came in to visit with Jack. "How is your dad, Carol Nan?"

"He's dying, Tom."

Tom turned and stumbled out the door. I knew he was crushed. He really did think a lot of my father. I raised my voice and added, "Tom, it's okay. He prayed to receive Christ."

Tom was silent.

It was about noon on Friday, February 8, 1991, when I called from Boston's Logan Airport to find out how Daddy was doing. Joe Bob answered the phone. "Gangi is gone."

"How is Mother?"

"She is fine."

"Let me talk to her."

The first thing she said was, "I'm not going to postpone your father's funeral like I did when Mother died."

"Yes, Mother." Mother's reminder was God's way of showing me how much damage I had done to my mother because of my insensitivity.

It was a big funeral, like "This Is Your Life, Carol Nan Everett." Both Jim Bob, my first husband, and Tom were there.

After the funeral I called to thank Tom for everything he had done for our family during Daddy's illness and death. This time Tom said to me, "I think of you often, and I pray for you, Carol Nan."

It was so special to hear Tom say those words. I knew he meant them.

"Tom, I want you to know I'm praying for you and Sandy. I want you to be happy."

After the funeral I spent some wonderful time alone with my mother. I came away with a whole new perspective of her: I did not see her as weak at all. She's strong and she's been very strong for years, and I couldn't see it.

I want to get to know her much better now. The jealousy between us is gone, maybe because Daddy isn't between us anymore.

God Is at Work

Things settled back down after Daddy's death, and I got back to work on the book as well as other things. Jack came in one day and announced, "Tom is agreeable to being interviewed about his part in the abortion and it being included in the book."

"I knew all along Tom was going to have his part in the book," I admitted.

I was anxious to hear the results of Jack's visit with Tom. In the interview Jack asked Tom, "What impact do you think the abortion had on your marriage?"

> I wasn't aware of any impact at that time. Now, I know it was devastating. But we didn't have a marriage, at least not a marriage as I understand marriage today. We had an agreed-upon arrangement.

The impact on the arrangement was minimal, however, because Carol couldn't talk to me about it.

She came in one day and said, "I'm pregnant." I didn't react or say anything. She proceeded to carry out our agreement. I didn't challenge it, but I wasn't comfortable with it, either. I couldn't tell her. I didn't stop it, though, because it was a part of my deal. We had agreed if she got pregnant, she would have an abortion. I believed both of us should uphold our part of the agreement. I'm still a little bit that way.

Both of us got married too quickly our first times because of crisis pregnancies. Carol Nan was pregnant and Susan, my wife-to-be, was too. We had children too early. Each of us believed marriage was forever, and we had failed in our first marriages. Both of us felt guilty for the mess we made with our first spouses.

I didn't want the responsibility of another child. We made the decision, as we knew it, with the heartache we had been through. But it was a mistake.

I guess every person plays the game of "what if," going back through their life. "What if things had been different?" I'm no different. A part of the reason why this reflection appeals to me now is the opportunity to learn more about building relationships based on trust. I've learned to trust people in my professional life, but I have been unable to trust in my personal life until recently.

Rather than carrying a shield to protect my past hurts, I want to trust, to be able to deal openly with all the cards dealt me. If only I had been able to let go and trust in my past, how much different my life would have been.

Carol and I were really volatile together in many respects. We couldn't work through our problems, and the baby was just another problem.

I have asked God to forgive me many times. The issue of children has been very confusing to me. Today, I clearly see what role children play in life. I have cheated myself out of the frustration and joy of raising children.

It is a control issue. I was in control. If it's really God's plan to give us children, then I've missed a part of my life. Remember, I do have a son, though. My life is not through. Children will surface again in my life.

I won't have any more biological children, but we will come up with more children in our lives. Maybe foster children. My wife is a teacher. She does really well with children. I don't know how good a father I'll be this time, though.

I've asked Carol to forgive me for it a couple of times, but I'm still not sure she has. Sometimes her actions still make me wonder. I can't go back and change what I did. I've asked God to forgive me.

"Tom, what message do you have for men who are facing their participation or the possibility of being a participant in an abortion?"

It comes back to an issue of control. Before you decide to terminate the pregnancy, it is important to understand why you are considering doing it. It is probably for reasons you are unable to voice. You may not be very risk-oriented, but having the baby is well worth the risk.

And I have some questions for men, like me, who've participated in abortions. Why did you participate? How has your value system changed since you aborted your child? What is your relationship with the person you were involved with in aborting the child? How do you deal with the fact your parents didn't abort you? How do you live with what you have done? These are some of the questions I have struggled with myself.

I can tell you I have made my bed, and now I live with the emptiness, amidst tears, particularly when I see the joy children bring to their parents and other people.

When I finished digesting Tom's remarks during his interview with Jack, I realized, *God is at work changing Tom, too.* I told myself I have to focus on the new Tom that is evolving, rather than the old Tom I knew in the past. I am so glad God doesn't freeze us in our past mistakes, but He warmly, lovingly changes us. I silently prayed, *Lord, help me to see and love the man You are making Tom into today.*

The world tells a woman there is something wrong with her if she has a problem with her abortion. After all, the woman is supposed to be liberated from having to carry a child for nine months when she has an abortion. So the woman tends to push her feelings of remorse after the abortion aside. She tries to convince herself "abortion is the best thing that ever happened to me." The denial period can last for years.

Think of what the man must go through. If the woman is not supposed to be hurt by the abortion, the man certainly is not supposed to be hurt. He, too, suppresses his feelings for years. Tom was no exception. It has taken him eighteen years to begin to work through his true feelings.

I could not finish this chapter without telling you how God has changed my heart toward Harvey Johnson. Yes, there was a time when I wanted to hurt Harvey as badly as he hurt me when he helped me kill my baby and when he blamed me for the problems at the clinic. Now, I know revenge is not mine. I know God is working with Harvey and Fredi, too.

"I am so glad God doesn't freeze us in our past mistakes, but He warmly, lovingly changes us."

I would like to see them come to know the Lord. I would love for Harvey to become a pro-lifer actively involved in fighting abortion with us. That may or may not happen. I know Harvey has a real Christian friend in Wayne Byles who has not given up on prayerfully trying to help him get out of the abortion business. I pray Wayne is successful.

I ask you to please indulge me now, while I write a few words to my daughter.

Heidi, I wish I could see you right now and hold you. But, for now I can only share with you what's on my heart.

I hope you like the name I've given you. Precious, you were hidden from me for seventeen years. I'm sorry it took me so long to acknowledge you.

Although you have never physically lived on this earth, you have lived for more than eighteen years in my heart. It is true your father and I had no place for you in our home, but you have always had a home in my heart. You will live there as long as I live. I wear my gold, "precious feet" pin everywhere I go to remind me of you.

Heidi, nothing can replace the loss of you. But I want you to know your death has not been without purpose. The love God has shown to me in forgiving me compels me to work hard telling every mother and father I can about my mistake. I try to help them hear the cry of their unborn child saying, "I want to live. I want to have the opportunity to grow to my full potential, too. Don't shut me out before I have a chance to share my life with you. Don't shut your heart to me."

I am also trying to help all of the families who have been damaged by abortion. I want them to discover the power of love I know today and continue to see working in our family.

Heidi, I look forward to seeing you in heaven, in your home. I know you and your Aunt Tooter, Gangi, and our other loved ones are already having a glorious time.

Heidi, you would be graduating from high school this year and preparing to go off to college. I would be helping you select a college just like I did with your brother and sister. They would be right in the middle helping us with your selection! You would really love Joe Bob and Kelly like I do.

I have a special request to make of you I think you can honor. Please sing a joyful song of thanksgiving to the Lord for me because of all His love shown to our family.

Heidi, I love you and miss you with all my heart. I can hardly wait to hug you and join you in our heavenly home.

To say I have been surprised by the events of the past two and a half years is an understatement. The greatest surprise is the miracle of how God has changed my heart and is working in all my relationships. He is creating the desire in me to love people I used to hate and to forgive others like He forgives me. This is indeed a miracle.

I trust you can see from reading my story, I have been blessed beyond measure from the moment I prayed with Jack, "God, I have been running my own life and have missed the mark You have for me to hit. Father, thank You for sending Your Son, Jesus Christ, to die for my sins. Thank You for raising Him from the dead and making Him living Lord over all. Come into my heart, Lord Jesus, and begin to reign over my life. Begin to love through me as only You can and make me a worker in Your vineyard. Amen."

I exchanged thirty-eight years of destructive living for life as a worker in God's vineyard. I thank You Lord for the privilege of being a tooth in Your threshing sledge to be used to cut abortion clinics out of our society.

Inside I hear a voice saying *The best is yet to be.*

ABOUT THE AUTHORS

C AROL EVERETT Is the director of the Pro-Life division of Marketplace Christian Network in Dallas, Texas, where she resides.
Ms. Everett is the mother of two grown children. She is currently
working on a book detailing the inside workings of an abortion clinic.

Ms. Everett's unique experiences of being a post-abortive mother
and an ex-abortion provider make her a sought-after speaker in the
pro-life movement.

JACK SHAW has twenty-eight years of pastoral ministry experience
and for the past fifteen years has been involved in business consulting,
executive counseling, and motivational speaking.

Mr. Shaw is the President of Marketplace Christian Network in
Dallas, Texas, where he lives with his wife, Gwen. Married for thirty-
one years, the Shaws have three grown children.

The typeface for the text of this book is *Caledonia* which was created by the talented type and book designer, William Addison Dwiggins. Dwiggins, who became acting director of the Harvard University Press in 1917, was also known for his work with the publisher Alfred Knopf and for his other type designs, notably *Electra*. The name *Caledonia* is the ancient name for what is now the country of Scotland and denotes that the type was originally designed to parallel *Scotch Roman* (sometimes described as a *Modernized Old Style*). In creating *Caledonia*, Dwiggins was also influenced by the type that William Martin cut in 1790 for William Bulmer. Thus *Caledonia* is a modification of *Bulmer* and *Scotch Roman*, yet it is more business-like and versatile than the two older types.

Substantive Editing:
Michael S. Hyatt

Copy Editing:
Cynthia Tripp

Cover Design:
Steve Diggs & Friends
Nashville, Tennessee

Page Composition:
Hewlett Packard *LaserJet III*

Printing and Binding:
Maple-Vail Book Manufacturing Group
York, Pennsylvania

Dust Jacket Printing:
Strine Printing Company
York, Pennsylvania